What's Wrong with Sin?

Sin in Individual and Social Perspective
from Schleiermacher to Theologies of Liberation

Derek R. Nelson

t&t clark

Published by T&T Clark International
A Continuum imprint
The Tower Building, 11 York Road, London SE1 7NX
80 Maiden Lane, Suite 704, New York, NY-10038

www.continuumbooks.com

British Library Cataloguing-in-Publication Data
A catalogue record for this book is available from the British Library

ISBN: 978–0-567–06713–5 (hardback)
        978–0-567–26676–7 (paperback)

Typeset by Free Range Book Design & Production Limited
Printed and bound in Great Britain by Athenaeum Press Ltd, Gateshead,
Tyne and Wear

To three mentors and friends who continue
to teach me with their words and their works:

Ted Peters, William C. Placher and Curtis L. Thompson.

May they know that whenever I think of sin,
I will always think of them.

LIST OF WORKS BY THE SAME AUTHOR

'Gerhard Ebeling's Critical Appropriation of Kierkegaard', in Jon Stewart, ed., *Kierkegaard's Influence on Theology*. Aldershot: Ashgate, 2009, forthcoming.

'Sins of Commission, Sins of Omission: Girard, Ricoeur and the Armenian Genocide', in Robert John Russell, Martinez Hewlett, Ted Peters and Gaymon Bennett (eds), *The Evolution of Evil*. Göttingen: Vandenhoeck and Ruprecht, 2008, 318–33.

'Encountering the World's Religions: Nathan Söderblom and the Concept of Revelation', *Dialog* 46:4 (2007), 362–70.

'The Vulnerable and Transcendent God: The Postliberal Theology of William Placher', *Dialog* 44:3 (2005), 273–84.

'The Indicative of Grace, the Imperative of Freedom: An Invitation to the Theology of Eberhard Jüngel', *Dialog* 44:2 (2005), 164–80.

CONTENTS

ACKNOWLEDGEMENTS

The research leading to the writing of this book took shape during my doctoral studies at the Graduate Theological Union in Berkeley, California. Then, as now, I took great delight in telling people that I was engaged in serious primary fieldwork on the topic of sin. The late Tim Lull oversaw the initial studies, and Ted Peters saw to completion the dissertation that gave rise to this book. An aspiring theologian could not ask for more enthusiastic, learned, or supportive *Doktorväter*. I wish to extend publicly my deep gratitude to them once again.

Many people have read all or parts of the manuscript: Claude Welch, Niels Gregersen, Richard Crouter, Andrew Dole, William Placher, Lynn Hofstad, Michael Aune, Joseph Dayam Prabhakar, Erik Samuelson, Bryan Wagoner and Natalie Dorfeld. Their specific editorial comments made this work more readable than it would otherwise have been, and did much to dissuade me from the frightening suspicion that I had gone intellectually haywire. To know that all of the remaining errors and theological missteps are mine is both humbling and true.

I would like to thank Richard Schenk, OP, Rosemary Radford Ruether and David Kelsey, who, along with Ted Peters, functioned as the examining committee for the dissertation. I have learned immensely from them over the years, and profited particularly from their helpful comments, probing questions and blessed assurances. A great many other teachers, too, helped make the book what it became by making me the theologian that I am. To list just a few, I am happy to register my gratitude to: Stephen Webb, Raymond Williams, David Blix at Wabash and the late Paul McKinney; Marilyn McCord Adams, Nicholas Wolterstorff, Miroslav Volf, Serene Jones, Gene Outka and George Lindbeck at Yale; Gregory Love, Claude Welch and George Griener at the GTU; and Thomas A. Brady at the University of California. I hope they can see some of themselves in whatever clarity I bring to this work.

My family, especially my parents, Rodney and Mary Nelson, and my sister, Gretchen Jerskey, have been a source of support and love, and I am humbled to thank them. Too many friends even to begin to name have provided companionship and encouragement at every turn, none more than Kelly Ayers, whom I am also pleased to be able to fondly thank here.

Thiel College was brave enough to take a chance on a very green professor and consequently has been the context of my scholarship and teaching for the last three years. Conversations with many colleagues and students have delighted and nourished me during my time in Greenville. I hope that this book's completion will let them see even more of me in the future.

During the time that the proofs for this book were being prepared, William Placher unexpectedly died. He was my first, and best, theological mentor. His enormous learning and his rootedness in the great theological and philosophical traditions made him more, not less, open to their critique and re-interpretation. This is the spirit in which many of his other students and I, too, work. I hope that this book, carried on largely in conversation with him, honours that commitment to tradition and openess to reconsideration. Those who have tried to write clearly on complicated topics know how difficult a task it is. Bill was one of the best at it. He will be sorely missed as one of the great teachers and scholars of his time.

ABBREVIATIONS

CD	Karl Barth, *Church Dogmatics*
CF	Friedrich Schleiermacher, *The Christian Faith*
ICR	Albrecht Ritschl, *Instruction in the Christian Religion*
JR I and III	Albrecht Ritschl, *Justification and Reconciliation*, vols I and III
LN	*Libertatis Nuntius*
LC	*Libertatis Conscientia*
RV II	Albrecht Ritschl, *Rechtfertigung und Versöhnung*, vol. II

Chapter 1

INTRODUCTION

A Statement of the Problem

Monsignor Gianfranco Girotti, who is Official of the Vatican's Supreme Tribunal of the Apostolic Penitentiary, recently issued a list of seven new 'deadly sins'. In an interview with the semi-official newspaper *L'Osservatore Romano*, Girotti outlined new ways that humanity breaches its relationship with God. Upon examining the list it is immediately obvious that most of these sins are prominently *social and corporate* in character, as opposed to the very individualistic traditional version of the seven deadly sins. Girotti says, 'While sin used to concern mostly the individual, today it has mainly a social resonance, due to the phenomenon of globalization.'[1] The new seven deadly sins are: 'bioethical' violations like birth control, 'morally dubious' experiments like stem cell research, drug abuse, polluting the environment, contributing to widening the divide between rich and poor, excessive wealth, and the creation of poverty.

Whether one is sympathetic to the new list matters little; what is beyond dispute is the fact that it represents an attempt to take seriously sin as a not strictly individualistic phenomenon. For a very long time in the history of most Western theology, sin has been easily localizable in the distorted will of the individual sinner. But it is very difficult to see how this view can square with something as interpersonal and systemic as 'contributing to poverty', or 'polluting the environment'. Those are *social* evils, and not much attention has been paid, theologically speaking, to their interpretation.

A scholarly consensus seems to have emerged that pointing out the hyper-individualistic focus of the doctrine of sin is a profoundly *new* approach. The critique of individualism appears most forcefully in Latin American liberation theologies and their heirs around the world, including feminist proposals. Critics of this approach protest that it diverges too radically with the inherited Christian traditions on sin. But the question remains: is the approach really so new?

As a way of entering into the question, consider a debate that sprung up among some theologians over the proper interpretation of a five-minute movie clip. A scene from the 1991 film *Grand Canyon* depicts a wealthy

---

1.   <http://www.catholicnewsagency.com/new.php?n=12031>, accessed 18 July 2008.

lawyer driving a sports car in a run-down part of Los Angeles. His car breaks down, and he calls for a tow truck on a pay phone. As the lawyer waits in his car, a group of young men pulls over in their own car, gets out and walks toward the stranded man. He becomes fearful and locks the doors, hoping they will go away. When they draw near to him, he insinuates that he hopes he will not be robbed or assaulted. In the ensuing confrontation one of the young men flashes a gun. Before anything drastic happens the tow truck driver arrives and mollifies the situation. In doing so, he delivers himself of a brief soliloquy on sin. 'All I know is,' he says, 'everything is supposed to be different than what it is. This guy's supposed to be able to call a tow truck to come get his car without you hassling him, and I'm supposed to be able to do my job without asking your permission. This is not the way it's supposed to be.' It is a powerful scene (not easily lending itself to a prose re-telling) and gets at what Christians mean by 'sin'.

The Reformed theologian Cornelius Plantinga wrote a book about sin, entitled *Not the Way It's Supposed to Be*, using the scene from this movie as his departure point.[2] Plantinga laments the demise in popular culture of the notion of sin, and shows how important it is to re-establish genuine responsibility in an age he feels is rife with people playing the victim of the sins of others or ignoring their complicity in sin altogether. Plantinga tries to offer a new way of describing sin in social, non-individualistic terms by seeing it as a rupture in God's shalom. We have an orientation to God's shalom which is deeper than sin, and this very orientation, when cultivated, allows us to see sin for what it is. It allows us to see the sin in a scene where, as Plantinga puts it, 'the attorney does manage to phone for a tow truck, but before it arrives, five young street toughs surround his disabled car and threaten him with considerable harm. Then, just in time, the tow truck shows up ... The toughs protest: the truck driver is interrupting their meal.'[3] We might ask, where is the sin in this scene? Plantinga's answer is unequivocal – the 'toughs' sin by threatening violence and harm. Though sin is social (i.e., is best named by the general statement 'it's not the way it's supposed to be' for all of us), sins are individual.

Another theologian wonders whether it is so clear. Stephen Ray, in a book called *Do No Harm: Social Sin and Christian Responsibility*, takes on Plantinga's views.[4] Ray thinks Plantinga ignores a critical element in the scene, thus exposing Plantinga's own sinfulness in trying to formulate a doctrine of social sin. Plantinga, who is white, simply *assumed* that the young black men who came to the lawyer's car were 'urban predators'. Yet this was not unambiguously clear in the film. Why not assume that the young men were coming to help the stranded lawyer, and that it is the lawyer who

2.   Cornelius Plantinga, *Not the Way It's Supposed to Be: A Breviary of Sin* (Grand Rapids: Eerdmans, 1995).
3.   Ibid., 7.
4.   Stephen H. Ray, *Do No Harm: Social Sin and Christian Responsibility* (Minneapolis: Fortress Press, 2003).

sins first in saying to his would-be helpers, 'Don't rob me or hurt me'? As Ray notes, 'It is only clear what the intentions of the young men are if one assumes that they ... are "urban predators". Certainly, this appears to be the lens though which the man in the movie, and Plantinga, for that matter, sees what is going on.'[5] Ray goes on to show how harmful such cultural assumptions can be when using the concept of sin to describe social realities. Social sin is dangerous, even if necessary, territory to cover.

Let us follow this debate about this five-minute movie clip one ripple wider. Ronald Stone notes in a review of Ray's book, a bit tongue in cheek, 'Ray criticizes what he sees as Plantinga's unconscious use of negative stereotypes, not the contours of his project as a whole. As Ray presents no evidence that Plantinga's use of the scene has actually harmed anyone, I am unable, from my limited perspective as a white, retired seminary professor, to judge his claim.'[6] The implication is that Ray has made the notion of sin so context-dependent that he has trivialized the whole point of a doctrine of social sin, which is to show our connectedness with each other, as well as our common lot and common hope. Others have criticized Stone for his remarks, and Plantinga, Ray, Stone and others have engaged in an extensive, multi-sided debate.

Of all this business a sober bystander can only ask, What on earth is going on here? How can five minutes of a mediocre movie prompt book after book and round after round of discussion of social sin? The innate combativeness of theologians notwithstanding, the theological interchange recounted above only scratches the surface of what is actually a deeply seated crisis in contemporary theology. Even highly traditional theologians like Cornelius Plantinga think that we simply must learn to discuss sin in a way that is not restricted to the individual level. Yet the proposals on offer for how to go about doing this are dizzying in their variety and practically riddled with conceptual incoherencies, theological cul-de-sacs, and even, as Ray argues, harmful social effects.

The last fifty years, and especially the years since Vatican II, have seen an incredible proliferation of doctrines of social sin. The theologians who espouse these views differ in countless ways, but they all agree that sin can no more be compellingly described in a purely individualistic way. Sin must no longer be conceived as a transaction between the individual self (or often, the individual *will*) and God, without reference to the effects this sin has on others. Put another way, advocates of social sin want to emphasize the ethical, as well as the religious dimension to sin. Sin is wrong because it hurts people, they say, and while it may well be against God, too, the horizontal, ethical facet of sin is most visible and consequently most immediately offensive. Yet this is such a challenge to traditional ways of thinking that a British theologian who has laboured intensively on the problems of social sin, Alistair McFadyen, is led to remark, 'It is the reductive reading of the

---

5. Ibid., 29–30.
6. Ronald H. Stone, Review of *Do No Harm*, *Theology Today* 61 (2004): 268.

language of sin in moral categories, the migration of theology to ethics (accompanied by that from the ontological to the social) which constitutes *the most pressing challenge* to sin as a theological language – *indeed to God-talk in general* – in contemporary culture.'[7] When as thoughtful a theologian as McFadyen makes a claim that sweeping, we had best pay attention.

More specifically, the challenge to conceive of sin in other than a strictly individualistic way has been raised perhaps most forcefully in the last five decades from the most important new perspectives in recent theology, namely the various forms of theologies of liberation. Theologians from these traditions have been uncommonly sensitive to the distortions individualism has had on notions of sin. Writing appreciatively of these perspectives, Theodore W. Jennings notes how clearly they see that 'one of the most remarkable transformations in the understanding of sin comes in the form of a transition from the prophetic view of sin as the deviation of *society and its elites* from the divine will for justice to an emphasis upon sin as the unrighteous act or attitude of *individuals*.'[8] With the help of the liberationists we realize that 'it is increasingly clear that the hegemony of Euramerican males drawn from the influential classes has greatly skewed our understanding of the brokenness and bondage of the human situation'.[9]

Thesis of This Book

The central thesis of this book can be stated fairly briefly. I argue that individualistic doctrines of sin can be corrected by (1) focusing attention on the social structures of sin and (2) by conceiving of the self in more appropriately relational terms. In sum, in what follows I *assume* that privatized and individualistic doctrines of sin are problematic and should be emended; I *demonstrate* that two primary schemes for their emendation were on offer in the nineteenth century; I *apply* those schemes as organizational principles for describing doctrines of sin in certain contemporary liberation theologies; and I *recommend* strategies for integrating corporate and individualist emphases in future doctrines of sin.

Guidelines of the Work's Unfolding

It is every bit as impossible for a theologian to be without a method as it is for a person to be without a mood. The specific nature of the method,

---

7.   Alistair McFadyen, *Bound to Sin: Abuse, Holocaust, and the Christian Doctrine of Sin* (Cambridge: Cambridge University Press, 2000), 19, my emphasis.

8.   Theodore W. Jennings, 'Reconstructing the Doctrine of Sin', in *The Other Side of Sin: Woundedness from the Perspective of the Sinned-Against*, ed. Susan L. Nelson et al. (Albany: SUNY Press, 2001), 113, my emphasis.

9.   Jennings, 'Reconstructing the Doctrine of Sin', 109.

however, is sometimes least apparent to the one supposedly operating under its auspices. If pressed to elaborate on my self-understanding of the philosophical presuppositions which have surely shaped this work, I would describe a kind of naïve nominalism on the concept of social sin. The term 'social sin' appears all over the last fifty years of theology. I ask, towards what is it said to point? And further, is the observable phenomenon so named the same among all those who employ this designation? Note that I am not asking whether social sin exists, nor am I interested in finding out *what it is really like* in these pages, though these would be fascinating questions. This book operates one level of abstraction behind those sorts of questions. Fact: theologians use words like 'social sin', 'systems of oppression', 'the relational self' and 'structural sin' all the time. Fact: recourse to such terminology is prompted by legitimate reservations regarding the viability of alternative traditional concepts, largely because these concepts are seen as inappropriately individualistic. When such new terms as those above replace old ones, one must ask whether their billing as 'new and improved' really holds up. Yet in order to do this, the specific proposals being offered need to be understood, in all their bewildering diversity. A map of this new terrain is needed before it is even conceivable to navigate through its deserts and meadows.

In addition to my functionally naïve nominalism, then, the method employed in the following pages is similar to Edmund Husserl's self-described phenomenological method. In the 1931 introduction to his *Ideas: General Introduction to Pure Phenomenology* Husserl compared the phenomenological philosopher to an explorer trying to chart new territory.[10] Whether this ground has been mapped, he does not know. He only knows it to be the 'trackless wilds of a new continent'.[11] He moves forward, plotting as he goes, noting what he sees, slowly building his map. When he is done, he will have no time for 'the refusals of geographers who judge the reports in the light of their own experiences and habits of thought, and on the strength of this exempt themselves from all the trouble of making a journey into the land proclaimed to be new'.[12] Husserl also knew the limits of his philosophical cartography, as I am all too aware of my own. 'The far horizons of a phenomenological philosophy, to speak geographically, have disclosed themselves ... The author sees the infinite open country of the true philosophy, the "promised land" on which he himself will never step.'[13]

In drawing my theological map I try to let the texts being considered speak both for themselves and to each other. Readers will not find here a highly original argument about the nature of social sin, partly due to my convictions about the importance of detailed theological examination of history, even

10.   Edmund Husserl, *Ideas: General Introduction to Pure Phenomenology*, trans. W. R. Boyce Gibson (London, Allen, 1931).
11.   Ibid., 22.
12.   Ibid., 23.
13.   Ibid., 29.

recent history, for subsequent creative theology, and partly due to what I take to be the next necessary steps in Christian theological reflection on sin and fallenness. What is needed on that last score, I think, is a thorough assessment of what has happened in theological reflection on sin since the sea-changes of modernity and, putatively, postmodernity. In fact, the impetus for this book grew out of the concrete experience of searching card catalogue after card catalogue in vain for just such a work. Regretting its unfortunate absence, this book seeks to fill that void. It will be for future explorers of this terrain to develop.

Overview of the Contents

As I noted above in the thesis statement, I will not be defending the claim that an overly individualistic doctrine of sin is in need of change. That this is so seems plain to me, though a defence of this position as well as an account of its development as a problem would be books in themselves. And the simple fact of the matter is that the theologians discussed in this book have indeed operated under this assumption (and have, to varying degrees, defended it, too), so a work examining the positions they prefer to individualism may safely bracket concerns over the correctness of rejecting individualism. What they have written, they have written, and this deserves attention on its own grounds. The question here considered, then, is not precisely in what way, or even whether or not, individualism is a problem in the doctrine of sin, but what ways around it are on offer.

Wide reading in nineteenth-century theology confirms the thesis that basically two such proposals have been tendered. In Chapters 2 and 3, I exposit and briefly critique these two proposals. One way of describing this is to call them two 'types' of rejection of individualism.[14] The first type is represented by Albrecht Ritschl, particularly in his criticism of Friedrich Schleiermacher. Ritschl found Schleiermacher's doctrine of sin to be too individualistic and tried to correct and go beyond it by focusing on sin's corporate and social dimensions. Specifically, Ritschl joined the language of the 'kingdom of sin' and the 'kingdom of evil' to more traditional formulations of individual sin in order to emend Schleiermacher's excessively individualistic focus. I regularly refer to this general strategy as the 'structural sin' type.

The second type of rejection of individualism in sin is called the 'relational

---

14.   Though this book is a good deal less sophisticated in its usage of a typology, the reader should know that the work of Ernst Troeltsch, H. Richard Niebuhr and Hans W. Frei is in the background of my thinking about these matters, especially these representative works: Troeltsch, *The Social Teachings of the Christian Churches*, 2 vols, trans. Olive Wyon (Louisville: Westminster John Knox Press, 1992); Niebuhr, *Christ and Culture* (San Francisco: Harper, 2001); and Frei, *Types of Christian Theology*, ed. William C. Placher and George Hunsinger (New Haven: Yale University Press, 1992).

self' type. This strategy seeks to show that an individual's sin is never the individual's alone, precisely because the 'self' emerges as an acting subject by relating to a whole host of other *relata* which are not the self. Thus if sin is to be understood aright, this whole network of relationships in which selfhood is forged must be considered. When only the will of the individual is considered theologically, the real dynamics of sin escape us. This second type is represented by the Reformed theologian John W. Nevin, particularly in his extensive criticisms of Charles G. Finney's doctrine of sin.

Once these two views have been scrutinized closely and demarcated clearly, we have a major conceptual tool in place with which to begin making sense of how social sin has been understood in the last five decades. The subsequent three chapters analyse and compare doctrines of social and individual sin in selected theologies of liberation. Chapter 4 deals with several Latin American liberation theologians, selected according to the criteria outlined below. Chapter 5 examines several feminist and womanist authors, and Chapter 6 studies Asian and Asian-American doctrines of sin, particularly Korean *Minjung* theology. After all of this new territory has been mapped out, the book concludes with a summary that makes recommendations for proceeding along the avenues of reflection opened up in the earlier analyses. Specifically, I assert that a future doctrine of social sin should include elements of *both* types of emendations to individualism, the structural sin type *and* the relational type. None of the theologians studied in Chapters 2 through 6 is able compellingly to integrate an appreciation of the extrapersonal, structural dimension of sin with a developed understanding of selfhood forged in relationship with other selves and other terms (creation, one's body, God, etc.) of relation. This lack manifests itself in conceptual imprecision regarding the object of sin (whether and how it is against God, creation, other selves, etc.), the status of sin as 'act' (given that structures and systems cannot 'act' in the way that a human person can), the relation between 'actual' and 'original' sin, and especially the extremely difficult problem of maintaining individual moral responsibility while admitting of the extrapersonal nature of sin.

Why these *Theologians?*

My principles for the selection of theologians whose views are discussed are not easy to enumerate. First, I have sought to balance influential theologians – whose views are well known but must nonetheless be addressed – with less known thinkers, whose work may deserve increased attention. This is particularly true in Chapter 4, where thinkers like the Mexican-American biblical scholar Juan Alfaro and the Argentine Methodist bishop Aldo Etchegoyen make appearances, and Chapter 3, where John Williamson Nevin's undeservedly neglected theology takes centre stage. Second, I have also tried to take a more global approach to the question of sin than is typical: the theologians considered in the following pages live or lived on six continents in dozens of countries. While I firmly believe in the principles of contextualization, there has not been ample space in the following pages to document the considerations of 'situatedness' that lay in the background of many of my judgements. My worries about the reductionism endemic to abuses of contextualization, to be perfectly honest about the matter, also figured into that decision. I trust, however, that I have shown sufficient sensitivity in such matters to escape censure, and the contexts have been thoroughly considered 'behind the scenes'.

Third, the political views of the first four authors were actually considered in some detail. I intend to show that the issue of unjust and sinful social arrangements is a matter of universal human concern. It is neither a 'liberal' hobbyhorse nor a 'conservative' patsy. Schleiermacher and Ritschl are both squarely in the liberal camp of European theology, and Nevin and Finney anchor American conservatism. I invite my readers, therefore, to become as uncomfortable as I am with stereotypes regarding the theological viewpoints assumed to be taken by thinkers of a given political persuasion.

Finally, the most important criterion in determining which views to take up has been the extent to which the central problematic of the book has been addressed by them. Many books have been written on sin in the last half-century which, while they were otherwise often fascinating, have comparably little to say about the interplay between corporate and individualist emphases. Again, some works, due to their influence, simply have *had* to be included.[15] On the whole, however, the less interesting thinker who has tried to think through systemic sin is more likely to be treated in these pages than the most brilliant individualist.

Scope of the Project

This book is not a survey of the doctrine of sin. No chapter in it is a survey of the areas it covers. This is an analysis of one major aspect of hamartiology in the last 150 years, particularly in the last fifty. The most obvious omissions are the thinkers often described as 'neo-Orthodox'. Barth, Tillich, Bultmann, Brunner and the Niebuhr brothers appear only sporadically in these pages. This omission compels a defence. There are two reasons for not dealing more closely with these theologians. First, the literature on the doctrines of sin in neo-Orthodox thought is so vast that one more book in that area seems superfluous. Second, whether to do so is right or wrong, these thinkers have been accused of tending too much towards individualism in their formulations of sin. I do not want to adjudicate that debate, but it is not hard to see why it would be hard to defend the neo-Orthodox on this point. For example, Reinhold Niebuhr may have appeared in 1932 to be thinking of something like a doctrine of social sin when he published his

---

15.   I have included in the bibliography many such works that did not make it into this book but which lie in the background of my thinking on the matter.

Moral Man and Immoral Society.[16] Yet when a decade later he gave an explicit theological description of sin in his *The Nature and Destiny of Man*, sin was articulated in nearly wholly individualistic terms.[17] Barth's emphasis on the centrality of the Christian community could be seen as an advance away from individualism, yet his explicit treatments of sin in *The Epistle to the Romans* and especially in Volumes III and IV of the *Church Dogmatics* are almost entirely individualistic. The reliance of Bultmann, Tillich and others on forms of existentialism, itself basically individualistic, gives them difficulty in describing sin in an importantly social fashion.

Thus, instead of offering what would have to be a superficial analysis of the neo-Orthodox theologians on sin, I have chosen another approach. One could think of this project as a set of bookends on neo-Orthodoxy. While I want to be clear that I am not arguing anything like an historical thesis, it is true that Ritschl and Nevin had offered extensive proposals on the social nature of sin before the early twentieth-century shift to the individual, and it is also true that much of the recent writings on sin have re-emphasized the social, extrapersonal dimension. Bracketing out the neo-Orthodox thus makes possible closer comparisons between the nineteenth-century 'types' and twentieth-century 'manifestations' of doctrines of social sin.

I want also to be clear that liberation theologians do not have a corner on the social sin market. Dozens of major works have been written by non-liberationist authors on this topic. Some of them have been deeply informed by liberation perspectives, and some register no such debt at all.[18] Works like these are omitted not because they are unpersuasive or irredeemably problematic, but because space would not allow for their inclusion, and also because the liberationist proposals differ much more widely than do the non-liberationist ones, thus making the need for a map through that terrain more pressing.

Why this Book?

The topic taken up in these pages is a significant one for several reasons. Three of these contributions are somewhat broad in scope, and five others are rather more specific. First, broadly speaking, simply the way the material is organized represents a profound contribution in making sense of where the doctrine of sin has gone in the last four or five decades. The presentation of such a diversity of material gives an indication of the richness of thought

16. Reinhold Niebuhr, *Moral Man and Immoral Society* (New York: Charles Scribner's Sons, 1932). I cannot resist reminding the reader that Niebuhr later rued the fact that the title was not *The Not So Moral Man in His Even Less Moral Communities!* Niebuhr, *Man's Nature and His Communities* (New York: Charles Scribner's Sons, 1965), 22.

17. Reinhold Niebuhr, *The Nature and Destiny of Man*, 2 vols (New York: Charles Scribner's Sons, 1941).

18. For a basic but reliable introduction to this topic, cf. Mark O'Keefe, *What Are They Saying about Social Sin?* (New York: Paulist Press, 1990).

that the desire to conceive of sin in non-individualistic ways has manifested. And the fact that it has not been possible to include even close to all of the relevant material testifies even more strongly to how heavily this problem weighs on the collective theological mind. Plainly what is needed is some way of making sense of this diverse theological shift. Grouping various strands of liberation theologies together under the rubric of structural sins and sins of relational selves will not, in the end, be a sufficient way of making sense of social sin. The project that does that will have to be much larger than this one. But the achievements of this book may well make that bigger one possible.

Second, many scholars and people in Christian churches have been concerned by the polarizing effects liberation theology has had in contemporary theological discourse. Advocates of liberationist models have often been so thorough in their rejection of traditional theological conceptualities that one wonders what possible continuity with the church's proclamation of and about Jesus Christ could possible endure. Critics of liberationist approaches have stressed its discontinuity with traditional theologies so much that one wonders if there could possibly have been any treatment of liberation themes before, say, Vatican II or Gutiérrez' *A Theology of Liberation*. This book takes a small but significant step towards some kind of rapprochement. Ritschl was no liberationist and would probably have decried 'reflection on praxis' as 'meditation on sinful action'. Nevin was no liberationist, and would have been appalled at a theological appropriation of Marxist, or even Marxian, social analysis. Yet the two share a common commitment to the theme liberation theologians care about more, perhaps, than any other; all of them are committed in their writings and in their lives to building up the *community* of the church, and when the concept of sin is thus implicated, that means correcting the vision of theological traditions from their individualist myopia.

Third, the book concludes with a brief and relatively general recommendation for future doctrines of social sin. Immanuel Kant laboured for decades to show clearly the limits and constraints within which speculative thought was legitimately located, and after the publication of his incredibly influential *Critique of Pure Reason*, his critics thought that Kant been so sceptical of the possibilities of human knowledge that he must have been misguided. He therefore published his *Prolegomena to Any Future Metaphysics* to assuage their anxieties that human knowledge was not really possible, and his later work showed positively that it was possible. As long as parallels are not drawn very closely between the author of that work and this one, I see my task along similar lines. Though I am at times highly critical of the forms that doctrines of social sin have taken, I remain convinced that an adequate formulation is possible, and the criticisms I make along the way of current attempts should not be read as attacks on the project of a social understanding of sin as such, but as an attempt to establish clearly the limits and constraints within which a doctrine of social sin can be located in Christian theology. Thus I will conclude with what I think is a third area of the book's significance by offering what might be termed a brief *Prolegomenon to Any Future Doctrine of Sin*. This is something more than a wish list of features that should be included, and something less than a full theory of how the difficulties in speaking of social sin can be avoided.

Aside from those broad contributions, this book makes some very specific theological advances. For a long time most theologians in America (as well as many in Europe) simply assumed that Albrecht Ritschl had really said what Karl Barth, Emil Brunner, Rudolf Bultmann and the rest of the neo-Orthodox theologians said that he said. That the neo-Orthodox picture is a distorted stereotype is now beyond doubt; Ritschl was far more subtle than his detractors gave him credit for, and good deal more concerned with sin and grace than one would gather reading *about* him rather than actually reading him. This state of affairs has, thankfully, largely changed. There has been a 'Ritschl Renaissance' of sorts in recent years. Works have appeared discussing much more positively his contributions to biblical scholarship, to the philosophy of religion, theological methodology, and many other doctrinal loci. But there has been no real contribution in the area of his doctrine of sin. Though Chapter 2 is intended mostly to set the stage for an analysis of twentieth-century doctrines of sin, it also has significant value on its own as an analysis of Ritschl's particular conception of sin and the Kingdom of God.

There has never been a John Nevin renaissance, because he was never remembered well enough to have been forgotten and then 'reborn'. This is a travesty of theological historiography. John Nevin and Phillip Schaff, the founders and greatest proponents of what came to be called the 'Mercersburg Theology', have always been held by qualified commentators to be the most brilliant minds of nineteenth-century American theology, but their thought has been almost completely neglected, and when taken up, has been characterized more by sycophancy than critical appreciation. Chapter 3 thus also makes a more balanced contribution to the secondary literature on the Mercersburg movement.

Despite the centrality of the concept of structural sin in Latin American liberation theology, there exists only *one* comprehensive essay and *zero* full-sized monographs on the subject.[19] I find this to be simply incredible. Although as I pointed out above, no chapter in this book is a 'survey' of the material it covers, Chapter 4 on Latin American liberation theology's views of structural sin is, on its own, one of the most developed extant treatments of this theme. Putting all of those theologians together in one place and letting their similarities and differences come into relief is thus in itself a modest but valid contribution.

The same may be said, in the fourth place, about the chapter on feminist and womanist theology. There are rich secondary materials on the topic of women and sin, but relatively few concentrate on the array of views women

---

19. Vitor Westhelle, 'O Tamanho do Paraiso: Presupostos do Conceito de Pecado na Theologia Latino-Americana', in *Estudos Teologicos* 38 (1998): 239–51.

hold on 'how sin looks' from their perspective, compared to the ones that ask 'how women sin'. While the second of those questions is an important one, it receives relatively little attention in Chapter 5. Finally, Chapter 6 makes a valid, stand-alone contribution to what was once a very exciting theology coming from Asia, the *Minjung* theology. Though I will not be explicitly defending the thesis that this theology has now run its course, this is the opinion of many experts, and Chapter 6 can be read as a kind of appreciative *in memoriam* for it. Too few Western theologians engaged the themes of *Minjung* theology, and its possible decline need not prevent us from mining its riches in the future.

Part I

Nineteenth-Century Types of Social Sin

With no further ado, let us embark in the spirit of Husserl's intrepid explorer through the wilds of social sin. Our first destination will be the rich, and too often disparaged, thought of that great Lutheran theologian Albrecht Ritschl, and his still-greater Reformed counterpart, F. D. E. Schleiermacher. Chapter 2 exposits briefly the salient points of Schleiermacher's view of sin, with particular emphasis on those aspects relevant to an understanding of social sin (though as Ritschl points out, these are relatively few). Once his basic view is in place, we see how Ritschl exposes many shortcomings in Schleiermacher's doctrine of sin, weaving together direct commentary from Ritschl on Schleiermacher's position and Ritschl's own constructive, less polemical suggestions for a better approach to social sin. This view pays careful attention to the social structures of sin, headed under the symbol of the Kingdom of sin, which stands in direct opposition to the Kingdom of God.

Chapter 3 takes exactly the same approach to two nineteenth-century American theologians. There is first an exposition of Charles Finney's views on sin derived from an examination of his doctrinal writings and from the position on sin implicit in his writings on revivals. We then analyse his work on some issues which should be prime candidates for counting as 'social sin', namely economic exploitation and slavery, as a means of testing our theory about the individualistic nature of sin in his theology. John Nevin is chosen as a representative critic of this position, and his thought aptly typifies the relational self type of rejection of individualism. I weave together both Nevin's explicit opposition to Finney's revivalism and his proposed alternative of the self-in-relation, derived in part from German Idealism. The chapters in Part II then take up this twofold scheme for looking at doctrines of social sin for the aim of assessing contemporary twentieth- and twenty-first-century doctrinal proposals.

Chapter 2

SCHLEIERMACHER AND RITSCHL
ON INDIVIDUAL AND SOCIAL SIN

Why Schleiermacher?

Friedrich Schleiermacher's *The Christian Faith* is admittedly an unorthodox place to begin a discussion of twentieth-century doctrines of sin.[1] He obviously is not from the time period, and he seems to have had little positive effect on the thinkers whose volumes fill the shelves of hamartiology over the last several decades. Reinhold Niebuhr – whose opinions about sin (whether one agreed with them or not) seemed to matter more than anyone else's in this century – considered Schleiermacher to be a Pelagian.[2] Niebuhr complained that Schleiermacher had conflated actual sin with the consciousness thereof, and that his notion of original sin too greatly delocalized sin from the will, situated as it was in a kind of ethereally distorted subjectivity.[3] While Karl Barth had deep respect for Schleiermacher's contributions to theology in general, his approval did not extend to the doctrine of sin.[4] In fact, it was precisely Schleiermacher's alleged confusion regarding sin and grace that led Barth to accuse Schleiermacher of 'destroying Reformation theology.'[5] Rather than locating sin entirely within the sinner, and grace entirely within Jesus Christ, Schleiermacher, according to Barth, made them piecemeal concomitants in the consciousness of the sinner. Thus, 'We are confronted at this point with an abysmal error in Schleiermacher's teaching.'[6] Still more vanguards of the neo-Orthodox, Paul Tillich and Emil Brunner, are

---

1.   F. D. E. Schleiermacher, *The Christian Faith*, trans. H. R. Mackintosh, et al. (Edinburgh: T&T Clark, 1989). This is hereafter cited as CF with section number. This is a translation of the second German edition, from 1830.

2.   Reinhold Niebuhr, *The Nature and Destiny of Man* 1:245–8 describes certain 'Pelagian Doctrines'.

3.   Ibid., 246–7. Niebuhr's prooftexts are CF 68–9.

4.   Cf. especially his *Protestantische Theologie im 19. Jahrhundert: ihre Vorgeschichte und ihre Geschichte* (Zürich: Evangelischer Verlag, 1947), 419–22, and idem, *The Theology of Schleiermacher*, trans. Geoffrey Bromiley (Grand Rapids: Eerdmans, 1982), 118–22.

5.   Karl Barth, *Protestant Thought: From Rousseau to Ritschl*, trans. Brian Cozens (New York: Harpers, 1959), 354.

6.   Karl Barth, *Church Dogmatics*, trans. G. Bromiley and T. F. Torrance (Edinburgh, T & T Clark, 1960), III/3:333.

likewise unimpressed with Schleiermacher's interpretation of the human condition.[7] Schleiermacher's detractors are not even limited to the neo-Orthodox. The German Catholic theologian Thomas Pröpper, for example, finds Schleiermacher's notion of sin to be shallow and harmless.[8] Further, Hermann Fischer, who would agree with Pröpper's claim regarding the shallowness of sin, holds that Schleiermacher's view of sin implies that sin is at its strongest transient, and at it weakest, merely illusory.[9]

Schleiermacher did have certain important admirers on this locus, such as Søren Kierkegaard (admittedly while writing under the pseudonym Vigilius Haufniensis). Kierkegaard praised Schleiermacher's method for discussing sin, noting 'Schleiermacher's immortal service to this science.'[10] But it seems that in terms of content, Kierkegaard was not indebted in any significant way to Schleiermacher.[11] Walter Rauschenbusch claimed to be a proponent of Schleiermacher's view of *original* sin, using Schleiermacher's insights to develop his own views of the transmission of original sin not by biological means but through social institutions. This does not, however, necessarily

7.   Brunner found Schleiermacher to be too 'naturalistic,' and thought sin to be nearly hypostatized in the inevitably obscured development of the (im)pious self-consciousness. Brunner nowhere, however, criticizes Schleiermacher for being too individualistic, and seems unaware of his language of social evil. Cf. his *Der Mensch im Widerspruch: Die christliche Lehre vom wahren und vom wirklichen Menschen* (Zürich: Zwingli Verlag, 1941), 82 and 259, for illustrative examples. Tillich is cautious in his dismissal, hinting that Schleiermacher's view is weak since sin could accordingly be overcome by a simple convergence of the human's biological and spiritual development. Cf. his *Perspectives on 19th and 20th Century Protestant Theology*, ed. Carl E. Braaten (New York, Harper and Row, 1967), 113–14.

8.   Thomas Pröpper, 'Schleiermachers Bestimmung des Christentums und der Erlösung', in *Theologische Quartalschrift* 168 (1988): 193–214

9.   Hermann Fischer, *Subjektivität und Sünde: Kierkegaards Begriff der Sünde mit ständiger Rücksicht auf Schleiermachers Lehre von der Sünde* (Itzehoe: Spur Verlag, 1963), 77–82. More representative examples of criticisms can be found in Maureen Junker, *Das Urbild des Gottesbewusstseins: zur Entwicklung der Religionstheorie und Christologie Schleiermachers von der ersten zur zweiten Auflage der Glaubenslehre* (Berlin: Walter de Gruyter, 1990).

10.   Kierkegaard, *The Concept of Anxiety*, trans. Reidar Thomte (Princeton: Princeton University Press), 20. In characteristic Kierkegaardian fashion, he goes on to lament that 'Schleiermacher was left behind long ago when men chose Hegel.'

11.   This would have to be qualified more carefully than is possible here. Schleiermacher and Kierkegaard are the two figures who do theological anthropology a great service by trying to dehistoricize the fall, which is significant. But the two ways of going about doing it are quite different. Each describes sin as a distortion in one's subjectivity. Kierkegaard's account in *Works of Love*, trans. Howard V. Hong and Edna H. Hong (Princeton: Princeton University Press, 1995) is thoroughly interpersonal; subjectivity is created in the presence of other subjects. Yet his more strictly dogmatic accounts of sin in *The Concept of Anxiety* and *The Sickness unto Death* are on the whole more individualistic despite his notion of interpersonal subjectivity. Something like the reverse is true for Schleiermacher; though the consciousness of the subject emerges in a social context, its 'subjectivity' is always there.

apply to the current project, since we are looking at the ways in which systemic, extrapersonal reality can be said to be actually sinful, not merely a cipher for a different conception of original sin.[12]

Given such vehement denunciation by so many noteworthy detractors, and such remarkably *muted* praise by so few supporters, what earthly reason could there be for a re-examination of Friedrich Schleiermacher's concept of sin? Could it be that those who have criticized him have largely missed the mark with their objections? No, I do not find that this is the case.[13] Could it be that his advocates saw in Schleiermacher's concept of sin a foundation which could support further reflection and development? No, I do not find this to be the case, either.[14] Ironically, I argue that a re-examination of Schleiermacher is relevant for the current project neither because his detractors were wrong nor because his admirers were right. Instead, looking again at Schleiermacher helps because the reasons given for the rejection of his analysis of sin were largely misdirected in the twentieth century.

One of Schleiermacher's more immediate theological descendants saw a much more important shortcoming in his formulation of sin. Albrecht Ritschl, the next great theologian in Germany after the deaths of Schleiermacher and Hegel, saw much more incisively into Schleiermacher's doctrine of sin than the neo-Orthodox were able. Ritschl's objections to Schleiermacher focus neither on a putative hypostatization of sin in the sinner, nor on an allegedly shallow appreciation of sin's gravity, nor on its transient or illusory character. Rather, Ritschl points out the ineluctably *individualistic* character of the doctrine. One of Ritschl's great achievements was gleaning relevant insights about the nature, task, form and even *possibility* of theology from Schleiermacher, without buying wholesale into the trappings of the content

---

12.   One particularly relevant citation is Walter Rauschenbusch, *A Theology for the Social Gospel* (Nashville: Abingdon, 1978), 92–3. Rauschenbusch's main point is that Schleiermacher's view of original sin as a social condition helpfully attracted attention away from the biological perspective shaping the *peccatum originale originatum*. The result was Rauschenbusch's positive statement that social arrangements, too, could transmit sin in history, but Rauschenbusch turned his attention away from Schleiermacher when trying to find a vocabulary for a social view of actual sin.

13.   One attempt at a vindication of Schleiermacher from these charges can be found in Robert Lee Vance, *Sin and Self-Consciousness in the Thought of Friedrich Schleiermacher* (New York: Mellen Press, 1994). Experts in the field have found the attempt unsuccessful. For one example, cf. Walter Wyman's review in *Religious Studies Review* 22:4 (1996), 334.

14.   John Hick holds that Schleiermacher's anthropology is valuable as a resource for developing a theodicy and conception of *evil*. But that is not the same thing as a doctrine of sin, and even Hick himself does not find Schleiermacher to be much of a guide at this point. Cf. his *Evil and the God of Love* (London: Macmillan, 1960), especially 323–4. Walter Wyman is perhaps more optimistic regarding the prospects for a Schleiermachian recovery in postmodernity, but even he is cognizant of the significant problems with such a project. Walter Wyman, 'Rethinking the Christian Doctrine of Sin: Schleiermacher and Hick's "Irenaean Type",' *Journal of Religion* 74:2 (1994), 199–217.

of his substantive theological claims.[15] Ritschl saw that Schleiermacher had attempted to go beyond the distorted consciousness of the individual which has been named by the Christian symbol 'sin' to a notion of sin which was at least trans-personal, and possibly even communal or social. But he had not gone far enough. Too many strands were left untied in what Schleiermacher had written, and too many mines for an effective vocabulary of social sin were left unexcavated in what he had not. Ritschl's proposed alternative was to discuss sin in terms of *both* the individual under the symbol of justification and reconciliation, *and* in terms of the collective under the symbol of the Kingdom of God.

Before adjourning to the specifics of Ritschl's position it will be helpful to examine in closer detail the particulars of Schleiermacher's formulation of sin. When doing so, I shall focus attention not on the shortcomings of the doctrine already pointed out by the neo-Orthodox and others in the twentieth century. With the exception of Niebuhr's labelling of Schleiermacher as a Pelagian, I view those criticisms to be largely on target.[16] Instead, I will focus attention where it should have been concentrated all along, and where Ritschl placed his attention over a century ago, namely, on the interplay between the social and individual aspects of sin and its theological description.

Development of Consciousness, Individual and Social

Schleiermacher was one of the first Christian theologians who did not think of the fall as a strictly historical event. The Garden of Eden had represented for Augustine, as for virtually all of those whom he influenced, an actual historical state of original perfection, wherein humans were possessed of their 'original righteousness'.[17] The fall of Adam and Eve was a fall from

15.   The most balanced treatment I am aware of regarding how important Schleiermacher's contribution was to the rethinking of the nature of doctrine in the modern period is Claude Welch, *Protestant Thought in the Nineteenth Century*, 2 vols. (New Haven: Yale University Press, 1972), 1:59–85. On Ritschl's relatively positive and generous appropriation of Schleiermacher on several aspects of doctrine, method, and critique, cf. the excellent work by Christoph Senft, *Wahrhaftigkeit und Wahrheit: die Theologie des 19. Jahrhunderts zwischen Orthodoxie und Aufklärung* (Tübingen: Mohr Siebeck, 1956), and the one-sidedly critical but still helpful Franz Courth, *Das Wesen des Christentums in der liberalen Theologie: dargestellt am Werk Fr. Schleiermachers, F.C. Baurs und A. Ritschls* (Frankfurt: Lang, 1977).

16.   Niebuhr's accusation misses the mark because he tries to fit Schleiermacher into his own Augustinian framework, instead of reading him out of his own Romantic (and in Hick's sense, Irenaean) framework. If Augustine is allowed unconditionally to set the terms for the doctrine of sin, Schleiermacher could be a Pelagian. If not, he is not.

17.   Augustine's first use of this concept comes in *De Peccatorum Meritis et Remissione*. Yet this is only one strand of Augustinian thought on the matter. Another strand names *concupiscentia* as original sin. Thomas Aquinas combined these emphases, merging the Anselmian-Augustinian tradition of original sin as the privation of original

this state to a sinful state, the state of original sin. That state issues inevitably in actual sin.

Schleiermacher's alternative vision, however, does not rely on the historicity of the passage in Genesis. Part of the reason for this is methodological; Schleiermacher does not think it is appropriate for a dogmatician to pronounce on an exegetical matter.[18] But more importantly, Schleiermacher simply thinks of 'original perfection' in quite a different way. To say that creation is 'good' is basically to affirm that God has made creatures that can come to know and love God. That is to say, goodness is not a state of moral activity, but a framework for moral possibility. Creation is 'perfect' when it is, in principle, perfectible.[19] However, on Schleiermacher's view, though God created humanity good, we are nonetheless left incomplete and in need of maturation. We develop and grow. In our early stages, we are basically like all the other creatures. We react more or less instinctively to the environment around us, according to what Schleiermacher calls our 'confused animal grade' consciousness.[20] But then we also come to have perceptions and feelings, and these perceptions and feelings are made known to us through our 'sensible consciousness'. After a while, we begin to reflect on our thoughts and feelings, and we begin to understand ourselves as consciously situated in the physical world. This creates a kind of self-transcendence and self-understanding. The final stage in this development is God-consciousness, wherein we begin to understand who or what God is as the 'whence' of our existence. Located in this integration of consciousness is the famous 'feeling of absolute dependence'.[21] It must be carefully noted that while this is a developmental view, it is not as though once the higher forms of consciousness emerge, the old ones fall away. To the contrary, the sensible consciousness and self-consciousness remain for all of one's life, and exist as the conditions of the possibility of God-consciousness. Before segueing into the properly dogmatic part of the *Glaubenslehre*, Schleiermacher hints at the 'evil condition' such an anthropology prefigures, later to be named sin, which is 'an obstruction or arrest of the vitality of the higher self-consciousness, so that there comes to be no union of it with

justice (in Anselm, cf. *De conceptu virginali* II.1 and XX.1) with the Lombard-Augustinian tradition of concupiscence (for Lombard, cf., among many other places, *Libri Sententiarum* II.Cap.198: 'Quod originale peccatum dicitur fomes peccati, id est concupiscentia'. Cf. *Summa Theologiae* IaIIae.82.3. Schleiermacher's and Ritschl's Protestant forebears tended to stress the concupiscence strand of this tradition.

18.   Schleiermacher writes, '[A]s regards the Mosaic narrative: in accordance with the limits which we have assigned to Dogmatics, that science cannot be expected to determine how the said record is to be interpreted, and whether it purports to be history or allegory. Without encroaching upon the work of exegesis or criticism, however, we can use the story ... in illustration of the universal process of the rise of sin as something always and everywhere the same.' CF 72.5.

19.   I am here summarizing CF 59–60.

20.   CF 5.1.

21.   CF 4.2 and 4.4

the various determinations of the sensible self-consciousness, and thus little or no religious life'. Schleiermacher then continues, saying, 'we may give to this condition, in its most extreme form, the name of *Godlessness*, or better, *God-forgetfulness*'.[22]

Sin as Distortion of Consciousness in an Individual

Sin fits into this anthropology in two ways: developmentally and socially. In the developmental sense, Schleiermacher locates sin in the bad habits one acquires when mired in states dominated by the sensible self-consciousness. He says that sin is made known to us as the power and work of the time before one's God-consciousness could arise and take root in the self. The sensible self-consciousness tends to dominate our willing and acting, for the exigencies of the material world are always close at hand and demand our attention. We should note at this point that this strength of the sensible self-consciousness is not necessarily bad. In fact, it is a good thing to have, both as a means to developing the higher consciousnesses and as a means of securing the basic needs of existence. Sin emerges, however, at the level of the individual when the self is unable successfully to integrate the 'higher' or religious self-consciousness with the lower ones. The power and intensity of the God-consciousness is limited or obscured. This disintegration of the pious self-consciousness both *is* sin and eventuates in further sin.

Schleiermacher compares his view to the apostle Paul's in Romans 7. On Schleiermacher's reading of Paul, the split self (flesh and spirit) knows what it should do but cannot muster the resources actually to do it. The flesh trumps the spirit. This could be interpreted two ways. First, there is the obvious sense of the power of the flesh (or the sensible self-consciousness) due in part to its developmental anteriority. The sensible self-consciousness may have the psychological equivalent of 'squatter's rights' on the territory of the self. Or in Schleiermacher's words, 'here the flesh has habit on its side as the real law in its members'.[23] But Schleiermacher also discusses this notion of the power of the flesh in a second, more subtle way as the disparity between 'will-power and insight'.[24] We can, by virtue of the gift of our God-consciousness, *see* farther down the road than our self is able to travel. From the standpoint of grace, our God-consciousness can fragmentarily recognize and know the pious life free from sin, but we cannot cooperate in the full realization thereof. Our will-power and our insight conflict at their intersection. Or as Walter E. Wyman puts it, for Schleiermacher 'were this not the case, human beings would be either brutes (unable to imagine anything they could not do), or "some kind of incomprehensible wonders" (able to turn the thought instantly

22. CF 11.2.
23. CF 68.1.
24. CF 68.3.

into deed)'.[25] Part of our created goodness is the possibility of the integration of God-consciousness with lower self-consciousness. The adverse side-effect of this good creation is that the insight afforded by the God-consciousness outpaces, at times, the gait of the sensible self-conscious will. We should be careful to note, however, that even though Schleiermacher sometimes speaks of the God-consciousness as though it existed independently, even when the God-consciousness does develop in the self, it is never 'fully' attained, in the sense that one could be conscious only and totally of God. It is a kind of conceptual abstraction, or even a kind of heurism.[26]

The development of the God-consciousness so described applies equally to corporate, as well as individual, structures. Put differently, in addition to the presence of a genuine development of the God-consciousness in the self, there is also a communal aspect to this development. The more ancient the culture, presumably, the less chance a proper God-consciousness had to be developed and cultivated. The 'higher' and 'lower' self-consciousness could not be adequately distinguished.[27] The development of the self must have some connection to the context in which the self is formed; Schleiermacher was no atomist – he saw that to be a self meant, in part, to become a self in the presence of already developed selves.

Given that there seems to be no conceivable way to avoid the structures which allow for the presence (and even dominance or integration) of the God-consciousness, it becomes perfectly natural to ask whether Schleiermacher has thereby hypostatized sin. On first glance, this looks like a tenable read, for it is hard to see how any human, given this developmental structure by God, could become anything but too firmly rooted in one's own lower self-consciousness. But Schleiermacher says that this view misunderstands the goodness of God's creation. What is good about the creation of humans is, as noted above, that the God-consciousness in the human is possible. It remains possible even after the incursion of sin. Schleiermacher's notion of creation

---

25.   Wyman, 'Rethinking the Christian Doctrine of Sin', 208–209. The texts Wyman cites come from Schleiermacher's sermon 'Christ the Liberator', in *Servant of the Word: Selected Sermons of Friedrich Schleiermacher*, trans. Dawn DeVries (Philadelphia: Fortress, 1987), 47–9. This sermon is wholly consistent, however, with the treatment of foresight and will-power in CF 68.

26.   'Finally, not only is the feeling of absolute dependence in itself a co-existence of God in the self-consciousness, but the totality of being from which … all determinations of the self-consciousness proceed, is comprehended under that feeling of dependence; and therefore all modifications of the higher self-consciousness may be also be represented by our describing God as the basis of this *togetherness* of being in its various distributions.' CF 30.1.

27.   CF 67.1 and 8.2. Part of Schleiermacher's analysis depends on a comparison of religions. The monotheistic faiths, according to Schleiermacher, 'evolved' from more primitive ones, and Christianity, in turn, from the monotheistic ones. I will of course not want to defend this assumption (in fact I think it is completely false), yet since it is not germane to the argument concerning social sin, I will not offer a full-scale refutation of it.

is not an original state that can be lost by Adam, but rather a durable, even permanent, structure of the world. The fact that it is not a state, I argue, should not count as evidence that the depths to which sin binds us are in fact quite shallow. On the contrary, as Schleiermacher writes, 'Throughout all the entire range of sinful humanity there is not a single perfectly good action, i.e. one that purely expresses the power of the God-consciousness; nor is there one perfectly pure moment, i.e. one in which something does not exist in secret antagonism to the God-consciousness.'[28] Sin understood from a developmental framework, as opposed to one based on a spatiotemporal 'fall' need not be seen as harmless.

So much for the developmental aspect of sin. There is also a social dimension to sin, even sin understood at the level of the individual. Humans do not develop in a vacuum. There are myriad outside influences that factor into our self-understandings, and therefore into our God-consciousness. This is the subject matter of §71 of *The Christian Faith*, which is one of the most powerful restatements of the doctrine of original sin I am aware of, and one of the most novel of all of Schleiermacher's theological novelties. In it Schleiermacher asserts three principal theses. First, original sin is indeed inherited, because sinful individuals beget sinful individuals inevitably (though not 'necessarily').[29] Just as a prize-winning rose will not grow in unfertilized dust, so too will a person not successfully integrate his lower consciousness with his God-consciousness when placed in a matrix of sin. The tradition calls this 'originated original sin'. Nevertheless, second, each person is still guilty of their sin, because they 'ratify' originated sin by making it a part of themselves, and in turn negatively influencing those around them.[30] This is called 'originating original sin'. This implies, third, that original sin is a universal affliction, and is, in Schleiermacher's haunting phrase, 'in each, the work of all, and in all, the work of each'.[31]

Sin is not sin simply because it is wrong to fail to integrate one's higher and lower consciousness. While the primary party offended by sin is, properly speaking, the God of whom we are not adequately conscious, there exists in Schleiermacher's analysis a 'horizontal' element to sin, as well. He writes, for example, that the sinner lives 'a self-enclosed life of feeling within a sensuous vital unity, to which all sympathetic feeling for others and for the whole was subordinated'.[32] Others will feel the effects of our sins, and those others experience our sin as evil. 'Evil' is the category under which Schleiermacher analyses the social aspect of sin, and so it is there we must turn to discover what Schleiermacher says about sin at the extrapersonal, non-individualistic level.

---

28.   CF 73.1.
29.   CF 71.1. Schleiermacher uses the word 'unfailingly' to describe how actual sin proceeds from original sin.
30.   For this way of putting the matter, I am indebted to Wyman, 'Re-Thinking the Christian Doctrine of Sin', 210.
31.   CF 71.2.
32.   CF 101.2.

Social Sin and Social Evil

If one understands 'sin' as basically the inability to integrate one's world-consciousness and one's God-consciousness, it might be possible to identify the ethical, or horizontal direction of sin with the wrongly asserted power of the world-consciousness, and the religious dimension with the absence of the God-consciousness. Schleiermacher does say that 'actual sin may be either more an expression of an appetite [world-consciousness], or more a positive obscuration, i.e. a vitiation of the God-consciousness'. However, this strategy will not get us very far, for he concludes that 'We cannot wholly separate the two, for the one evokes the other.'[33] Therefore Schleiermacher chooses to frame the issue of the social effects of sin not according to their ethical cast, but rather under the rubric of sin and evil.

Schleiermacher is somewhat less than perfectly clear on the distinction between 'sin' and 'evil', so a decision must be made at the outset as to how these concepts are to be compared.[34] I shall operate under the assumption that in Schleiermacher's system, the concept of sin presupposes an *agent*, or at least human action, and that the concept of evil primarily presupposes a *patient*. A sinner 'performs' sin but undergoes evil.[35] Traditionally, evil has been divided into two types. Moral evil is the suffering which results from human action, and natural evil is suffering caused by non-human events. This further distinction is not hard and fast, of course; the same event could be experienced as both moral and natural evil. The recent flooding in the American South could be one example. The 'natural' event had both natural and human causes,[36] and the resulting suffering both natural and moral causes.[37] Schleiermacher does not divide evil among natural and moral,

33.   CF 74.2. While Schleiermacher does assert that the religious and ethical aspects of sin should be kept together in conversation, it would be almost impossible to read CF without noting that the religious side is doing most of the talking.

34.   I am grateful for a clarifying conversation with Andrew Dole on this matter.

35.   I think this is a good approximation of Schleiermacher's position, but slippage and overlap burden this distinction generally in the history of theology. Barth, for example, differentiates by the object; sin is against the Creator, evil against the creature. CD III/3:311. (He later equivocates, saying that, for example, evil is 'adverse to grace', and therefore presumably is against God. CD III/3:353.) One fascinating and directly relevant recent study which does justice to the need to think 'performing' and 'undergoing' into each other in the context of sin and evil is Marilyn McCord Adams, *Horrendous Evils and the Goodness of God* (Ithaca: Cornell University Press, 2000). See also the dated but learned essay by Walter Kasper, 'Die Lehre der Kirche vom Bösen', in *Macht des Bösen und der Glaube der Kirche*, ed. Rudolf Schnackenburg (Düsseldorf: Patmos, 1979), 68–84. The helpful distinctions of Christof Gestrich lay also in the background of my thinking on this matter, esp. 'Homo Peccator und Homo Patiens', in Gestrich, *Peccatum: Studien zur Sündenlehre* (Tübingen: Mohr Siebeck, 2003), 1–29.

36.   Among its 'human' causes would be the changes in weather patterns caused by human pollution.

37.   On the human side would be such factors as the public policy issue of the funding and construction of proper levees.

but rather natural and *social*, types.[38] 'Now, anything that gives rise to obstructions in human life so far as it is independent of human action we call *natural* evil; while what in bringing about such obstructions is really due to human action, we call *social* evil.'[39] Does this imply that Schleiermacher means the same thing by 'social evil' that was meant traditionally by 'moral evil'? For if so, then we would have no real advancement in viewing sin and evil as something more than individualistic concepts. One cannot merely change the name of an individualistic concept to 'social' and expect the meaning of its content to change, too. Let us then take a closer look to determine whether Schleiermacher can be of help in expanding the doctrine of sin from its overly individualistic bent.

Recall that in the situation of sin, the 'predominant factor is not the God-consciousness but the flesh', and so consequently

> every impression made by the world upon us and involving an obstruction of our bodily and temporal life must be reckoned as an evil, and the more so, the more definitely the moment of experience terminates solely in the flesh apart from the higher consciousness; the reason being that there is then a repression of the only principle which could in such a case restore the harmony [namely, the God-consciousness].[40]

Since the stultification of the God-consciousness can be understood as a function of the development of social systems (recall that genuine God-consciousness was, in Schleiermacher's view, only possible through the 'evolution' of Christianity from the 'lower' forms of religion), so too can the experience of sin as evil (as opposed to the origin of sin, or the act of sinning) be rightly said to be social in character. 'The world ... appears otherwise to man [sic] than it would have appeared had he had no sin.'[41] The very facticity of the experience of sin leads to a snowball effect. Sin is caused by a failure to integrate one's God-consciousness with one's lower consciousness, which is caused in turn by one's failure to identify and act rightly within the basic subject–object relations of the world. When the matter is further complicated by sin's ability to *distort* those subject–object relations, the sinner is at even more of a disadvantage to integrate his or her competing consciousnesses. Thus 'social evil' is not exactly a mere heading under which the experiences of the sins of others is cast, but also names a factor in perpetuating sin.

However, just as soon as Schleiermacher makes the assertion that social evil is a factor in perpetuating sin, he takes it halfway back. He discusses one possible view, that future sin is caused by past evil, but then rejects it. 'To advance this view ... would imply that the ultimate ground of sin lies wholly

---

38.   Schleiermacher himself is uncomfortable with the distinction, however, noting that the spread of a disease, for example, could have both natural and human causes. CF 75.2.

39.   CF 75.2.

40.   CF 75.1.

41.   Ibid.

outside of human activity, in an original ordainment of evil independent of such activity; and this would mean that sin was ... in the first instance the work of an external nature wherein evil was supposed to have its basis.'[42] This is wrong. Sin is logically and ontologically prior to evil. Evil depends on sin, not vice versa. 'In opposition to all this we record our consciousness that in the connexion between sin and evil, sin is always the primary and original element, and evil the derivative and secondary.'[43] This does not mean that evil is somehow less real than sin, just as a child is not less real than its parents. It does, however, mean that while there can be something called social evil, there can not really be anything like social sin, as we shall see below.

Schleiermacher asserts that the relationship of sin to evil is not so simple as to say that one person sins and then 'pays' for his or her sin by experiencing evil, like a glutton with a bellyache or an adulterer with syphilis. Since religion is an irreducibly social phenomenon (and since, accordingly, so is the consciousness of sin), Schleiermacher can say, 'The dependence of evil upon sin ... can be empirically established only as we consider a communal life in its entirety; on no account must the evils affecting the individual be referred to his sin as their cause.'[44] It is inappropriate, Schleiermacher concludes, for the theologian to make evil the cause of sin. While the effects of sin as evil are always present as a part of the context in which future sinning takes place, its presence there is coincidental, not causal, with respect to ensuing action.[45] This makes Schleiermacher's view of sin and evil even less promising as a remedy to individualism. The point of this passage quoted immediately above seems to be that there may not be a one-to-one correspondence between the 'amount' a single person sins and suffers. This is probably a difficult judgement to make empirically, but it seems reasonable enough. He clarifies a bit further on that, saying, 'only the merest fraction of the common evil may fall upon the author of much common depravity'.[46] Or again, 'as regards social evils: were these to be apportioned to each individual according to his share in the collective wrong-doing, we should often, as if by some magic process, have to find justice in injustice'.[47] But when a communal group as a whole is considered, Schleiermacher thinks, the two do basically equal out. It is tempting to affirm this with Schleiermacher. In some ways, after all, it seems logical to say that the health of a group waxes and wanes according to the health of its members, and it makes sense that one could construe this in religious terms just as well – that a group's suffering would, in general, vary directly with its sins. But this mindset leads Schleiermacher to make what must be seen as a truly abhorrent claim. Following the logic of his position

42.   CF 76.1.
43.   Ibid.
44.   CF 77.
45.   CF 76.2–3.
46.   CF 76.2.
47.   Ibid.

to its most uncomfortable end, he actually writes, 'We shall next be able to say of every nation, and indeed of every social class in it, so far as it seems to stand by itself, that the measure of its sin will be also the measure of the evil it suffers'.[48] Thus any group's experience of suffering is God's punishment for the sin of its members.[49] And this is where the logic of Schleiermacher's position proves itself to be of very little use in naming the structures of sin and evil as such, as the experience of suffering only serves to convict the sufferers further of their sin.

The question remains to be asked, 'why are the evils evil?' Or rather, what makes them 'evil'? Whereas, as we shall see below, Ritschl, borrowing from Kant, is comfortable using the language of an impersonal force, named as the kingdom of evil or the kingdom of sin, Schleiermacher practically disallows any notion of such a force abroad in the world when he describes, 'the unchristian or rather the wholly irreligious nature of a certain other view – namely, that it is evil alone which, from the outset, has evoked all the human activity that goes to subjugate nature and to form social life'.[50] Instead, with respect to evil, Schleiermacher answers, 'Both kinds [natural and social] ... are evils only because they either diminish the wealth of stimuli which further men's [sic] development or make the world less tractable to human effort.' He goes on further to say, 'Of the former class are the evils of scarcity and want, of the latter those of oppression and antagonism; and everything that from our point of view may be regarded as evil, together with all the deadening and derangement of our spiritual powers in consequence of sin, must be traceable to these two types.'[51] Anticipating, in a way, the twentieth century's preoccupation with and emphasis on the 'social' sins of oppression and group antagonism, Schleiermacher thinks that 'the measure in which sin is present is the measure in which evil is present, so that, just as the human race is the proper sphere of sin, and sin the corporate act of the race, so the whole world in its relation to man is the proper sphere of evil, and evil the corporate suffering of the race'.[52] But as should now be clear, the once promising language of sin as the 'corporate act of the race'[53] does not look so promising anymore, for it only refers to the relevant social context of individuals sinning, and the effects it produces are held only to be the cold but just suffering of the guilty. In Chapter 4 I discuss the situation of extreme poverty in South America which Gustavo Gutiérrez found he had to name as 'social sin'. If we were to take Schleiermacher's point of view on what 'social sin' is, the response a theologian would have to give to the abjectly poor in

---

48.   CF 77.1.
49.   The thesis of CF 76 reads, 'All evil is to be regarded as punishment for sin, ... social evil directly as such.'
50.   CF 78.3.
51.   CF 75.2.
52.   CF 75.3.
53.   This term, as far as I can tell, is nowhere actually defined in Schleiermacher's writings.

South America who suffer so greatly from the economic tyranny of the first world is, 'You deserve it.'

Sin Known in Its Overcoming

That is a harsh judgement to make, of course. And yet it is the logical conclusion of Schleiermacher's statements on evil and sin in *The Christian Faith*. Schleiermacher did indeed write many other volumes, and there are reasons to temper such judgements based on his other work. But it is also true that his vast influence has been primarily mediated through his *Glaubenslehre*, and so if we are to find more resources for a non-individualistic notion of sin, we really should look therein and not someplace else. In this very brief section, then, I will try to sketch how some other aspects of Schleiermacher's system mitigate the sustained critique I have been making, though I do not think he can be exculpated totally, or even mostly, from the charges of individualism.

Sin is, in Schleiermacher's theology, known in its overcoming. We cannot see with unredeemed eyes that human frailty, fallenness, or baseness is *sin*. We could know by instinct that it was painful, or criminal, or even immoral. But we could not know it was sin. We need the perspective of the pious consciousness for that. In this sense, then, there is a way for Schleiermacher to appear less individualistic, for if the perspective of sin is known only in the redeemed consciousness, and if the redeemed consciousness is communal rather than wholly individual we have taken some steps forward. So we must ask, is sin known in its overcoming? Schleiermacher responds, 'We are conscious of sin as the power and work of a stage when the disposition to the God-consciousness has not yet actively emerged in us. In the stage to which the consciousness of sin points back, sin was not present in us in the same ways we are now conscious of it.'[54] Or again, Schleiermacher answers in the affirmative: 'Sin in general exists only in so far as there is a consciousness of it; and this again is conditioned by a good which must have preceded it and must have been just a result of that original perfection.'[55] And this 'good' is the redeemed pious consciousness. As Schleiermacher scholar Robert Vance puts it, 'Only the subsequently pious self will be able to broaden the horizons of philosophical reflection to pursue a philosophy of religion, and thereby be able to point out precisely how and why the self's former sinful interests were limited to the worldly dimension of consciousness, in exclusion of the God-consciousness.'[56] This is true because 'the character of sin is not known by one within the state [of sin] however, just because it is a disjointed and expendable stage, which will be comprehended only when it has been

54.   CF 67 (thesis).
55.   CF 68.2.
56.   Robert L. Vance, 'Sin and Consciousness of Sin in Schleiermacher', in *Perspectives in Religious Studies* 13:3 (1986): 242.

disallowed and overcome by the stage which is to follow'.[57] There is some
reason to assert that this new viewpoint is decidedly communal. There are
the earlier axioms on the sociality of all religion, for example. But there is
more, too. Schleiermacher makes a fairly famous analogy in paragraph 100
regarding soteriology. Imagine, says Schleiermacher, that there is a group of
people who live near one another but who have not yet formed a community,
strictly speaking. One thing that could happen is that the consciousness of
just one person in the group could start to understand the group as a cohesive
model. Eventually, this mindset could catch on, and the group would thus
begin to understand itself in a different way, namely as a community bound
together by this new consciousness. This may have been true of, say, some
early British colonists in America. A person in Savannah and maybe one
in Boston and another in Baltimore stopped thinking of themselves as
'Georgian' or 'a member of the Massachusetts Colony' or 'a Marylander',
and started to think of themselves as Americans.[58] This new consciousness
can be contagious. The result is, as Schleiermacher puts it, 'not only that
there arises among them a new corporate life, in complete contrast to the
old, but that also each of them becomes in himself a new person – that is
to say, a citizen'.[59] Something like that happens to the Christian community
when it encounters the perfectly integrated consciousness of Jesus Christ.
This surely reveals in Schleiermacher's notion of sin something other than
an individualistic concept.

But even in describing the new point of view from which the pious
consciousness is able to see sin as such, Schleiermacher succumbs to
individualism. Schleiermacher also asserts, 'The recognition of such a
condition [named earlier as "God-forgetfulness"] undeniably finds a place
in all *religious communions*. For the aim of all penances and purifications
is to put an end to the consciousness of this condition or to the condition
itself.'[60] The penances and purifications are themselves distorted, for the
sinner does not have the critical distance on sin, afforded by grace, to know
of what it is repenting, what it is purifying, or what the production of works
of penitence are for. 'A description of the sense of sin as the exclusive content
even of merely detached portions of life … could find no verification in the
Christian consciousness itself; such a description would therefore be no
doctrine of faith.'[61] Yet all of these formulations are themselves essentially
individualistic. Few categories in Schleiermacher's thought are as focused
on the individual experience as is 'faith', so we see even more focus on the
individual in a passage like this: 'Thus, owing to faith, the consciousness of
sin becomes the consciousness of forgiveness of sin.'[62]

---

57.   Ibid., 248.
58.   Though this is not Schleiermacher's example.
59.   CF 100.3.
60.   CF 11.3.
61.   CF 64.1.
62.   CF 109.2. In fact, the vast majority of references in pars. 108–111 regarding the
consciousness of sin attained in the 'state' of grace are couched in individualistic terms. It

Brief Summation of Schleiermacher

The person looking for help from Friedrich Schleiermacher for constructing something other than a strictly individualistic view of sin will be frustrated on three counts. First, in Schleiermacher's conceptual framework there is simply no real way to describe social structures or arrangements or experiences as sinful. Sin is so thoroughly housed in the various consciousnesses of the individual that the concept cannot expand much outside of that sphere. Second, when Schleiermacher does attempt to consider the social effects of sin, he does so with the concept of social evil, which is basically the same as the older concept, itself basically individualistic, of moral evil. The place where 'social evil' differs from moral evil is a step backward towards more individualism, as he views social evil as the just suffering of some for the sins of themselves and others. Finally, we see in Schleiermacher a disengagement of the concepts of corporate sin and corporate grace. Though he made important headway in seeing grace as an aspect of the pious consciousness of the redeemed community, he could not use this perspective to see that the state from which the community was redeemed was sinful in non-individualistic ways. Let us then turn to a deeper and more thorough critique of Schleiermacher on this matter, found in the profound and massive work of Albrecht Ritschl.

Albrecht Ritschl's Critique of Schleiermacher on Sin

Here is one plausible way to interpret the origins of sixteenth-century Protestant theology. Martin Luther discovered a radical new way to think about humanity's relation to God, namely that by the merits of Jesus Christ the sinner is able to receive the grace of God in the power of the Holy Spirit, apart from any action or intent on the behalf of the believer. In principle and in articulation this was a deep break from the former means of conceiving of the God–human relationship. So deep was the break in this new view of the 'vertical' dimension of human existence, the 'horizontal' implications of the God–human relationship for human–human affairs were not fully comprehended by Luther.[63] He arguably made significant headway in this direction, developing an ethic of faith active in love, a notion of freedom for service to neighbour in one's vocation, and an escape from the perceived legalism of the age just prior to him. But Luther and his immediate

---

should be noted in fairness that although Schleiermacher's explication of the concept comes across as individualistic, the actual experiences which this theology interprets in terms of the individual happens in community (and happened for Schleiermacher himself there, too).

63.   Even as sympathetic an interpreter as Paul Althaus admits as much. Cf. his *The Ethics of Martin Luther*, trans. Robert C. Schulz (Philadelphia: Fortress, 1972), 143–7 on the matter of the shape of social order based on an ethic of justification by faith.

contemporaries were not able fully to address the new requirements of social ethics that this religious shift required. John Calvin, however, did have sufficient distance on the Reformation *Durchbruch* of Luther to reflect more adequately on the social ethics implied in the re-conception of human, church and world of Luther's doctrine of justification. Calvin's subtler ecclesiology, elaborate theology of the state and his codification of the morality of interpersonal relationships reflect this ethical emphasis.[64]

Here is one plausible way to interpret the origins of nineteenth-century Protestant theology. Friedrich Schleiermacher discovered a radical new way to think about humanity's relation to God, namely that God becomes known to our consciousness as the 'whence' of our existence, upon which all else in our lives depends. While this conscious experience presupposes and entails certain objective realities, the theological emphasis is primarily one of subjective feeling, thinking and doing. Schleiermacher could not see that this new way of thinking about God implied a quite different articulation of a theocentric social ethic, and Albrecht Ritschl had sufficient distance on Schleiermacher's insights both critically to appropriate them as well as to shore up what he held to be a critically weak emphasis on the ethical dimensions of the Kingdom of God. It is therefore reasonable to conclude that the Lutheran Ritschl played Calvin to the Calvinist Schleiermacher's Luther!

The Relation of Schleiermacher to Ritschl's Thought

Though I will be highlighting the ways in which Ritschl critiques and goes beyond Schleiermacher, Schleiermacher is for Ritschl no simple foil. In fact, the matter of Ritschl's dependence on Schleiermacher is quite complicated, and warrants some attention.[65] The easy way to determine the relationship would be simply to listen to what Ritschl says about Schleiermacher. In 1874 Ritschl

---

64. This is, incidentally, the basic view of Ernst Troeltsch, who saw not Luther but Calvin as the first modern thinker. Luther was too trapped in the thought forms of the medieval period and its emphasis on the *lex naturae* and 'church-type' to conceive appropriately of the social teaching implicit in the so-called new 'religious idea'. Cf. his *The Social Teachings of the Christian Churches*, 2:523–624.

65. To cite just two examples of wildly diverging estimations of their relationship (there are many more), Alfred E. Garvie thought Ritschl founded a completely new school by breaking wholly from Schleiermacher (*The Ritschlian Theology, Critical and Constructive* (Edinburgh: T&T Clark, 1902)), whereas Karl Barth, in characteristic Barthian hyperbole, referred to Ritschl's 'spasmodic concentration' of Schleiermacher's theology! (CD I/1:276). It is, I think, largely to Barth's discredit that he cannot adequately distinguish between Ritschl and Schleiermacher even on sin. Though he discusses the emendation of Schleiermacher's doctrines of sin and grace by Ritschl's recourse to the kingdoms of sin and God, Barth wrongly views the kingdom of sin in Ritschl to be simply another way of describing subjectivity, which as I shall show below, it emphatically is not. Cf. *Church Dogmatics* IV/1, 376–83.

wrote a short book entitled *Schleiermachers Reden über die Religion und ihre Nachwirkungen auf die evangelsishe Kirche Deutschlands.*[66] Throughout the book Ritschl is quite dismissive of the influence of Schleiermacher. He writes, for example, 'In my youth each student of theology was compelled to work through Schleiermacher's *The Christian Faith*. I have not gained anything for my system from this labor.'[67] Or again, 'If it be necessary for theological work that at the outset of one's study one must give one's complete confidence to a single master, it should not be done with Schleiermacher.'[68] Sideways and dismissive references to Schleiermacher in Ritschl's letters and in his son Otto's biography would count as further evidence for the thesis that Ritschl simply rejected Schleiermacher.[69] However, I shall defend the somewhat more postmodern thesis that any writer is in no better position to pronounce on the influences on her or his work than is anyone else who has read it. Though reading Ritschl with the intent of excavating his influences is harder than simply reading his words about his influences, the result is a more complete picture of his relationship to Schleiermacher.[70]

Areas of Convergence between Ritschl and Schleiermacher

I identify three areas of significant overlap in Ritschl's and Schleiermacher's general theological projects and three deep ruptures between them. The first area of convergence is methodological. Orthodox Protestant theologians in the seventeenth and eighteenth centuries tended to use primarily the *loci* method for writing systematic theology. This took various forms, some following Philip Melanchthon's organization from the order of doctrines touched on in Romans, or sometimes following Lombard's Sentences, and sometimes inventing a novel order in which to treat the major loci.[71] The other 'branch' of Protestant thought in these centuries, the Pietists, tended to write less systematically. Much of their writings took the form of epistolary moral exhortation, devotional literature and sometimes exegesis.[72] But Schleiermacher broke this mould, choosing instead a method enunciating a single grand theme at the outset of his work, and allowing that theme (of

66.   (Bonn: Adolph Marcus, 1874).

67.   Ibid., 19.

68.   Ibid., 20.

69.   Daniel L. Deegan cites many of these in his essay 'Ritschlian School: The Essence of Christianity and Karl Barth', in *Scottish Journal of Theology* 16 (1963): 390–414.

70.   James K. Graby comes to similar conclusions in 'The Problem of Ritschl's Relationship to Schleiermacher', in *Scottish Journal of Theology* 19 (1966): 257–68.

71.   The best resource outlining the relationship between doctrine and method in this period remains Robert D. Preus, *The Theology of Post-Reformation Lutheranism*, 2 vols (St Louis: Concordia, 1970). The first volume is, in fact, a study exclusively of the systematic prolegomena to typical Loci theologies.

72.   Johannes Wallmann, *Der Pietismus* (Göttingen: Vandenhoeck & Ruprecht, 1990), 88–94.

the pious consciousness) to unfold and work itself out in the ensuing pages. Ritschl shares this method to a great extent. This is of particular import for a doctrine of sin. Luther, Melanchthon and Calvin wrote about sin so widely, and their successors in the period of Protestant scholasticism did as well, that they could avoid systematic discussions of the topic. Calvin's *Institutes* contains a fairly lengthy entry on the doctrine of original sin, but his thoughts on actual sin are spread out on virtually every second page of the work, which has led in part to the great proliferation of doctrines of sin in the Reformed tradition.[73]

The second area of overlap involves the emerging understanding of the communal nature of religion. Though this understanding had not been lacking in previous theologies, Ritschl thought Schleiermacher had done a great service in re-emphasizing it. The first volume of Ritschl's three-volume great work, *The Christian Doctrine of Justification and Reconciliation*, is a massive history of the development of those doctrines, and Schleiermacher merits an entire chapter.[74] There he is explicit about his debt for the fact that 'Schleiermacher has established the much more general truth, that the religious moral life of the spirit cannot at all be conceived of outside of the *fellowship* that corresponds thereto, and that, in reciprocal action and reaction therewith, the individual attains his peculiar development.'[75] This is an outgrowth of what Ritschl interprets as Schleiermacher's genuine Christocentric approach to theology.[76] Since all of what must be said about God must come from the perspective of the redeemed pious consciousness, and that consciousness takes shape in the Christian community, Schleiermacher has 'proven the necessity for every religion having the character of fellowship', most particularly Christianity.[77]

Finally, Ritschl is indebted to Schleiermacher's notion of Christianity as *teleological*. At the outset of *The Christian Faith* Schleiermacher describes religions according to two types: aesthetic and teleological. A religion is aesthetic when it is concerned primarily with nature, and secondarily with action. 'This form of piety, in which each moment of spontaneous activity, simply as a determination of the individual by the whole of finite existence

73.   John Calvin, *Institutes of the Christian Religion* (1559 edition), II.1–3.
74.   Albrecht Ritschl, *A Critical History of the Christian Doctrine of Justification and Reconciliation*, trans. John S. Black (Edinburgh: Edmonston and Douglas, 1872), 440–512, hereafter cited as JR I. The original was published in 1870. Volume II, from 1872, is a treatment of the biblical basis for justification and reconciliation, and Volume III, from 1874, is Ritschl's masterful constructive proposal. They will be cited as RV 2 and JR III, respectively (Volume 2 has never been translated out of *Rechtfertigung und Versöhnung*).
75.   JR I, 443–4.
76.   Schleiermacher has not normally been read in North America as being particularly Christocentric, but that may be changing. One important study that shows the Christological emphasis is Richard R. Niebuhr, *Schleiermacher on Christ and Religion* (New York: Charles Scribners Sons, 1964), though this has unfortunately remained a minority view of sorts.
77.   JR I, 448.

[i.e., nature] and thus as referred to the passive side, is taken up into the feeling of absolute dependence, we will call *aesthetic* Religion.'[78] Islam and ancient Greek religion are cited as examples. On the other hand, a teleological religion is one in which 'the passive states ... become simply an occasion for the development of a definite activity which can only be explained as the result of a God-consciousness of that particular description'.[79] Thus the genuine significance of action in religion, and therefore of ethics in theology, was seen by Schleiermacher by calling Christianity, along with Judaism, a teleological religion.

Areas of Divergence in Ritschl from Schleiermacher

However, Ritschl thinks that while Schleiermacher 'saw' this, he did not fully 'grasp' it.[80] In fact, Ritschl says that as soon as Schleiermacher made his point about the importance of the ethical moment in dogmatic theology he promptly forgot about it! According to Ritschl, 'No topic receives less justice in the general argument of his *Glaubenslehre* than what he admits to be the teleological character of Christianity.'[81] To be fair to Schleiermacher, this fact, while in my opinion true, is not without good reason. Whereas many theologians influenced by Schleiermacher chose to fold together their treatments of ethics and dogmatics, Schleiermacher himself thought it best to separate the two in practice, even while holding them together in theory. This is why Schleiermacher wrote his *Sittenlehre* as its own free-standing volume, rather than having a section on 'the Christian Life' within the *Glaubenslehre*.[82] James M. Brandt goes so far as to make the case that Ritschl is completely misguided in his critique of Schleiermacher on this matter, because he thinks Ritschl may not ever even have read the *Sittenlehre*.[83] If he had, his critique would not have been so harsh. He may have seen that the separation of ethics from dogmatics need not imply a diminution in importance. In a suggestive image, Brandt compares the fact that the *Sittenlehre* is its own book to the decision to separate conjoined twins to improve the health of the weaker sibling by giving it some independence.[84] Whether Brandt is

---

78. CF 9.
79. Ibid.
80. JR III, 11.
81. JR III, 9.
82. F.D.E. Schleiermacher, *Die christliche Sitte nach den Grundsätzen der evangelischen Kirche im Zusammenhänge dargestellt*, in L. Jonas, ed., *Friedrich Schleiermachers sämtliche Werke*, I.12 (Berlin: G. Reimer, 1843).
83. James M. Brandt, 'Ritschl's Critique of Schleiermacher's Theological Ethics', in *The Journal of Religious Ethics* 17 (1989): 51–72, at 54. Brandt's essay is a good one on the specific matter of the Ritschl–Schleiermacher exchange, but for a better look at Schleiermacher's ethics in general, cf. James Duke, 'The Christian and the Ethical in Schleiermacher's Christian Ethics', in *Encounter* 46 (1985): 51–69.
84. Ibid., 58.

right in his assessment need not be determined at the present, for it is not, strictly speaking, relevant whether Ritschl was correct in his appraisal of Schleiermacher's ethical lacuna. What is more important is that, practically speaking, Schleiermacher and his followers had had virtually no impact whatsoever in the matter of theological ethics. No matter Schleiermacher's intent: the entire excision of ethical deliberation from the most influential theological text of the century was, in Ritschl's view, inexcusable.

The second main departure Ritschl makes from Schleiermacher lies in his critique of Schleiermacher's subjectivity. Since Schleiermacher's entire system can be considered part of the typically modern 'turn to the subject', Ritschl's criticism thereof is accordingly wide-ranging. When discussing Schleiermacher's soteriology, for example, Ritschl considers him to be a kind of Abelard *redivivus*. Abelard of course had taught that Jesus Christ saves humanity not by placating a bloodthirsty tyrant, but by so living his life in obedience that the repentant sinner would be drawn back into fellowship with God.[85] That could make it sound like the salvation of the sinner *depended* on the subjectivity of the sinner in enacting that fellowship.[86] So too did Schleiermacher sound at times, to Ritschl's ear anyway, as though the Christian subject was the maker of his or her own salvation. Another aspect of Ritschl's critique of Schleiermacher's subjectivity is methodological. Schleiermacher taught that the starting point of dogmatic theology was reflection on the experience of absolute dependence as a kind of *Gefühl*. Ritschl found this to be overly Romantic and even dangerously ambiguous. Ritschl asserts to the contrary that dogmatic theology ought to begin with the objective fact of the revelation of God in Jesus Christ as this fact is attested in the New Testament.[87]

Finally, we come to the most important divergence from Schleiermacher's thought. This is Schleiermacher's deficient understanding of what was to become the central theological concept in Ritschl's thought, namely the Kingdom of God. Ritschl thought that Schleiermacher had made a very important contribution to theology by restoring the concept of the Kingdom of God to a place of importance in theology. It was undisputedly the centre of Jesus' preaching, which had been recognized long before Ritschl's son-in-law, Johannes Weiss, wrote his book *Die Predigt Jesu vom Reich Gottes*.[88] However, there was no consensus as to the proper dogmatic construal of the Kingdom. Ever since Augustine the concept had been used, at least in part, as a cipher for the dominion of the church.[89] Luther had thought

85. Peter Abelard, *Commentaria in Epistolam Pauli ad Romanos, II.3*. (On Romans 3:19–26).

86. Although Abelard himself was careful to note that it was God's prevenient love that made it all possible.

87. JR I, 466–76.

88. (Göttingen: Vandenhoeck and Ruprecht, 1892).

89. *De civitate Dei*, xx. 9 represents a turning point in his thought, where he decides that Jesus' promise to be present with his disciples in Matt 28:20 implies an at least partial temporal reign in the present church.

of the Kingdom of God as a kind of eschatological, or even apocalyptic, reign, and there was always a strand of Christian theology which held the Kingdom of God to refer simply to the way things were in heaven.[90] Even more varied and then diffuse usage followed in later theologies, and eventually the concept played very little role in Protestant thought. Ritschl appreciated that Schleiermacher established the idea that the Kingdom of God was the 'highest good' which, as Philip Hefner puts it, 'motivates man's action and which serves God's own highest good as expressed in the idea of the kingdom'.[91] However, there was a serious problem with this otherwise laudable presentation of the kingdom: it was not a part of Schleiermacher's ethics. As we will see below Ritschl was always at pains to make the Kingdom a simultaneously religious *and* ethical concept. As Claude Welch aptly puts it, 'Schleiermacher first identified the teleological character of the kingdom as decisive for Christianity. For this we should be grateful. Yet the significance of this discovery of the ethical had not been fully exploited. That was the task Ritschl set for himself.'[92] The religious and the ethical co-inhered for Ritschl, and the trick to dogmatic theology in general, and the doctrine of sin in particular, lay in keeping the ethical and the religious in balance. The slogan of many medieval philosophers was 'qui bene distinguit bene docet': the one who distinguishes well teaches well. But Ritschl's own personal motto was 'qui bene distinguit et bene comprehendit bene docet': the one who both distinguishes *and combines* well teaches well.[93] Teaching well on the doctrine of sin meant combining many things – the Kingdom of God, the meaning of justification and reconciliation, the religious and the ethical, the present and the future, and as we shall see in the next section, it meant joining Rothe and Kant.

If one were to begin to list all the influences on Ritschl's thought there may be no end to the inventory. Since Ritschl was such an able historian, he deeply researched and was forced to come to some conclusion about nearly every major figure in Christian history.[94] Luther,[95] Calvin and Melanchthon

---

90.   On Luther and the eschatological Kingdom of God, cf. Jane Strohl, 'Luther's Spiritual Journey', in Donald McKim, ed., *The Cambridge Companion to Martin Luther* (Cambridge: Cambridge University Press, 2003), 159–60. I am also indebted to conversation with Joshua McGuffie on the matter of Luther's ecclesiology and the kingdom.

91.   Philip Hefner, 'Albrecht Ritschl: An Introduction', in idem, ed., *Three Essays* (Philadelphia: Fortress, 1972), 22.

92.   Welch, *Protestant Thought in the Nineteenth Century*, 2:18.

93.   Otto Ritschl, *Albrecht Ritschls Leben*, 2 vols. (Freiburg im Breisgau: Mohr, 1892), 2:167, my emphasis.

94.   The importance of the method of his historical investigations for his constructive dogmatic proposals is convincingly shown in Philip Hefner, *Faith and the Vitalities of History: A Theological Study Based on the Work of Albrecht Ritschl* (New York: Harper and Row, 1966).

95.   Luther's thought could be said, in a way, to dominate Ritschl's own. Cf. David W. Lotz, *Ritschl and Luther: A Fresh Perspective on Albrecht Ritschl's Theology in Light of His Luther Study* (Nashville: Abingdon, 1974).

would have to be on such a list, as would nearly all of the major church fathers[96] and the early figures of the Middle Ages. For a discussion of the interplay between individual and social sin, however, and the emergence of Ritschl's controlling insight into the Kingdom of God, the two figures which simply must be mentioned are the philosophers Immanuel Kant and Richard Rothe.

Immanuel Kant and Ritschl

Ritschl gleaned three major ideas from his study of Kant. The first was the richness of his concept of the will. Often when Ritschl criticized Schleiermacher on sin, he did so by pointing out the secondary importance that the will had in his doctrine. Ritschl thought that the Enlightenment and its heirs (including Schleiermacher) had become soft on sin, on the one hand, by reducing 'man's obligation towards God's law to the relative criterion of their internal and external situation, and on the other hand by denying all internal conviction of guilt'.[97] Kant is not guilty of this, for 'That conception of the absolute obligation of the moral law which Kant developed in accordance with the notion of the free will provides him with the means of establishing on a surer basis than was afforded by the old Protestant doctrine of original sin, the corresponding subjective consciousness that we are in effect guilty in the eyes of the law.'[98] This means of securing guilt by reference to the absolute moral law entails, in Ritschl's eyes, an incredible advance over other Enlightenment and old Protestant Orthodox descriptions of the human condition.

The second area has been mentioned already, which is that Kant, even before Schleiermacher, had seen the necessity of the concept of the Kingdom of God. He did not interpret it in terms which were sufficiently religious, but he did see its ethical import. Kant's vision of the Kingdom of God was one of the ethical community wherein all people were perfectly ruled by virtue and the power of their consciences. In his reinterpretation of Christianity in *Religion within the Bounds of Reason Alone* Kant positively links this notion to the development of a 'moral faith' from the then regnant so-called 'ecclesiastical faith'. If this were to happen, according to Kant, then we could say that 'the Kingdom of God is come unto us'.[99] Kant seems to have equivocated as to whether this was in reality possible or not, but the

---

96. Ritschl's first major work was on patristic theology. *Entstehung der altkatolischen Kirche: Eine kirchen- und dogmengeschichtliche Monographie* (Bonn: Adolph Marcus, 1850).

97. JR I, 387.

98. JR I, 388.

99. Immanuel Kant, *Religion within the Bounds of Reason Alone*, trans. Hoyt Hudson and Theodore Green (New York: Harper, 1960), 113.

immediately relevant point is that his description of this 'kingdom of ends' had great effect on Ritschl and his emerging concept of sin.[100]

Finally, there is the idea of radical evil. This is a notoriously difficult to understand aspect of Kant's thought, developed late in his life and in seeming contradiction to some of his earlier writings. Kant defends an 'inclination' to evil (*Neigung*) in human nature that can be explained only by reference to the will. 'We are speaking of a propensity to genuine, that is, moral evil; for since such evil is possible only as a determination of the will, and since the will can be appraised as good or evil only by means of its maxims, this propensity to evil must consist in *the subjective ground of the possibility of deviation of maxims from the moral law.*'[101] Yet this last thing is exactly what is disallowed in the *Groundwork of the Metaphysics of Morals*. We are therefore in the presence of paradox when attempting to describe evil. Kant concludes that evil must be seen as 'inextirpable' (*nicht zu vertilgen*) by human powers, thus opening the door, in Ritschl's hand, to an account of the Kingdom of God as the extirpation of the kingdom of evil towards which the inclination to evil tends.[102]

Richard Rothe and Ritschl

Richard Rothe (1799–1867) was a student of Schleiermacher whom Ritschl met when the latter was a student and the former a professor at the University of Heidelberg.[103] Rothe is hard to fit into any of the usual categories of his time (liberal, conservative or mediating, left- or right-wing Hegelian, etc.), leading Claude Welch to remark that this is perhaps why Rothe nearly always warrants a whole chapter to himself in nineteenth-century religious

---

100. The eminent Kant scholar Allen Wood, for example, argues on the basics of Kant's statements in *Groundwork of the Metaphysics of Morals* that the kingdom of ends is not attainable, since 'A kingdom of ends would actually come into existence through maxims which the categorical imperative prescribes as a rule for all rational beings, *if these maxims were universally followed*' which, Kant goes on to say, they will not. Cf. Allen Wood, *Kant's Moral Religion* (Ithaca, NY: Cornell University Press, 1970), 126–7. On the other hand, many scholars maintain that Kant always meant to hold up the possibility that all people could in fact uphold the moral law, citing in this regard Kant's arguments from the *Critique of Pure Reason* that moral perfectibility was a postulate required by reason for moral deliberation. Cf. Roger J. Sullivan, *Kant's Moral Theory* (New York: Cambridge University Press, 1989).

101. Kant, *Religion*, 24.

102. Ibid., 32.

103. On Rothe generally, cf. Dietrich Rössler, 'Richard Rothe', in Martin Greschat, ed., *Theologen des Protestantismus im 19. und 20. Jahrhundert* (Stuttgart: Kohlhammer, 1978), 74–83, and specifically on his relationship to Schleiermacher, cf. Matthias Heesch, 'Transzendentale Individualität? Schleiermacher und sein Schüler Rothe im Streit um das Wesen des Endlich-Gegebenen', in *Neue Zeitschrift für Systematische Theologie* 35 (1993): 259–95, and on Ritschl, cf. Christian Walther, 'Der Reich-Gottes-Begriff in der Theologie Richard Rothes und Albrecht Ritschls', in *Kerygma und Dogma* 2 (1956): 115–38.

historiography.[104] His thought was extremely innovative and profound, and he probably deserves to be better remembered both in European and North American religious thought. Yet there is only one key insight in his massive corpus that must be highlighted as being of importance for Ritschl's view of the Kingdom of God and sin, and that is his view of the historicality of the Kingdom of God. Rothe picked up from Hegel, by way of Fichte, that the practical upshot of the Protestant Reformation was that the church could be overcome by the Kingdom of God.[105] Far from linking the two, which had been done since Augustine at least, Rothe tried to separate them nearly completely. He thought that the Christian church was simply a means of Christianizing the world, and that once this was done, the Kingdom of God would be present and there would be no more need for the church.[106] 'Christianizing' the world meant that all areas of life: its social and civic, its artistic and scientific aspects, would come to their appropriate balance according to the aims of God.[107] Hegel's word for this balanced whole was 'the State', though by this he did not mean merely political organization, nor did Rothe, who adopted it from him.[108] Jesus was accordingly not merely a religious figure, but a priestly king who had laid the foundation for God's kingdom, conceived as a gradually developing ethical-religious community devoted to the fulfilment of the kingdom. He had instituted the church as a kind of necessary means to this greater end. When the end had been achieved, the church would no longer be necessary, or even desirable.

We thus see in Rothe a powerful application of the Hegelian view of history to the concept of the Kingdom of God. The Kingdom is not immanent, as in the late patristic view (at least on Rothe's read of that period), nor is it primarily eschatological, as in Luther's thought. It exists in history as the process of history unfolds in its constitutive ethical and religious arrangements.[109] As we now turn to Ritschl's constructive proposal regarding the Kingdom of God and sin, we will do well to keep Rothe, Kant and Schleiermacher in mind as the subtle background of Ritschl's deceptively simple formulations becomes clearer.

---

104. Welch, *Protestant Thought in the Nineteenth Century*, 1:282.

105. For a brief treatment of the history of this idea, cf. Wolfhart Pannenberg, *Systematic Theology*, 3 vols., trans. Geoffrey Bromiley (Grand Rapids: Eerdmans, 1998), 3:54–5.

106. In one of Rothe's earlier books he noted how prior to Cyprian, this had in fact been the dominant ecclesiology. Rothe, *Die Anfänge Der christlichen Kirche und ihrer Verfassung* (Wittenberg: Zimmerman, 1837).

107. Richard Rothe, *Theologische Ethik*, 3 vols. (Wittenberg: Zimmerman, 1845), 3:206ff.

108. Welch, *Protestant Thought in the Nineteenth Century*, 1:290.

109. On this, cf. Walther, 'Das Reich-Gottes-Begriff', 117–28.

Ritschl's Doctrine of the Kingdom of God as summum bonum

Now that we have become clear on the major influences on Ritschl regarding his doctrines of the kingdoms of God and sin, we shall be able, in relatively brief compass, to look at his own constructive synthesis of these doctrines. We will treat the Kingdom of God first. This is perhaps *the* most frequently misinterpreted aspect of Ritschl's constantly misconstrued theology, which is due in part to the lack of care taken in examining the genetic development of the relevant forerunners, as well as a myopic view of Ritschl based exclusively on one or another small sections of his massive corpus.[110] But now that we have clarified the available options and shown the critiques of why he did not choose certain other ones, his own position will become quite clear.

The Ethical and Religious Foci of Christianity

Though he did not actually employ it all that often, the image for which Ritschl is best known is the ellipse. Christianity, according to Ritschl, is like an ellipse with two foci.[111] The foci are named varyingly, but they correspond on the one had, basically, to divine action, reality and becoming, and on the other hand to human action, reality and becoming. The one focus is religious, the other ethical. The one focus is faith, the other love. The one focus is justification and reconciliation, the other the Kingdom of God. The two can, when necessary, be distinguished, but they must never be separated. We know God in our neighbour, and we know our neighbour *as* neighbour (and not, say, as enemy) only because we know God. The religious may not be reduced to the ethical. This is where Kant went wrong, in Ritschl's view – he claimed to be able fully to translate theological doctrines into ethical principles without distortion or remainder.[112] One way of putting this is to say with Ritschl that 'The Kingdom of God is the divinely ordained highest good of the community founded through God's revelation in Christ; but it is the highest good only in the sense that it forms at the same time the ethical ideal for whose attainment the members of the community bind themselves to each other through a definite type of reciprocal action.'[113]

---

110. Though it is not limited to Barth, since his voice was so strong he is one of the major reasons for the near constant misapprehension of Ritschlian thought today. His sharpest critique comes in the shamefully brief treatment (c. ten pages; even Novalis warrants forty!) in Barth, *History of Protestant Thought in the Nineteenth Century*, trans. John Bowden and Brian Cozens (Valley Forge, PA: Judson Press, 1972), 655ff.

111. JR III, 11. Of course, every ellipse has two foci.

112. This aspect of Kant's thought eventually caused Ritschl to become famously critical of the role of metaphysics in theology, though not only for this reason. Cf. his 'Theology and Metaphysics', in *Three Essays*.

113. Albrecht Ritschl, 'Instruction in the Christian Religion', in Hefner, ed., *Three Essays*, 222. Hereafter cited as ICR.

In Ritschl's doctrine, the Kingdom of God comes to us as *both* gift and task, *both* objective reality and subjective charge, *both* religious statement and ethical ramification. In Ritschl's words, 'The kingdom of God is the *summum bonum* which God realizes in men; and at the same time it is their common task, for it is only through the rendering of obedience on man's part that God's sovereignty possesses continuous existence. These two meanings are interdependent.'[114] While the religious must constantly be conceived in close reference to the ethical, it is not as though the religious character of Christianity could be interpreted in just any old ethical scheme. The scheme chosen must be a thoroughly communal one.[115] That is to say, the horizontal dimension of the Christian faith necessitated by its particular vertical cast must be comprehended in a community structured in mutual love, love being further understood according to what Jesus had taught it to be. For Ritschl,

> Christianity is the monotheistic, completely spiritual and ethical religion, which, on the basis of the life of its Founder as redeeming and establishing the kingdom of God, consists in the freedom of the children of God, includes the impulse to conduct from the motive of love, the intention of which is the moral organization of mankind, and in the filial relation to God as well as in the kingdom of God lays the foundation of blessedness.[116]

This definition implies that the Kingdom of God is the highest good not only for humanity and the rest of creation, but for God, too. That is to say, the Kingdom of God exists both on earth and as a part of God's will as love. In fact, Ritschl goes so far as to say that 'God's decision to establish the community of the kingdom of God was decreed even before the foundation of the world.'[117] The Kingdom of God as *summum bonum* is a reality in God and on earth, though in different ways in each.

Two more points must be made at this time. First, we must note that the kingdom is both present and absent in important ways for Ritschl. This is another way of naming the ethical and religious poles, or in other words, a way of conceiving of Paul's already-but-not-yet eschatology. 'The presence of the kingdom is always invisible and a matter of religious faith', but still the kingdom 'exists in the world as the present product of action motivated by love'.[118] Note that the second half of the articulation does not imply that the Kingdom of God is present only when acts of love are performed from within the church or from Christian consciousness, as Schleiermacher would have phrased it. *Any* loving act 'counts'. Here is clear evidence of Rothe's influence on the widening of the kingdom from its previously narrow identification with the church, and the more open view of history Ritschl

---

114. JR III, 30.
115. Recall the influence of Schleiermacher on this point, noted above.
116. JR III, 13.
117. ICR, 226.
118. ICR, 233–4.

embraces. God works out God's Kingdom in all cultures and at all times, though the Kingdom was in fact founded by Jesus and maintains its clearest expression in Christianity. As Ritschl puts it elsewhere, 'those who believe in Christ are a church in so far as they acknowledge in prayer their faith in God the Father and present themselves as human beings well pleasing to him through Christ. Those who believe in Christ are a kingdom of God in so far as, without observing the differences of sex, class or nation, they act reciprocally toward one another out of love.'[119]

This leads us to the second point, which is that the Kingdom of God is not to be correlated *too* closely with any particular social group. The Kingdom of God rightly understood transcends those. In fact, Ritschl even makes the fairly radical point that the very *telos* of human life is 'the moral society of nations'.[120] But Ritschl has been roundly criticized for equating the Kingdom of God with the bourgeois culture of the Prussian Empire, and later the new German state, of his time. Some of that criticism is probably deserved, though it should be pointed out that Ritschl, in my opinion, never meant to equate the two. He simply saw the affluent society around him, with its 'high culture', incredible scientific advances (it is not irrelevant to note that the Göttingen of Ritschl's time was perhaps the premier university in Europe for the *Naturwissenschaften*), and seeming 'progress in history' touted by the left-wing Hegelians, and assumed that the Kingdom of God was particularly present there. Even if he may have been imprecise in explaining just how the Kingdom of God concept related to his own particular social situation, it seems excessive to claim, as some neo-Orthodox epigones did, that the political reality of Germany in 1919 (i.e., after the catastrophe of World War I) obviated the theological approach taken by Ritschl and his followers around the turn of the century. It is hard for us now, with our vision obscured as it is by the 'Barthian spectacles' which colour the theological historiography of the period, to see what Ritschl actually taught: the Kingdom is *both* a future reality as the *summum bonum* for humanity, and a current reality as the *summum bonum* of Godself, instantiated as it is in concrete acts and structures of love and justice.[121]

Lebensideal *and* Lebensführung

Those acts and structure must take a certain shape. Ritschl described that shape by recourse to a pair of fascinating concepts: the *Lebensideal* and the *Lebensführung*. Part of the notion of the kingdom as both gift and task is that the Christian has been charged with living out his or her life as an

---

119. JR III, 271.
120. JR III, 10.
121. Michael B. Aune has made some important first steps in clearing up our vision on this point. See his series on 'Removing the Barthian Spectacles', in *Dialog* 43 (2004): 223–32 and 44 (2005): 56–68.

appropriate (ethical) response to the gift of (religious) salvation. But the form of that response is a gift, too, for God has ordained that each person have his or her own ethical vocation (*der sittliche Beruf*) which can serve as the medium for ethical living and gratitude. The essence of Luther's doctrine of Christian vocation, Ritschl believed, was 'the practical expression for the fact that Christianity was not world-denying but world pervading'.[122] When Jesus founded the Kingdom, he revealed the ideal way one could live (*Lebensideal*) in it. The *Lebensideal* has both objective and subjective character. It is the positive declaration of God on how one is to live in the world (objective), and the experience of this reality *feels* a certain way (and thus is subjective). When that feeling is apprehended, one must act out of it. This eventuates in the concrete way in which one does in fact lead one's life (*Lebensführung*). As we should by now have come to expect from Ritschl, several more dialectical partners compose the ellipse of the *Lebensideal/Lebensführung*. The religious aspects which we see perfected in Jesus' exemplification of the ideal Christian life are faith, humility, patience and prayer. Ritschl writes, '[R]econciliation with God through Christ is exercised through faith in the loving providence of God, through the virtues of humility and patience, and finally through prayer, and through this last one receives communal expression.'[123] Ethically, the ideal of life is made into the leading of life in the concrete realms of love and justice to neighbour is harder for Ritschl to formulate theologically, because as a Lutheran he has been trained to shun formulations of ethics which even sniff of works-righteousness.[124] Ritschl's answer as to the ethical imperatives implicit in the *Lebensideal* is nonetheless fairly clear: freedom (understood again as both gift and task), self-control and conscientiousness, and kindliness, thankfulness and justice.[125]

The Kingdom of God, therefore, has both social and individual levels. The individual is called to acts of love, while the community is called to structures of justice. Sin, as we will see shortly, thus *must also have both social and individual character*. Of this social level in the Kingdom of God, Ritschl writes,

> Justice is the communal activity of those who belong to the kingdom of God. It is the obedience through which the dominion of God exercised through Christ becomes effective. The public good of being obedient to God's will is the plant which emerges out of the seed through the encouraging power of the proclamation of the kingdom

122. Ritschl, '"Prolegomena" to *The History of Pietism*', *Three Essays*, 87.

123. JR III, 670. It is worth mentioning that Ritschl always stressed Luther's conception of faith primarily as *fiducia*, and only very rarely as *assensus*.

124. For the full story of Ritschl trying affirm the interpenetration of the religious and ethical in neighbour love while denying its contribution to justification, cf. JR III, 485–535. This is also an excellent example of Ritschl's magisterial grasp of sixteenth-century theology.

125. ICR, 248–9. I have emended the list slightly to harmonize ICR paras 66–9 with JR III, 507–23.

of God. And both the general and the particular moral order, which are equivalent to peace, are the fruit to which the individual who acts justly contributes in various capacities, and from this contribution either a few or many will benefit, and from it the moral community will either receive its regular lease on life or gain a vigorous new impulse.[126]

Ritschl genuinely hoped for that 'vigorous new impulse' which could renew society. But he also thought that the society in which he lived was, on the whole, doing just fine. This tends to make Ritschl, as Philip Hefner notes, 'a curious blend of conservative and liberal, even though he is invariably (and rightly so) viewed as a figure in the history of German liberal theology'.[127] Yet it is also true, as Mark Chapman puts it, that 'however much Ritschl might have seen God as the Prussian paterfamilias, and however much he might have equated worldly vocation with the status quo, he nevertheless provided the basis for subsequent attempts to reform the present for the sake of the future, to bring love as the highest motivation for action to its concrete realization'.[128] Thus we have in Ritschl a serious tension. There is both a genuine hope for real and imminent transformation of present struggle into future blessedness, as well as a hard-headed realism about the reality of structures, habits of vice and human forces which resist such conversion. In Ritschl's own words, 'As a member of the Christian community one is called to the kingdom of God as man's highest good and his highest common duty, because it is the final purpose of God himself. At the same time, however, by the very recognition of this destiny there comes an increase of the feeling of guilt and separation which arises from our own sin and our solidarity with the sin common to all men.'[129] We now move to the final doctrine of Ritschl to be considered in this chapter (though it has been presupposed and partially revealed in the foregoing), his doctrine of sin as both individual and corporate.

Ritschl's Constructive Doctrine of Sin

One could do worse in explicating Ritschl's doctrine of sin than simply to re-describe the Kingdom of God in its social and individual, in its temporal and eternal and in its religious and ethical moments and then conclude:

---

126. RV II, 292–3, quoted in Hans Schwarz, 'The Centrality and Bipolar Focus of Kingdom: Ritschl's Theological Import for the Twentieth Century', in Darrell Jodock, ed., *Ritschl in Retrospect* (Minneapolis: Fortress Press, 1995), 106.

127. Hefner, 'Albrecht Ritschl: An Introduction', in *Three Essays*, 37. On this point, cf. also Rolf Schäfer, *Ritschl: Grundlinien eines fast verschollenen dogmatischen Systems* (Tübingen: J. C. B. Mohr, 1968), 123–8.

128. Mark Chapman, 'The Kingdom of God and Ethics: From Ritschl to Liberation Theology', in Robin Barbour, ed., *The Kingdom of God and Society* (Edinburgh: T&T Clark, 1993), 148.

129. ICR, 236.

'Sin is only NOT that!' This is true because Ritschl, following a long line of Christian theologians, implies that sin is best, or perhaps only, known as the shadow side of redemption, as the negative imprint of the signet ring of salvation. Sin is, for Ritschl, one of the many 'value-concepts' (*Werthbegriff*) which must be accepted axiomatically in Christian theology. It is known in its fullness by the redeemed Christian community 'in light of its opposites, namely the Kingdom of God, the good, forgiveness, and the Christian ideal of life manifested supremely in Jesus Christ'.[130] But to stop here and leave sin only as a negative concept is not enough; deeper insights reward the seeker of more subtlety in Ritschl's thought, both in terms of Ritschl's historical investigations into this matter in dogmatics, his searching interpretation of relevant biblical materials and in his constructive proposal for the doctrine of sin.[131]

Sin in its personal expression is mistrust of God or unbelief, as well as the actions that this distorted orientation toward God entails. 'Luther first, and after him Calvin, maintained that hatred of sin proceeds from love of the good, a love which entirely coincides with faith in reconciliation through Christ.'[132] Sin is therefore primarily religious, but importantly, even if secondarily, ethical. Ritschl opposes Augustine and much of the subsequent Protestant tradition which taught that the relationship of our 'first parents' and us with God is mainly couched in legal terms. Luther saw the relationship rather as one of personal trust, and sin is likewise the failure of this trust to obtain. Jesus manifests the trust again in such a way that the appropriate *Lebensideal* becomes clear once more. We see the 'trust in God, by which we rise superior to sin'.[133] This religious aspect has its direct analogue in an ethical component to personal sin, which is defined negatively as any action not 'prompted by love towards our neighbor and tending to produce that fellowship which, as the *summum bonum*, represents at the same time the perfected good'.[134]

Although this sounds vaguely reminiscent of Schleiermacher, for whom as we saw above individual sin was the inability to integrate one's higher and lower consciousnesses such that the neighbour would be served by one's acts, Ritschl thinks that Schleiermacher has not understood even the full gravity of individual sin, to say nothing of the fact that he has no way of naming social sin as such. He writes that we cannot, with Schleiermacher, view sin 'merely as hitherto unattained moral perfection', but rather we should

---

130. David L. Mueller, *Introduction to the Theology of Albrecht Ritschl*, 70.

131. I should note that in some ways Volume II of *Rechtfertigung und Versöhnung* (which is the biblical basis of the doctrines) is the most important. It aided significantly in the recovery of the Kingdom of God as an eschatological concept in Jesus' preaching emblematic of the scholars in the (primarily second) quest for the historical Jesus. But since this chapter is essentially about Ritschl's rejection of Schleiermacher, which was not, for the most part, based on exegetical grounds, I have minimized reference to volume II.

132. JR III, 329.

133. JR III, 333.

134. Ibid.

'regard our imperfection as sin, in order to awaken in our minds the longing for redemption and perfection'.[135] Personal sin is active opposition to the good, not the passive refraining-from-seeking the good, which Ritschl holds Schleiermacher should have seen.[136] Rather, 'sin is active striving, desiring and acting against God'.[137] Elsewhere Ritschl describes sin as 'the perverted attitude which the sinner adopts towards God'.[138]

Ritschl tends to focus on the personal and individual aspects of sin more when he is discussing sin as a religious rupture. Conversely, sin is seen more in its corporate or social expression when Ritschl discusses the ethical and moral focus of sin. But we should be careful not to divide what Ritschl merely distinguishes, for the social and individual aspects of sin are always seen together.[139] As Ritschl puts it, 'sin can not be completely represented either within the framework of the individual life, or in that of humanity'.[140] David Mueller notes that 'this derives in part from his axiom that man is a social being and that religion is always social. It follows from this there is something like a corporate kingdom of sin and evil paralleling the Kingdom of God and the good.'[141]

What, then, are the basic features of this 'kingdom of sin?' It is, in the first place, the product of human action. 'The subject of sin, rather, is *humanity as the sum of all individuals*, in so far as the selfish action of each person, involving him as it does in illimitable interaction with all others, is directed in any degree whatsoever towards the opposite of the good, and leads to the association of individuals in common evil.'[142] It is the sinful association of individuals whose actions found the kingdom of sin. However, the kingdom of sin is not accordingly reducible to individual actions. It is a new thing. It takes on a kind of life of its own. It can influence and redirect subsequent human activity. The kingdom of sin slowly wears down the moral agent, as Ritschl says, 'blunting our moral vigilance and our moral judgment'.[143] Further, 'this sinful federation with others, however, affects everyone, at least in this way: that we become accustomed to standing forms of sin, at any rate in others, and acquiesce in them as the ordinary expression of human nature'.[144] Ritschl can thus speak of 'this whole web of sinful action and

135. JR III, 380.
136. JR I, 535–6.
137. JR III, 348–9.
138. JR III, 334.
139.   The most successful integration of these twin concepts in Ritschl I have found is in Poul Juul Nicolaisen, *Samfund og individ i Albrecht Ritschls teologi* (Copenhagen: G. E. C. Gad, 1972), 38–46. The title means 'collectivity and individual in Ritschl's theology'. It is also an excellent work on a critical aspect of Ritschl's thought, and one that deserves more attention.
140. JR III, 335.
141. Mueller, 72.
142. JR III, 335, emphasis original.
143. JR III, 338.
144   Ibid.

reaction, which presupposes and yet again increases the selfish bias in every man'.[145]

The Kingdom of God is always becoming. That it never unequivocally *is* implies the co-presence of that which is not the Kingdom of God. The Kingdom of God 'is therefore mingled at all points with the opposing currents of evil springing up on every side'.[146] It should be noted that this presence of evil in the kingdom of sin does not, in any strict logical sense, make subsequent human sin *necessary*, but rather only possible or probable.[147] Even though sin is universal, it is not due to necessity. 'The fact of universal sin on the part of man [sic] is established ... by the impulse to the unrestrained exercise of freedom, with which everyone comes into the world and meets the manifold attractions to self-seeking which arise out of the sin of society.'[148] Society presents options among which the innately free moral agent may choose; sin is universally chosen, the effect of which is to further curtail the options available for the next moral agent to choose among, and so on. Thus, 'the cooperation of many individuals in these forms of sin leads to a reinforcement of the same in common customs and principles, in standing immoralities, and even in evil institutions'.[149] Ritschl does not, unfortunately, go into more detail about what an 'evil institution' might be. When he discusses them, they have the character not of *acting*, as such, but he does say that they can 'influence human action' in the form of temptation. 'So there develops an almost irresistible power of temptation for those who with characters yet undeveloped are so much exposed to evil example that they do not see through the network of enticements to evil. Accordingly, the kingdom of sin, or the (immoral, human) world is reinforced in every new generation.'[150] If I may be permitted a fairly imprecise analogy, the image which comes most to mind in thinking about this part of Ritschl is that of a web spun by an incompetent spider. The spider, who perhaps had never spun a web before, is created able to do it, and is probably able to do it well. But for reasons which later seem inexplicable, mistakes are made, leaving the spider stuck with a half-broken, wholly functionless web. It is the spider's own fault, for no one else made the web for it. Yet every time it tries to free itself, it simply gets more and more stuck, wrapped up in its own imprisoning silk, and the web is more and more broken. This is not God's intent for the spider, yet God has willed to create spiders that are free to make their own webs. With that (admittedly coarse) image in mind, consider the following quotation from Ritschl: 'Corporate sin [*die gemeinsame Sünde*], this opposite of the kingdom of God, rests upon all as a power which at the very least limits the freedom of the individual with respect to the good. The limitation

145. JR III, 350.
146. ICR, 232.
147. Ibid.
148. ICR, 233.
149. Ibid., 233.
150. Ibid.

of the freedom of the individual for the good, by his own sin and by the entanglement with the common condition of the world, is, strictly speaking, an absence of the freedom to choose the good [*Unfreiheit zum Guten*].'[151]

We thus have in Ritschl a powerful statement of the full reality of sin, in both its roots in the individual and its far-reaching limbs in the Kingdom of sin. The Kingdom of sin is not run by the devil, is not accorded agential status to perpetuate itself, and is not seen merely as a heuristic device to describe in another way a phenomenon otherwise reducible to the individual level. It is real, it exists *as* a structure organizing human social arrangements, and it is contrary to God's will of establishing the Kingdom of God on earth. It is therefore genuinely sin. Ritschl concludes the extensive discussion of sin in *Justification and Reconciliation* Volume III with a succinct summary thesis of the whole of this doctrine, the terms of which should, following the extensive preceding analysis, now be quite clear.

> Sin, which alike as a mode of action and as a habitual propensity extends over the whole human race, is, in the Christian view of the world, estimated as the opposite of reverence and trust towards God, as also the opposite of the Kingdom of God – in the latter respect forming the kingdom of sin, which possesses no necessary ground either in the divine world order or in man's natural endowment of freedom, but unites all men with one another by means of the countless relations of sinful conduct.[152]

Conclusion: Ritschl and Schleiermacher

There has been a kind of Ritschl renaissance in the last three decades. We no longer see him and his work the way we did during the ascendancy and reign of the neo-Orthodox theologians. To take just one example of this 'sea-change', we could look to the Scottish Barthian James Richmond, who after a deep re-reading of Ritschl's theology is forced to conclude, 'Ritschl, perhaps more than anyone in the Christian tradition, wrestled with the problem of significantly relating the Kingdom of God and human action to the fabric of Christianity.'[153] This is high praise, and as the foregoing should have indicated, I am much in sympathy with its sprit. This is especially true when seen from the perspective of individual versus social sin. A theologian in the twenty-first century trying to develop new and adequate ways of naming extrapersonal structures, social arrangements and even transpersonal forces as *sin* have a great friend in Albrecht Ritschl, and a compelling doctrine of sin for this century will have to contend with his formulations of a century and a quarter ago. His position is not without its limitations, however. The Kingdom of sin is defined in basically negative terms, as that which stands opposed to the Kingdom of God. While that is a legitimate approach to take

151. ICR, 233–4.
152. JR III, 383–4.
153. James Richmond, *Ritschl: A Reappraisal – A Study in Systematic Theology* (London: Collins, 1978), 271.

in part, it seems lacking when not coupled also with a more detailed social analysis of what is concretely contrary to the Kingdom of God. Further, the positive formulation of the social arrangements of the Kingdom of God cannot be the same for Ritschl as for us. On this topic, his many detractors have a point.

Nonetheless, I have offered a read of Ritschl that takes a fairly new perspective on his setting in nineteenth-century theology by focusing on his massive, and quite successful, critique of the individualism implicit in his predecessor Schleiermacher's theology. Before pronouncing judgement on the adequacy of Ritschl's proposed alternative, however, we need to cover some more ground. The language of the Kingdom of sin is certainly not the only 'type' of way around the individualist problem. There is also the strategy of the relational self 'type'. Despite its near-faddish currency in contemporary circles, the relational self has been formulated at least as early as 1843 as a way to avoid excessive individualism in doctrines of sin. We thus look now at a second pair of nineteenth-century theologians, John Williamson Nevin and Charles Grandison Finney.

Chapter 3

FINNEY AND NEVIN ON INDIVIDUAL AND SOCIAL SIN

Charles Finney's Concept of Sin

As the discussion in the previous chapter made clear, Friedrich Schleiermacher was a liberal, and was the most influential religious figure in Germany in the first half of the nineteenth century. His individualistic notion of sin was corrected by someone thought to be, in a way, even *more liberal* than he was, in the person and work of Albrecht Ritschl. Charles Grandison Finney would by today's standards have been considered a conservative evangelical, and may have been the most influential religious figure in the United States in the middle half of the nineteenth century.[1] His individualistic notion of sin was corrected by someone thought to be, in a way, even *more conservative* than he was.[2] This figure is the now nearly forgotten Reformed theologian John Williamson Nevin. As I have shown above, Ritschl's preferred corrective to individualism was to recover the vocabulary of an extrapersonal structure, called the Kingdom of sin, which was named as sinful and in need of reconciliation to God, yet was not accorded agential power, and was not held to exist without and apart from the experience of individual human beings. Accordingly, the Christian symbol of the Kingdom of God was endowed with its proper ethical (that is, horizontal, as opposed to strictly religious or vertical) features.

Finney's conception of sin, while not nearly as nuanced as Schleiermacher's, was perhaps even more myopically individualistic, and Nevin's critique as subtle as Finney's doctrine was blunt. Nevin had his work cut out for him in criticizing Finney on sin, for scarcely few theologians in the history of Christianity have thought about sin as much or used the concept of sin more

1.   This is a somewhat contentious claim, admittedly, but certainly not a rare one. Cf. the near-grudging admissions of Sydney Ahlstrom, *A Religious History of the American People* (New Haven: Yale University Press, 1972), and Claude Welch, *Protestant Thought in the Nineteenth Century* (New Haven: Yale University Press, 1972), 1:129fn, 1:144 and 1:192. More recently, Charles Hambrick-Stowe comes to a similar conclusion in *Charles G. Finney and the Spirit of American Evangelicalism* (Grand Rapids: Eerdmans, 1996). Even among non-theological historians, Finney is estimated as being among the 'greats' of his time, as in Richard Hofstadter, *Anti-Intellectualism in American Life* (New York: Knopf, 1966), 277–9.

2.   Though this one datum does not prove the point, I advocate the stance that theological attention to social sin does and should transcend 'conservative' and 'liberal' positions.

centrally in their theology than Finney. The result of this extended reflection on the power and nature of sin in the Christian is as remarkable for its incredible consistency as it is for its astonishingly individualistic character. I have read nearly everything Finney ever published, as well as some of what he wrote but did not publish. In all of that investigation, I cannot find a single passage where sin is described as anything besides the voluntaristic act of the sinner in direct and wilful contravention of the moral law of God. In his exegetical, homiletic, theological, philosophical and personal writings, Finney conceives of sin in the same way: the sinner, who has not yet come to repentance and conversion, decides not to act in accord with the law of God.

So now that we have seen and examined in some detail Schleiermacher's and Ritschl's description of the human condition and its distortion in the individual in the clutches of sin, we can begin to compare them to Schleiermacher's near contemporary, Finney, who was not only a Reformed theologian but also a great revivalist, educator, showman.[3] I first present his concept of sin in relatively brief compass, giving special attention to its setting in early to mid-nineteenth-century theology and religious life, then look at the implementation of this doctrine as it appeared in the revivals and various movements known as the Second Great Awakening, and conclude with some 'test cases', namely slavery and economic injustice, to see whether Finney is even able, if willing, to conceive of sin in something other than an individualistic way.

Finney's Doctrinal Elaboration

One way to view Finney's characteristic contribution to an individualistic notion of sin is to focus attention on typically Old School and New School ways of formulating the problematic in mid-nineteenth-century Presbyterianism.[4] The Old School tended to focus on the 'destiny of estrangement' which describes the state of postlapsarian humanity. Unaware of the new conception of the non-historical fall being articulated by their

---

3.   On the issue of Finney's relation to the theatre arts and Christian theatrical experience in the revivals, I have learned much from Anthony Barrett Kendall, 'Riding the Anxious Bench: Enthusiasm, Conversion and Performance in Early American Revivals', unpublished PhD diss., Stanford University, 2008. It may be relevant to keep in mind that after Finney's career as an itinerant evangelist was drawing to a close, he retired to New York City to live and preach in a converted theatre on Broadway.

4.   Though now slang, these were once technical theological terms. No substantial work exists which traces the development of these fundamentally oppositional wings of Presbyterianism through to the present day. The 'schools' split in 1837, were reunited in 1869 and split again in 1936. A simple history of the movements can be found in James H. Smylie, *A Brief History of the Presbyterians* (Louisville: Geneva, 1996), and a slightly more thorough, if tendentious, treatment is David F. Wells, ed., *Reformed Theology in America: A History of Its Modern Development* (Grand Rapids: Eerdmans, 1995).

contemporaries Kierkegaard and Schleiermacher in Europe, Old School Presbyterians viewed the fall in quasi-biological terms, such that all humans, as inheritors of their 'natures' from the first pair, were unable not to sin (*non posse non peccare*).[5] The inability not to sin was twofold: the will not to sin was lacking, as was the power not to sin even if one so willed.[6] This meant, practically speaking, a doctrinal emphasis on the power of original sin, over against actual sin. The New School Presbyterians, of whom such disparate figures as Nathaniel Taylor, Albert Barnes, Lyman Beecher and Charles Finney were notable exponents, objected to this emphasis. These thinkers, as David Weddle puts it, 'tended to see in the human story the epic grandeur of free acts', wherein one 'located the value of the person precisely in the unique configuration of actions by which one is differentiated from others within that common substance or history'.[7] This led to a corresponding emphasis in formulations of sin on *actual*, and emphatically not on *original*, sin. Yet there was not uniformity in the New School as to how this emphasis should be articulated. Let us then take a closer look at Charles Finney's writings on sin (which are, incidentally, practically coterminous with Finney's writings in general) to see how actual sin is understood.

Finney seems not to have strayed much from a definition of sin he employs in his massive *Lectures on Systematic Theology*. There Finney writes,

> What is sin? Sin is a transgression of the law. The law requires benevolence, good-willing. Sin is not a mere negation, or a not-willing, but consists in self-gratification ... Sin consists in choosing, willing, intending. Sin must be voluntary; that is, it must be intelligent and voluntary ... The fact is, there either is no sin, or there is voluntary sin.[8]

Sin is identified as a wilful contravention of God's objective law by a knowing, thinking, selfish subject. For Finney, theology in general and especially the doctrine of sin had to be understood under the grand metaphor of two self-involving concepts: moral law and moral government.[9] These

---

5.   Illustrations of this position are legion, and are nearly uniform across the Old School. Representative examples can be found in Ezra Stiles Ely, *A Contrast between Calvinism and Hopkinsianism* (New York: S. Whiting, 1811), 74–8, and Lewis Cheeseman, *Differences between Old School and New School Presbyterians* (Rochester: Darrow, 1848), 117–21, or for an earlier statement of the views on sin which later became predominant, Moses Hemmenway, *Vindication of the Power, Obligation, etc., of the Unregenerate to Attend the Means of Grace, against the Exceptions of Samuel Hopkins in His Reply to Mills* (Boston: Kneeland, 1772).

6.   On this, see the perceptive analysis of E. Brooks Holifield, *Theology in America* (New Haven: Yale University Press, 2003), 152.

7.   David Weddle, *The Law as Gospel: Revival and Reform in the Theology of Charles G. Finney* (Metuchen, NJ: Scarecrow Press, 1985), 152–3.

8.   Finney, *Lectures on Systematic Theology*, ed. J. H. Fairchild (Grand Rapids: Eerdmans, 1957), 122.

9.   The first three lectures in Finney's *Systematic Theology* are, incidentally, entitled 'Moral Law', 'Moral Government' and 'Moral Obligation.'

terms had gained widespread usage in the theology of Finney's day, in what was basically the American equivalent of the continental Reformed emphasis on God's sovereignty. God was conceived as, above all else, the moral governor of creation.

The moral law held the primary metaphysical status in Finney's thought.[10] Founded in divine reason, God's law was so powerful that even God must obey it. The reason for obeying the law, both on God's and on humans' parts, was nothing less than 'the intrinsic well-being of God and the universe'.[11] Rather than making the typically Lutheran move of contrasting the law with the gospel in order to keep the two in creative tension, Finney instead asserted that the very purpose of the gospel was to instantiate and support the moral law. For Finney, robust freedom is the logical precondition for any kind of moral responsibility. The moral law is therefore simply the structure in which this freedom is operative. And moral government is the name given to the dealings God has with humans in the religious sphere. The moral law has several attributes. It is at once *intelligible* (and therefore known or knowable by all reasonable persons), *practical* (in the sense that one must be able to act on it; Gk. πράγμα = action), *fitting* (in the sense of being accommodated to human capacities and thought-structures), *impartial, universal, immutable, unified* (in the quasi-Thomistic sense of simplicity or indivisibility), *expedient* (because following the moral law hastens happiness to the obedient one) and *exclusive* of all other laws. The characteristic of the moral law most difficult to grasp is, finally, its *independence*. Finney describes the moral law as the 'eternal and necessary idea of the divine reason. It is the eternal, self-existent rule of the divine conduct, the law which the intelligence of God prescribes to himself.'[12] It is independent because it is decoupled from God's will and God's desire. The moral law is not a decree of God, nor is it properly speaking the will of God. It is, rather, the order of the universe as God has irrevocably created it.[13]

God's moral government therefore names the matrix which organizes divine and human interactions. God's 'relation to the universe and our relations to him and to each other, render it obligatory upon him to establish and administer a moral government over the universe'.[14] Since God is an

---

10.   It is also not irrelevant to note that Finney had his life-altering conversion experience while reading the Bible, which he was reading because he was studying the development of religious law as a part of his apprenticeship towards becoming a lawyer. Cf. his account of this experience in Charles G. Finney, *The Autobiography of Charles G. Finney*, ed. Helen Wessel (Minneapolis: Bethany House Publishers, 1977), 13–25.

11.   Finney, *Lectures on Systematic Theology*, 75.

12.   Ibid., 3.

13.   Had Finney been better educated, one might rightly point out the affinities of Finney's notion of 'natural' law and the Stoic (and perhaps early Christian) worldview. It is possible that Finney knew something of Greek philosophy, but he does not anywhere cite the ancients, and given that he did not have much formal education, it seems more likely that the resemblances are coincidental.

14.   Finney, *Lectures on Systematic Theology*, 8.

infinitely wise governor, Finney's argument goes, the well-being of created moral agents is best served by obedience to the moral law by all parties.[15] It should be clear by now that sin must be couched in voluntaristic terms. The human is created, and remains, free. The moral law of God is known by all, and able to be followed by all. Any violation of that law must of necessity be wilful on the part of the moral agent. Or as Finney puts it in one of his sermons, 'this is the very essence – the true idea of sin: it is deliberate, intelligent, and intentional rebellion against God'.[16]

Sin is, for Finney, malevolence – evil willing. Obedience or righteousness is, then, benevolence – good willing. Finney goes one step further and bases his ethics on the concept of a '*disinterested* benevolence'. Willing the right thing, that is, rationally intending to act objectively in accordance with the moral law, could still be sinful, for one's motives in so willing must be scrutinized. Is it not possible, Finney asked, that one might, say, obey God's Sabbath injunctions not out of proper reverence, but because one was exhausted by the work week and sought gain in one's own rest? In a similar vein Finney uses the example of a man who meets on the street a beggar in a most dreadful state. Moved to 'paroxysm' by the sad sight of the beggar, the man empties his pockets and gives the poor man all that he has. Has the man acted according to the moral law? Absolutely not. Finney writes, '[T]here is no virtue, no benevolence in it. It is a mere yielding of the will to the control of feeling, and has nothing in it in the nature of a virtue.'[17] There was not any intellectual deliberation about the reasons for willing to help the beggar, and so the action was not produced by disinterested benevolence, and was therefore sin. While this view can seem objectionably harsh, Finney is at pains to show the depths of humankind's self-deceptive selfishness. What is done in the name of the neighbour's well-being for her own sake and out of obedience to the moral law can really be simply the desire of the moral agent to feel better about him or herself. Charity given out of guilt still saves lives, but Finney finds it to be a diminished form of Christianly interaction with the world. It is, in fact, *sinful* to the extent that it is *selfish*.[18] On the relation of sin to selfishness, Finney argues, 'It is important that we should get at the fundamental or generic form of sin, that form which includes and implies all others, or, more properly, which constitutes the whole of sin. Such is *selfishness*.'[19] An analogous way of putting this, vaguely reminiscent of Schleiermacher, is that 'Sin consists in being governed by impulses of the

15. On this see the enlightening discussion and critique by David L. Weddle, *The Law as Gospel*, 142–5.

16. Finney, 'The Wrath of God', in *So Great Salvation: Evangelistic Messages* (Grand Rapids: Kredel Publishing, 1965), 49. The book contains several of Finney's more famous sermons from his later years (after 1858).

17. Finney, *Lectures in Systematic Theology*, 188.

18. It should be pointed out, however, that self-love is not necessarily sinful. One must love oneself to the extent that, and precisely because, God orders care and respect of the self in the moral law.

19. Finney, *Lectures on Systematic Theology*, 198–9.

sensibility, instead of being governed by the law of God, as it lies revealed in the reason.'[20]

Theologically speaking, then, Finney is able to describe a phenomenon as sinful if and only if the following conditions are met: a rational, intelligent moral agent, who knows the moral law of God, intelligently and voluntarily wills to contravene that law in the sphere of moral government, such that his or her actions are characterized by something other than disinterested benevolence. Since a group is not collectively intelligent and does not, in Finney's conception, have any kind of will apart from the wills of its members, there can be no group action, and therefore there can be no group or social sin.

Finney's Practical Application: The Idea of Sin in Revivals

In a way it is unfair to consider Finney's doctrines so closely, since he sometimes bragged about his 'amateur' status as a theologian. He often emphasized his own lack of theological training, and though he was a lawyer, a college professor and later president of Oberlin College, he only attended school for about three years in his whole life. For a Presbyterian theologian, he took inordinate pride in never having read the Westminster Confession. We shall be well served, therefore, to examine with even greater care the way in which Finney spoke and conceived of sin in the revivals for which he is so justly famous.

Finney's revivals, which took place all over the northeastern and middle parts of the United States, from New York to Ohio, West Virginia, Kentucky, Pennsylvania and elsewhere, were designed to create a renewed devotion to the evangelical Christian faith. Centred predominantly in rural areas and small urban centres, revivals were a logical form for religion to take. Most rural congregations would not have had the resources to pay a full-time minister, and smaller towns representing multiple denominations found it impossible to fund a separate minister for each congregation. Rather than rearing their children in a stable, highly programmed congregation which could be the focus of day-to-day or week-to-week life, Christians in rural middle America found that the pattern of recurrent revivals better suited their resources and exigencies.

Itinerant revivalist preachers could travel from town to town, giving settlers heavy, episodic doses of the proclamation they needed, and the attendant social renewal they desired. Thus, relatively few clergy could serve a relatively large geographic area. The non-theological emphasis of the preaching, coupled with a new form of 'liturgy' largely devoid of particular confessional emphases, meant that denominational affiliation posed less of a problem for church attendance and participation in the spiritual life of the community. The focus of the preaching, especially Finney's, was simple: bring

20.   Ibid., 181.

the unregenerate sinner to an awareness and hatred of his or her sinful ways, then demand contrition, and finally provide an atmosphere conducive to producing a profound and ecstatic conversion experience which could make the sinner more aware of the moral law. Ideally, such an experience would draw the convert's willing *permanently* in line with the moral law. In the right context, after all, Finney did believe in the perfectibility of the human's moral nature.[21] If this did not happen, then at least the convert could be counted on not to 'backslide' into his old ways for a while, at which time another revival could reawaken and reconvict him. Many so-called 'New Measures' were instituted into the liturgies of the revivals to produce just such an atmosphere of intense self-reflection and ecstatic conversion. These measures included the assembly praying by name for sinners who were present, so that they might come to heightened self-awareness and sorrow. The most famous of the new measures was the 'Anxious Bench'. Sinners who were thought to be near a conversion experience were herded together and seated on the pew nearest the preacher. There the preacher and his assistants would hover over them, berate them for their immorality and offer the chance to repent and be saved. A closer look at some reflections of Finney's on how sin should be conceived in this setting, given the needs of the communities Finney was serving, exhibits an intensification of the individualistic, voluntaristic view of sin developed in his dogmatic writings.

Finney had no time for notions of sin which were generalized or thought to be somehow a social, and not an individual, problem. To take just one example from his writings (there are hundreds more), Finney writes,

> Examine your sins one by one. Don't just glance over your life, see that it has been full of sin, and then go to God and make a general confession. That isn't the way. You must examine your sins one by one. Take a pen and paper and write them down as they occur to you; Go over them as carefully as an accountant goes over his books and whenever you remember a sin, add it to the list. General confessions of sin will never do. Your sins were committed one by one, and as best as you can they should be reviewed and repented of one at a time. Now, begin.[22]

As this passage makes clear, it is not as though Finney thinks that social sin cannot be repented of for some reason; rather, he thinks that it simply does not exist. Sins are committed one by one by individuals. Conscientious individuals will, with enough effort, be able to name and repent of every sin they have committed. Finney writes, 'Unless you examine your sins one by one, you can never grasp the amount of your sin. You should go over

---

21.   Finney, *Lectures to Professing Christians* (New York: Fleming H. Revell, 1878), 358ff. Finney's view of perfectionism was markedly different from any kind of Wesleyan 'second blessing', or even his Oberlin colleague Asa Mahan's vocabulary of 'total sanctification'. For Finney, what was perfected was one's *will*, and nothing else. For a reliable and brief discussion, cf. Holifield, *Theology in America*, 366–8.

22.   Finney, *Lectures on Revival* (St Paul: Bethany, 1988), 31. This was first published in 1835.

your life as thoroughly as you would prepare for judgment.'[23] Let one more quotation suffice to make the point. When the preacher knows the sinner, and knows what he has done, Finney advises, 'Bring up the individual's specific sins. Talking in general terms against sin produces no results. You must make the person feel that "he means *me*!"'[24]

Finney also, in his reflections on revivals as well as his sermons during them, locates sin exclusively as an interaction between the sinner and God. If a neighbour is harmed in a sinful act, the act is sinful only because it is against God's moral law, not because of the objective harm done. Finney asks, for example, 'You all agree that a killer or thief isn't a Christian. Why? Because he habitually disobeys God.'[25] Murder and theft may create victims, but in those acts only God is sinned against. In more subtle cases, too, Finney is at pains to note the strictly vertical cast of sin. Willing good for the neighbour, for example, is a sin when the motive behind the willing was not disinterestedly benevolent (as was noted above). Finney argues how this, too, is sin against God, even if the neighbour is served by it. While praying for a loved one's conversion might accord objectively with the moral law, it could still be selfish. On this, Finney writes, 'Women sometimes pray for their husbands because they feel it would be nice to have their mate with them at church. They never think beyond themselves. They are blind to the way their husbands dishonor God by their sins and how God would be glorified in their conversion.'[26] The wife has also sinned against God, Finney goes on to say, even in her apparently moral act of prayer, by allowing her will to be activated by motives that run contrary to the divine ordination.

Prayer, too, should likewise be individualized, and preferably not corporate. Prayer does not change God with respect to the community, but rather 'prayer produces a change in *us* [meaning in each contrite individual] that makes it fitting for God to do what would not have been fitting otherwise. When a sinner repents, that state of heart makes it proper for God to forgive him … The sinner's repentance renders His forgiveness right.'[27] Even if prayer had to be done corporately during a revival, the whole point of that corporate prayer must be to bring each individual to a greater consciousness of his or her individual sins. On this, Finney writes,

> Sinners feel awful as soon as Christians pray as they should. Sinners don't understand spirituality because they have no experience of it, but when living prayer ascends, they know something is real. They know God is in it and it brings them near to him. It makes them feel terribly solemn and they can't endure it. The impact doesn't stop there. When Christians pray in faith, God pours out His spirit and sinners melt and are converted on the spot.[28]

23.   Ibid., 35–6.
24.   Ibid., 108.
25.   Ibid., 77.
26.   Ibid., 42.
27.   Ibid., 38, emphasis original.
28.   Ibid., 85.

The last sentence of that quotation implies that an act of God in the Holy Spirit also contributes to the conversion of the repentant sinner. This is a point that warrants some clarification. Careful to differentiate his views on salvation from a kind of self-saving Pelagianism which had no role for God in salvation other than being the author of the moral law which convicts sinners (thus requiring salvation), Finney allowed for both divine and human willing in the act of conversion. To explain the convergence of these different kinds – or better, different levels – of willing in the moment of conversion, Finney uses an extended parable. Imagine, he writes, that a man is not paying attention to where he is walking, and is about to walk right over Niagara Falls (Finney grew up in upstate New York). Just before he does, a man at some distance hollers, 'Stop!' The man comes to his senses, realizes his imminent danger, and finds his way back to the right path. In Finney's view, it is correct to say that three different 'agents' conspired to save the man's life. First there is the man who yelled. Had he not said anything, the man would surely have died. Second there is the word 'stop'. Had the man not understood what it meant, and had the word not rung in his ear for a time with a kind of power, the man would have died. Finally there is the man himself. Had he not exercised his free will in deference to the other person's command and in respect of the spoken word's meaning, he could not have survived. It is not wrong to attribute salvation to any of the three 'agents'. So too, in conversion, is it legitimate to argue, Finney thought, that the repentant sinner, the providence of God, and the efficacious saving word of proclamation save the sinner's soul.[29]

On a related theme, Finney notes that some people who have never had a conversion experience wonder about the efficacy of the Holy Spirit in their lives. In the traditional theology of Old School Presbyterianism (and of virtually all of the Christian West), one need not have had a conversion experience to affirm that the Holy Spirit may objectively act in the world and in one's own life. But Finney's subjectivism and individualism extend so far that he writes, 'Some, even people who claim to know Christ, say, "I don't know anything about this [the dependence of real faith on an experience of the Holy Sprit]. I've never had that experience; either it isn't true or I am completely wrong". No doubt you *are* all wrong if you know nothing about the Spirit's leading in your life.'[30] Participation in the community who knew of the Spirit's activity was not enough. Either one's faith was secured by a profound conversion experience or it was worthless. Finney's denial of the validity of communitarian participation in faith extended itself in other ways. Far from any kind of appreciation of the sacraments, for example, as a consistent and reliable aid in the growth in faith and as an objective place for

29.   Ibid., 128–9. Finney took his preaching with the utmost seriousness. He once wrote, in fact, 'We must have exciting, powerful preaching, or the devil will have the people; except what the Methodists can save.' Cited in Whitney R. Cross's still-unsurpassed classic *The Burned-Over District: Social and Intellectual History of Enthusiastic Religion in Western New York, 1800–1850* (New York: Harper and Row, 1965), 335.

30.   Finney, *Lectures on Revival*, 73.

meeting with God, Finney has a very peculiar understanding of the 'means of grace'. Most Protestants mean by the phrase 'means of grace' sacraments, rites instituted by Jesus or the apostles, and the communal proclamation of the word. The concept was intended to describe the continuing religious and theological development of the community of the church and its members, on the one hand, and the sustenance of the Christian life on the other.[31] Finney makes this communal, developmental concept into an individual one. 'All the means of grace aim directly at converting sinners. You should pray that they would be *converted there* – not that they should be awakened and convicted, but converted on the spot.'[32]

All of these factors – the anxious bench and the new measures, the abandonment of sacraments and catechesis, the temporary, episodic nature of revivalist religion – served to inculcate and intensify a notion of sin as strictly voluntaristic and individualistic. Finney has no way to talk about his listeners' social relationships that names their distortion as sinful, save for viewing their 'social' suffering as a context rich for individual conversion.

> Distinguish between an awakened sinner and a convicted sinner. When a person feels open to Christianity don't assume he feels conviction of sin and thus neglect to show him his sin. Circumstances such as sickness, a thunderstorm, epidemic or death in the family, disappointment and so on often awaken people. They feel their need. If you find a person awakened – by whatever – lose no time pouring light in on his mind.[33]

That is to say, distortion of one's social arrangements are not sin, but rather opportunities for conviction of one's other voluntary sins.

Testing the Doctrine: Finney on Slavery and Economics

Thus far we have analysed Finney's notion of sin as it appears in both his dogmatic writings and in his application of that doctrine to the concrete situations of religious revivals and preaching. Until this point, Finney's view of sin seems utterly individualistic. In fact, it seems so atomistic in its outlook that one might reasonably assume that Finney could have nothing to say about what we might call the systemic, or social sins of his time. In the twenty-first century, our tendency is to look at issues like slavery, sexism, racism, global war and economic oppression as interpersonal and social distortions. One might suspect that an individualist like Finney could not, in such a context, have anything to say. But this is not the case. Actually,

31.   As in, for example, Phillip Melanchthon's Augsburg Confession, art. V, Wesley's view of the means of grace as both Works of Piety (including the sacraments) and Works of Mercy (including attention to social evils), or on the Reformed side, the Shorter Westminster Catechism, questions 88–9.

32.   Finney, *Lectures on Revival*, 93.

33.   Ibid., 108.

Charles Finney was one of the most outspoken critics of his time on issues of systemic distortion. I propose to look briefly at two such systemic problems, slavery and economic domination, in order to see how Finney's voluntarism fits into such social issues.

Finney was an avid abolitionist. He regarded slavery as 'always and unalterably wrong'.[34] He was not just a lone crusader on the frontier, giving sermons and making speeches against slavery, though he did do that. More importantly, according to Glenn Hewitt, Finney 'actively encouraged the various reform societies of his day, especially through his close association with the wealthy New York philanthropists Arthur and Lewis Tappan'. Yet, incredibly, 'in Finney's opinion social reform would occur only as *individuals* realized their responsibilities as Christians and pursued the reform of society through private efforts'.[35] Slavery was not wrong as a kind of systemic distortion of human society,[36] but rather due to the distorted wills of individual sinners.

> Slavery or any other evil, to be a crime, must imply selfishness ... That slaveholding, as it exists in this country, implies selfishness, at least in almost all instances, is too plain to need proof. The sinfulness of slaveholding and war ... will appear irresistibly, if we consider that sin is selfishness, and that all selfishness is necessarily sinful.[37]

As slavery was a thoroughly individualistic ill, it had a correspondingly individualistic remedy. Finney thought that slavery could be abolished (and its abolition ought to be pursued) not through ordinary governmental means of legislation, referenda, and so on. Instead, Finney held that the elimination of slavery would be a necessary after-effect of a more general revival of religion. If slaveholders could be rightly converted, they would see the error of their selfish motives in keeping their slaves, and they would free them.[38] Part of Finney's insistence on this track (nearly unparalleled in the abolitionist movement of his time) was that there could only be legitimate renewal of society when that renewal was carried out by fully regenerated individuals. In Finney's view, every person was either sinner or saint; if sinners sought social change, it could only be from an impure motive. When the saint wanted to reform society, his or her motive could be trusted.[39]

---

34.   Finney, *Lectures on Systematic Theology*, 227.

35.   Glenn Hewitt, *Regeneration and Morality: A Study of Charles Finney, Charles Hodge, John W. Nevin and Horace Bushnell* (Brooklyn: Carlson Publishing, 1991), 37.

36.   As it was for most abolitionists.

37.   Finney, *Lectures on Systematic Theology*, 227–8.

38.   On this, cf., for example, Finney's letter to Theodore Weld, July 2, 1836, cited in Gilbert Barnes, *The Antislavery Impulse*, 1830–44 (Gloucester: Peter Smith, 1957), 162. Barnes' book was one of the first to advance the thesis that the roots of the Abolitionist movement lay most decidedly not in the hands of the enlightened New England secularists who thought of themselves as having no need of religion, but rather in the growing religious consciousness of the Second Great Awakening.

39.   Finney, *Lectures on Systematic Theology*, 102–103 on the possibility of motives in sinners and saints, and on the role of the individual in social renewal, cf. ibid., 214–21.

Finney was also a champion of the fight against poverty. One of his lasting contributions to religion in the United States was his ban on the practice of 'pew rentals' at his revivals. In efforts to raise money, revivalists before Finney had charged a fee to sit in the better parts of the church (or tent), much like selling tickets for a sporting event. Finney opposed this, arguing that it stratified the congregation into the rich and the poor. He wanted to convert as many people as he could, and since pew rentals risked alienating the masses who could not afford them (and thus might not be converted), Finney disallowed the practice. He also insisted that people not wear their finest clothes to his revivals, lest those not as well dressed fear embarrassment.[40]

Finney opposed economic disparity even when the success of his revivals was less clearly at stake. He was a strong advocate for aid to unwed mothers, urged increase in aid to students seeking an education on the frontier, and opposed the outbreak of the American Civil War on the grounds that it would be a boon to the wealthy merchants of the North at the expense of the poor. And yet, even on all of these 'social' economic issues, Finney argues that the problem resides exclusively and wholly within the individual will. Let one fairly extensive quotation provide a flavour of Finney's views on economic or political oppression and its overcoming. Finney writes:

> I am happy to say that some business people do their jobs with integrity. Sinners hate them for it. They yell in barrooms that they would never buy anything from so and so – such a hypocrite will never touch a dollar of theirs. But then they go and buy from them because they know they will receive honest treatment. This is a testimony to Christianity's truth listened to from Georgia to Maine. Suppose all Christians acted this way. What would result? Christians would corner the country's business, and then the world's. Some Christians argue heatedly that they won't be able to compete if they don't do business on the same principles as the rest of the world. This is a lie. Make it your unbreakable rule to do business God's way, and you will control the market. The ungodly will be forced to conform to your standard if they want to compete. Indeed, the church could regulate the world's commerce if they themselves maintained perfect integrity. And if Christians did the same in politics, they could sway nations' destinies without getting involved in the corrupting strife of parties. If Christians united to vote for honest candidates of pure morals – apart from political opinions – no one could run who wasn't honest and pure. Within three years newspapers would ask the same questions: how good is the candidate? How moral? How devout? And no political party would ever run a known Sabbath breaker, gambler, swearer, fornicator or rumseller as their candidate.[41]

Just as the solution to slavery was a general religious revival that renewed morality all across the land, prompting individual slaveholders to release their slaves, so too was the solution to oppressive business practices seated

---

40.   Timothy L. Smith catalogues Finney's influence on social and economic reform movements in his excellent work *Revivalism and Social Reform: American Protestantism on the Eve of the Civil War* (Baltimore: Johns Hopkins University Press, 1980).

41.   Finney, *Lectures on Revival*, 100–101.

in the will of the individual merchant. In the elegant words of Timothy Smith, 'Good men and women are, in his [Finney's] understanding of biblical promises, bound to work in every way for a righteous society.' This is true because 'They know that mere understanding of social problems or human laws prescribing technical justice cannot bring *shalom*. Peace and wholeness for humanity require men and women who are willing to go those millions of second miles that Christians must travel to relieve the hurts and angers that no legislation can heal.'[42] That is a compelling, if romanticized, twentieth-century defence of Finney's notion of sin and its contribution to an understanding of social evil. But is it true? Is the source and cure of everything evil in the world to be found in the individual human will? An even subtler and more compelling critique of Finney's views of sin tell a different story. Let us then turn to Finney's greatest nineteenth-century opponent, the founder of the Mercersburg Theology, John Williamson Nevin.

Nevin's Critique of Finney on Sin: The Relational Self

To date there exists no full-length treatment of the history of American theology. The eminent historian Sydney Ahlstrom devoted about ninety pages to a sketch of what such a project would look like,[43] and more recently Ahlstrom's former student E. Brooks Holifield has written a much larger work on the history of theology from 1636 to the dawn of the American Civil War.[44] Partly because the historiography of the phenomenon is so lacking, there is, consequently, no consensus on just what exactly the import and influence of John Nevin has been for American theology. He is, at the very least, too little remembered at the present time, and nearly all specialists in nineteenth-century thought who encounter Nevin's theology remark on its incredible depth and insightfulness. To take just two notable representatives, B. A. Gerrish finds Nevin to be unsurpassed on either side of the Atlantic as an interpreter of Calvin's sacramental theology,[45] and that

42.   Timothy L. Smith, 'A Higher Law: Finney's Social Vision', in *Sojourners* 13 (March 1984): 19.

43.   Sydney E. Ahlstrom, 'Theology in America', in James W. Smith, et al., eds, *The Shaping of American Religion* (Princeton: Princeton University Press, 1961), 232–321. I am grateful to Michael B. Aune for this reference.

44.   E. Brooks Holifield, *Theology in America: Christian Thought from the Age of the Puritans to the Civil War* (New Haven: Yale University Press, 2003). I should note that while Holifield is extremely impressed by the quality of Nevin's thought, the Mercersburg thinkers do not fit very well into Holifield's schema, which is dominated by an account of the development of the evidentialist apologetic and the role of reason in theology. Nevin's thought is therefore couched in terms of 'communal reason' which highlights appropriately Nevin's emphasis on the ecclesial nature of theology, but provides a less than perfectly fitting framework for the actual content of his thought.

45.   B. A. Gerrish, *Grace and Gratitude: The Eucharistic Theology of John Calvin* (Minneapolis: Fortress, 1993), 3–6, 170.

on matters of grace, forgiveness and the regeneration of the self, 'in America, no Christian thinker delved more penetratingly' than did Nevin.[46] And perhaps the greatest living historian of nineteenth-century Christian thought, Claude Welch, writes, 'In its breadth of theological horizon and its degree of interrelationship, the work of Nevin ... was unparalleled in America and hardly matched in England and Germany.'[47]

Introduction to Nevin's Life and Work

Since Nevin is not nearly as well known as the three previous figures who have been discussed, I will provide a rough outline of the major events in Nevin's life, in order to see how he fits into the broader conversation regarding sin and grace in nineteenth-century theology. Nevin seems to have garnered many intensely loyal devotees, many of whom reflected at length on their former teacher, so there is no shortage of biographical material on Nevin.[48] John Williamson Nevin (or MacNevin, in previous generations) was born in 1803 in Shippensburg, Pennsylvania to a pious Scotch-Irish Presbyterian family. Educated in the classics at Union College in Schenectady, Nevin became distressed at the revivalism that was striking upstate New York at that time. During a probing but restrained sermon by Asahel Nettleton,[49] Nevin experienced (though he later inveighed that he was 'forced to experience') a fairly dramatic conversion there, even though he had been reared in a devout and humble home, and did not, on the face of it, have anything particularly dramatic of which to repent. He went on to Princeton where he studied with and came under the influence of Charles Hodge. Princeton at that time was deeply divided between the Old School and the New School factions. Though Nevin and Hodge would later disagree on much, Nevin was glad to have the brilliant Hodge on his side against the revivalists. Nevin became a linguist, mastering Hebrew so quickly that he was able to cover for Hebrew classes when Hodge left on sabbatical. He was also fluent in French and German, which had much to do with his later facility in interpreting late eighteenth- and early nineteenth-century continental philosophy to American theologians, who at that time (1830s–1850s) tended

---

46.   B. A. Gerrish, *Tradition and the Modern World: Reformed Theology in the Nineteenth Century* (Chicago: University of Chicago Press, 1978), 70.

47.   Claude Welch, *Protestant Thought in the Nineteenth Century*, 1:228.

48.   The fullest biography is Theodore Appel, *The Life and Work of John Williamson Nevin* (Philadelphia: Reformed Church Publication House, 1889). For a shorter version, cf. Scott Francis Brenner, 'Nevin and the Mercersburg Theology', in *Theology Today* 12 (1955): 43–56.

49.   Nettleton was one of the most effective revivalists of the Second Great Awakening, though he did not use such measures as altar calls or the anxious bench, and tended to stay in each community for much longer than the western itinerant revivalists. For a good summary of his contribution, cf. James Ehrhard, 'Asahel Nettleton: Forgotten Evangelist', in *Reformation and Revival* 6 (1997): 62–79.

to slander or completely dismiss, for example, German Idealism.[50] It was in this regard that he came also to read one of the fathers of modern church history, Augustus Neander, who impressed upon him the vast resources of the catholic, particularly patristic, traditions, as well as the developmental character of doctrine and dogma.

Nevin then accepted a professorship at Western Seminary in Pittsburgh, a Presbyterian school, where he taught for a decade before making what was, in every respect, a truly bizarre move. The only seminary in the country of the German Reformed Church, in backwoods Mercersburg, Pennsylvania, asked Nevin, a Scotch-Irish Presbyterian Old Testament scholar, to come and be president and professor of systematic theology there. Nevin accepted, changed denominational affiliation, and moved to Mercersburg, where he was fully one-third of the faculty. A colleague there, Frederick Augustus Rauch, was pioneering the field of psychology in America, and he and Nevin became fast friends. Educated under the right-wing Hegelian philosopher Karl Daub, Rauch was thoroughly steeped in Kantian and Hegelian thought, and influenced Nevin greatly in that area, the specifics of which occupy much more space below.[51] Shortly thereafter, Nevin was able to convince an up-and-coming Swiss historian of dogma, Phillip Schaff, to leave the greatest theological centre of the world in the University of Berlin, and come to Mercersburg to teach. Nevin and Schaff collaborated on a great many projects, founding what is known as the Mercersburg Theology. They were evangelical catholics with a deep appreciation for the ecumenical Christian texts and a very high view of the church. Their publications of the 1840s, while radically counter-cultural, were discussed everywhere by serious theologians. Nevin became quite ill from overwork in 1851 (he had to teach mathematics one year, as the college was too poor to hire another teacher), and Schaff went on to a more famous career at Union Seminary in New York, and so the Mercersburg Theology drew to a close by the mid 1850s. But Nevin continued to write brilliant theology for two more decades, and he died in 1886 as one of the better known religious thinkers of his day.

This theological movement is one which needs increased attention for several reasons. First, the growing body of scholarly work on Nevin and Schaff focuses nearly exclusively on themes closely related to ecclesiology. Nevin is justly famous for his most important book *The Mystical Presence*,[52] which is, *prima facie*, an account of the nature of Christ's presence in the Eucharist. But the book is much more than this. It offers an account of salvation-in-community that touches on nearly all of the doctrines of systematic theology, not just the sacraments and the church. Reading the

---

50.   Just prior to Nevin is of course the apex of the influence on American theology of Reidian epistemology, and its 'common sense' analogues.

51.   Daub came late to Hegel. His sequential and total allegiance first to Kant, then to Schelling, and finally to Hegel earned him the nickname 'Talleyrand of Idealism'.

52.   John W. Nevin, *The Mystical Presence: A Vindication of the Reformed or Calvinistic Doctrine of the Holy Eucharist* (Eugene, OR: Wipf and Stock Publishers, 2000), originally published 1846.

work from the perspective of individual and social sin and salvation offers a fresh take on a classic of American theology. But this is not the only reason for engaging Nevin's work. He was probably the most articulate and nuanced objector to the theology underwriting the spirit of revivalism.[53] Scores of theologians objected to the worship *style*, finding it undignified or too subjectivist. Those who objected on theological grounds usually did so by charging the evangelists with a blasé and rehearsed Arminianism, to be rejected on the same grounds that Edwards had rejected it generations before. Nevin's subtler objection to revivalism, that its exclusive focus on the individual ignored perilously the web of relationships in which the individual was created, offers profound insights into the problem of sin and the relational self which occupies not just the present project but many others as well. The section on Nevin proceeds in three parts. Following this brief contextualization, I carefully recount Nevin's critique of Finney. Second, I develop Nevin's notion of selfhood, which is heavily indebted to German Idealism, and which is manifested in the central doctrine of Nevin's thought, the Incarnation. Finally, I offer an evaluation of the success of Nevin's critique and counterproposal, with an eye toward a re-appropriation of these thoughts for the contemporary theological problem of individual and social sin.

Nevin's Critique of Finney in The Anxious Bench

In 1843, alarmed that the popularity and prevalence of evangelistic revivals seemed to be following him from New York to New Jersey and into Pennsylvania and beyond, Nevin wrote a book called *The Anxious Bench*.[54] The anxious bench, as was mentioned above, was a seat or row of seats in the front of a revival worship service upon which were seated those persons who had not yet experienced conversion but who were deemed likely candidates for such an experience, either by themselves or at the request of their family or acquaintances in the parish. Nevin's contention was not just with this particular 'measure', but for the whole outward form of religion it signified. Salient objections to Finney's system of New Measures can usefully be grouped into five types. These types are: the misunderstanding of the relationship between the inner essence and the outward form of religion, the impracticality of the system, its inability to

---

53.   Ahlstrom calls Nevin's the 'most inspired movement to repair the havoc which revivalism was working on Reformed church life in America', and that *The Anxious Bench* 'consists chiefly of a series of closely knit arguments calculated to demonstrate that the ground principles of this radical experiential emphasis were not only superficial but subversive to the Faith.' Ahlstrom, 'Theology in America', 267, 268.

54.   John Williamson Nevin, *The Anxious Bench*, 2nd edn (Chambersburg, PA: Publication Office of the German Reformed Church, 1844; repr. Wipf and Stock Publishing, 2000). Pagination is cited according to the reprint.

produce social renewal, its Pelagian character, and especially the erroneous notion of selfhood and community which it presupposes. We will examine representatives of each type of criticism in turn. Whereas with Finney we began with his theological lectures and investigated how the theory played out in their application to revivals, with Nevin the opposite order is followed; the practical critique comes first, and the theory which underlay his critique (which was, incidentally, developed much more deeply after 1843 anyway) is exposited second.

In some sense, the debate over revivals and their place in American Christianity was an aesthetic issue. The question was, what is religion supposed to *look* like? This is a question about the outward form which faith takes on. Nevin called the replacement of the proper form by an improper one *quackery*. The form is held to have the power which it can, in reality, only *signify*. 'Quackery consists in pretension to an inward virtue or power, which is not possessed in fact, on the ground of a mere show of the strength which such power or virtue is supposed to include.'[55] Finney makes promises about the forgiveness of sin that cannot be sustained. No matter how intense the experience of the liturgical form of forgiveness, if it is not connected to some kind of reality in God, the forgiveness is a sham. This is not to say that faith should not take some particular form in liturgy (and, for that matter, in social arrangements, ethics, patterns of religious experience, and so on), as formless worship is unthinkable. Indeed, according to Nevin,

> religion must have forms, as well as an inward living force. But these can have no value, no proper reality, except as they spring perpetually from the presence of the living force itself. The inward must be the bearer of the outward. Quackery, however, reverses the case. The outward is made to bear the inward. The shrine, consecrated with the proper ceremonies, *must* become a shechinah. Forms have a virtue in them to bind and rule the force of things. Such forms may be exhibited in a ritual, or in a creed, or in a scheme of a religious experience mechanically apprehended; but in the end the case is substantially the same. It is quackery in the garb of religion without its inward life and power.[56]

Sometimes the presence of this power in revivals was held to be attested to by the astonishing 'success' of preachers to coordinate conversion experiences. In fact, one of Finney's defenders, a preacher named William Davis wrote 'A quack may preach a sermon and make a long prayer, but it takes something more than a quack *so* to preach the truth that sinners will *immediately* come forward to the anxious bench.'[57] Nevin was unconvinced, and replied, 'Right bravely spoken, but the very dialect of quackdom itself.'[58]

Religion is perhaps most vulnerable to such confusions, since the effects promised by revivals cannot really be verified *ante mortem*. Quacks selling

---

55. Ibid., 26.
56. Ibid., 28–9.
57. 'Davis' Plea', in *Lutheran Observer* 12 (1843): 32.
58. *Anxious Bench*, 25.

elixirs can be confronted; either his medicines work or they do not. But a
theology based on the *signa* of outward forms, and not their *significatum*,
lacks the efficacious promises of God's forgiveness of sin. Nevin writes,

> [Q]uacks ... meet us plentifully in every direction. We need not be surprised, then, to
> find the evil fully at home also in the sphere of religion. Indeed it might seem to be
> more at home here than anywhere else. Here especially the heart of man, 'deceitful
> above all things and desperately wicked', has shown itself most ingenious in all ages
> in substituting the shadow for the reality, the form for the substance, the outward
> for the inward.[59]

Far from delivering the afflicted conscience from debilitating sin, in Nevin's
view Finney's system compounds the problem by adding the idolatry inherent
in religious quackery to the list of sins committed. It was no doctrinaire
stodginess that made Nevin nostalgic for traditional liturgy, but rather a
developing historical consciousness that saw in the continuity of the church's
outward forms a hint of the externalization of the ideal church into the
actual.[60] The traditional forms, Nevin thought, could still deliver the goods.
He summarized their possibilities glowingly:

> Sinners will be awakened and born into the family of God. Christians will be builded
> up in faith, and made meet for the inheritance of the saints in light. Religion will
> grow and prosper. This is the true idea of evangelical power. But let a preacher be
> inwardly weak, though ambitious at the same time of making an impression in the
> name of religion, and he will find it necessary to go to work in a different way. Old
> forms must needs be dull and spiritless in his hands. His sermons have neither edge
> nor point. The services of his sanctuary are lean and barren. He can throw no interest
> into the catechism. He has no heart for family visitation and no skill to make it of any
> account. Still he desires to be doing something in his spiritual vocation, to convince
> others and to satisfy himself that he is not without faith.[61]

The second type of objection Nevin makes of Finney in *The Anxious Bench*
has to do more simply with the impractical and indeed self-defeating nature
of revivals. Nevin and Finney agreed in their intent; each man wanted to
see the religious sensibilities of Americans heightened and sharpened so
that sin, in all its myriad forms, could be better resisted. But Nevin thought
that revivals would in fact do just the opposite. They had the effect of
compartmentalizing religion into something that 'happened' episodically
and for a short time, and could then be quickly forgotten. People who come
to Christianity through the bench 'fill the Church with lean professors, who
show subsequently but little concern to *grow* in grace, little capacity indeed
to understand at all the free, deep, full life of the "new man" in Christ Jesus.

---

59.   Ibid., 27.
60.   These are Nevin's preferred replacements for the Reformation terminology of the
visible and the invisible church. The idealism implicit in such a formulation is discussed in
detail below.
61.   Ibid., 29.

Such converts, if they do not altogether "fall from grace" are apt to continue at least babes in the Gospel, as long as they live.'[62]

The corollary goods ideally co-present with the Christian faith, such as education and social services, also would wane. In the system of the bench, Nevin argued,

> The attention of ministers will be turned away from more important, but less ostentatious methods of promoting religion. Preaching will become shallow. The catechism may be possibly still treated with professed respect, but practically it will be shorn of its honor and force. Education may be considered to some extent necessary for the work of the ministry, but in fact no great care will be felt to have it either thorough or complete. Ignorance, sciolism, and quackery will lift up the head on all sides and show themselves off as the 'great power of God'.[63]

Specifically with respect to the effects of revivalism on ministers, Nevin writes, 'Study and the cultivation of personal holiness will seem to their zeal an irksome restraint; and making their lazy heartless course of preparation as short as possible, they will go out with the reputation of educated ministers, the blind leading the blind, to bring the ministry into contempt.'[64] Even when the minister was well-meaning in his preparation and pastoral labour, the system of the bench fundamentally opposed the long-term promotion of religion. 'But it calls for comparatively little power for a man [sic] to distinguish himself as a leader in periodical religious excitements, where zeal has room for outward display, and wholesale action is employed to discharge within a month the claims of a year.'[65] In such a system, the pastor is less a shepherd of a faithful flock than a roving repairman of the broken faith of individuals.

Nevin objects, third, to the implicit Pelagianism of Finney's theology and practice. Although as I noted above, Finney had a fairly nuanced view of human willing and the determination of human salvation by God's word, in revivalism it seemed quite obvious (to a scholar like Nevin who was deeply knowledgeable of sixteenth-century debates over the relationship of faith to works) that each 'converted' sinner was simply saving herself. What was needed was merely a decision to be saved, and the salvation was accomplished. Nevin complains, 'All stress is laid upon the energy of the individual will (the self-will of the flesh) for the accomplishment of the great change in which regeneration is supposed to consist.'[66] In a coeval debate with the great New England Congregationalist theologian Horace Bushnell, Nevin would begin to describe this kind of concept as an inappropriate form of *naturalism* in theology. 'Salvation' was then nothing more than the gradual working out of an impulse which was always already naturally 'in' the sinner.

62. Ibid., 58.
63. Ibid., 33.
64. Ibid.
65. Ibid., 31.
66. Ibid., 60.

Grace could accordingly not come *extra nos* as a supernatural reality, could not be definitively 'in' the person of Jesus Christ, and could not even be really gracious. Instead, Nevin contends, in Finney's theology regenerating grace is 'apprehended mechanically as the result of a spiritual process which begins and ends with the sinner himself'.[67]

This has extremely important consequences for a doctrine of sin. As salvation is, in Nevin's view of Finney, simply pulling oneself up by one's bootstraps and going through the motions of a conversion, so too is sin accordingly a strictly individual phenomenon. One can decide not to do it anymore. This approach is compatible with such sins as theft or murder, but seems incompatible with what might be called systemic or social sins. One cannot simply decide no longer to participate in sexist or racist structures. One cannot decide to eradicate institutionalized poverty. These are inter-subjective, systemic distortions. Finney's system cannot address them, according to Nevin.

> Finneyism is only Taylorism reduced to practice, the speculative heresy of New Haven actualized in common life. A low, shallow, pelagianizing theory of religion runs through it from beginning to end. The fact of sin is acknowledged, but not in its true extent. The idea of a new spiritual creation is admitted, but not in its proper radical and comprehensive form. The ground of the sinner's salvation is made to lie at last in his own separate person.[68]

In addition to its 'quackery', its impracticality, and its Pelagian tendencies, Nevin raises two final related objections. He thinks, in the fourth place, that the larger renewal of society in general cannot be attained by Finney's system, and this is because, lastly, its view of the self is so atomistic that it cannot address the individual as she actually exists, which is in a network of other selves, with particular histories, social locations, community roles, and so on. Nevin writes,

> It is a different system altogether that is required to build up the interests of the community in a firm and sure way. A ministry apt to teach; sermons full of unction and light; faithful, systematic instruction; zeal for the interests of holiness; pastoral visitations; catechetical training; due attention to order and discipline; patient perseverance in the details of the ministerial work; these are the agencies *by which alone* the kingdom of God may be expected to go steadily forward, among any people.[69]

---

67. Ibid., 60.
68. Ibid., 59. 'Taylorism' refers to the style of theology characteristic of Nathaniel Taylor and the 'New Haven' theology that advocated a reinvigoration of preaching and revivals, but tries to harmonize this emphasis with the maintenance of traditional Reformed teaching regarding the objectivity of God's election. He altered the meaning of election, however, to refer not to a division between the elect and the reprobate, but to God's decision to elect a moral order to the world, its inhabitants then to be judged with justice, at least, and perhaps mercy. He was accused (probably rightly) of Arminianism.
69. Ibid., 61, my emphasis.

While Nevin is here placing perhaps too much weight on the shoulders of the clergy for effecting social change, the point is that only when one's religious outlook is broader than the status of the individual's soul, only when a commitment is made for the long-term health of particular community by particular persons of faith can that community thrive. Nevin believes in the ability of the local minister to marshal available resources for the betterment of the community, not just the soul. He concludes, 'Where these are fully employed, there will be revivals; but they will be only as it were the natural fruit of the general culture going before, without that spasmodic, meteoric character which too often distinguishes excitements under this name, while the life of religion shows itself abidingly at work.'[70] Prefiguring in a way some of the liberation theologians discussed in detail in Chapters 4–6 of this book, Nevin always thought that real salvation implied the salvation of the *whole person*, not just the soul in some distant future. Bringing the gospel to unbelievers meant bringing food and clothing, too. Sharing one's faith was not to be practised apart from sharing one's money. This kind of holistic faith was the only viable chance for true social renewal. One's relationship to God would determine one's social ethic almost completely. 'No wonder that the religion which is commenced and carried forward under such auspices [as the bench] should show itself to be characteristically coarse and gross. Wanting true reverence for God, it will be without true charity also towards men [sic].'[71] Nevin goes on to argue,

> As this [catechism] theory of religion is the ground of all deep experience in the case of the individual Christian, so it gives rise to the more vigorous and comprehensive action, on the part of the church, for carrying into effect the provisions of the gospel ... In proportion exactly as it is understood and felt, will such action display itself in all of its proper forms; and under no other circumstances can any agency be employed for the same end that will be entitled to take its place.[72]

The church could be the agent of real social change. As opposed to Finney, Nevin sought the abolition of slavery through ecclesial avenues, and many of the issues on the table when Nevin led synodical gatherings of the German Reformed Church were aspects of social ethics. Finney's ecclesiology was so lacking, in the view of Nevin, that the church so conceived could not be a leaven in the bread of the surrounding culture. Somewhat tragically, in the revivalist ecclesiology, 'All is meant to hang methodistically on sudden and violent experiences belonging to the individual separately taken, and holding little or no connection with his relations to the Church' and the view of the church as the community of believers is lost.[73]

Nevin's final objection to Finney falls along similar lines, and is the one most important for the current project, for it has to do with the

70. Ibid., 62.
71. Ibid., 57.
72. Ibid., 67.
73. Ibid., 68.

gross mischaracterization of the self which disallows any notion of non-individualistic sin. The fact that Nevin would infer that there must be some deeply erroneous theological notion underlying all of what he perceived to be the immoral practices of the system of the revival is not surprising, for Nevin always insisted on the intimate connection, indeed inseparability, of theory and praxis.[74] The self addressed in the practice of revivals was a sham, a chimera. The self implicit in the theology of revivals (and indeed, Nevin likely would have said that this deficient view of selfhood plagued American theology generally) was so fractured that it could never be wholly addressed or even met. Primarily, this meant that only the emotions of the individual were considered in revivals, not the intellect, not the body, not the community, and so forth.[75] Nevin writes,

> Commonly indeed those who deal in the anxious seat rely far less upon the presentation of truth to the understanding than they do upon other influences to bring persons forward. Pains are taken rather to raise the imagination, and confound the judgment. Exciting appeals are made to the principle of fear. Advantage is taken in every way of the senses and nerves.[76]

Nevin was not against any kind of feeling in religion, as he is sometimes accused of teaching.[77] He was simply concerned that in order for a conversion to be genuine, it must be the whole self which is converted, not simply the emotions, or only the will, and so on. Such one-dimensional conversions would not last and would indeed prove detrimental to the health of the church. It would be better to address the real emotions of Christians as part of a more comprehensive view of the self.

> It is well indeed that sinners should bind themselves by an inward resolution to seek the Lord, while He is to be found; and it is right that they should be urged to do this on all suitable occasions. But such a resolution, to be of any account, must proceed from intelligent reflection and inward self-possession; and it can have no salutary

---

74.   Writing in the context of revivalism, Nevin asserts, 'I have denominated the system a *heresy*, not inconsiderately or for rhetorical effect simply, but with sober calculation and design. In religion, as in life universally, theory and practice are always inseparably intertwined in the ground of the soul. Every error is felt practically; and wherever obliquity in conduct comes into view, it must be referred to some corresponding obliquity in principle.' *Anxious Bench*, 59.

75.   I contend that Nevin derived his insistence on the wholeness of the self from Rauch. Nevin edited the second edition of Rauch's masterwork, *Psychology, Or a View of the Human Soul* (New York: Dodd, 1841), the principal thesis of which is that the human body is the outward expression of an eternal organic law allowing for the participation in the whole by the part. 'Personality', which Rauch developed as the central anthropological theme long before Bushnell, was the co-inherence of the generic life of humanity and the consciousness thereof in any individual.

76.   *Anxious Bench*, 23.

77.   John Winebrenner, who promoted a revivalist sect within the German Reformed Church, and his followers frequently levelled this criticism of Nevin and Schaff.

force, except as entertained in the consciousness of God's presence and God's authority, to the exclusion comparatively of all inferior references.[78]

Indeed, 'True religious feeling is inward and deep; shrinks from show; forms the mind to a subdued humble habit.'[79]

How does all of this relate to sin? The answer is that the whole person, in all of her social and historical relationships, must be addressed in conversion, because sin is accordingly a problem that afflicts the *whole* self. Finney was wrong to locate it in the individual only, and wrong further to seat it so squarely in the will of the sinner. Instead, according to Nevin:

> In opposition to this [to Finney], the true theory of religion carries us continually beyond the individual, to the view of a far deeper and more general form of existence in which his [sic] particular life is represented to stand. Thus sin is not simply the offspring of a particular will, putting itself forth in the form of actual transgressions, but a wrong habit of humanity itself, a general and universal force, which includes and rules the entire existence of the individual man from the start. The disease is organic, rooted in the race, and not to be overcome in any case by a force less deep and general than itself.[80]

A concept of grace involving the perfecting of the will *by* the will simply would not do. The will, weakened by sin, is not strong enough to withstand the collective force of sin acting upon it. The overcoming of sin must therefore come wholly from without, or as the sixteenth-century reformers put it, salvation comes *extra nos*. Nevin, though in the 1850s he flirted with converting to Catholicism and was forever being accused of 'Puseyism', was more truly Protestant than the Presbyterian Finney.[81] The following passage reads like something Luther or Calvin might say about grace (although only after having read Hegel!). According to Nevin,

> The particular subject lives, not properly speaking in the acts of his own will separately considered, but in the power of a vast generic life that lies wholly beyond his will, and has now begun to manifest itself through him as the law and type of his will itself, as well as of his whole being... From first to last it is a power which he does not so much apprehend as he is apprehended by it, and more comprehended in it, and carried along with it as something infinitely more deep and vast than himself.[82]

---

78.   *Anxious Bench*, 47.
79.   Ibid., 56.
80.   Ibid., 65.
81.   Edmund B. Pusey was one of the Oxford Tractarians who attempted to bring the Anglican church more in line with historic Catholicism, especially with regard to their sacramental theology and ecclesiology. Pusey became the leader of the group after J. H. Newman's conversion to Rome, though he himself never converted. Pius IX is supposed to have said something to the effect of, 'Pusey rang in the Roman Church in England, but failed to follow the sound of the bell himself.'
82.   *Anxious Bench*, 65–6.

In order for genuine salvation to occur and be experienced,

> man *must* be wrought upon by a force, deeper and more comprehensive than his
> separate self. Great purposes and great efforts appear only when the sense of the
> general overpowers the sense of the particular, and the last is constrained to become
> tributary to the tendencies and purposes of the first ... To acquire, in any case, true
> force, it must fall back on a power more general than itself. And so it is found that in
> the sphere of religion particularly, the Pelagian theory is always vastly more impotent
> for practical purposes, than that to which it stands opposed.[83]

This is true because, to reiterate, 'The ruin of man and his recovery rest in
a ground which is beyond himself as an individual.'[84] The knowledge, or
consciousness, of this fact is made clear by the fact that when one realizes
that one is a sinner, the forms that one's sin takes is made clearer by
understanding the web of relationships that has been distorted by the sin.
Nevin concludes,

> Conviction of sin is never deep and thorough, till it comes to a clear consciousness,
> with the sinner, that his sinful life is rooted in a sinful nature, older and broader
> than himself, which he has no power to renovate or control. Nor is the Christian
> salvation rightly understood, till it is felt that it must be something more deep and
> comprehensive than the will of the individual subject himself, in whom it is to
> appear.[85]

The life of the soul must stand in something beyond itself. Religion involves
the will; but not as self-will, affecting to be its own ground and centre.
'Religion involves feeling; but it is not comprehended in this as its principle.
Religion is subjective also, fills and rules the individual in whom it appears;
but it is not created in any sense by its subject or from its subject. The life of
the branch is in the trunk.'[86]

Nevin on Idealism

I have laboured in depth in the preceding pages over the completeness of
Nevin's rejection of individualism. Charles Finney and the anxious bench
were singled out for particular censure, but this is merely an instance of
synecdoche, for Nevin was actually reacting to the whole ferment of mid-
nineteenth-century theology. His tireless critique may have seemed protracted
and tedious, and my exposition thereof may regrettably have shared these
qualities. But the points were crucial to make, for at least two reasons.
First, Nevin's communitarian voice is nearly a solo in the cacophony of
individualists of his time. The Mercersburg movement was counter-cultural

83.   Ibid., 66.
84.   Ibid., 67.
85.   Ibid., 66–7.
86.   Ibid., 60.

in many ways, but perhaps principally in its rejection of individualism.[87] Second, Nevin's preferred alternative to the 'solitary will' view of the self, the self considered in its constitutive relationships, seems utterly prescient given the course of recent theology. That the self is to be conceived in the context of, or even as the product of, its social relationships has become practically axiomatic in contemporary philosophical and religious thought. Yet there is no consensus as to how this is to be practically undertaken. The fact that Nevin was thinking through these issues already in 1840 is remarkable and potentially instructive. What remains, then, is to connect the dots of what kind of relationality Nevin had in mind in his view of human selfhood. To do this requires a fuller examination of the role German idealism played in Nevin's thought.

Asking about the self means asking what is *real*. The simplest explanation that can be given, in general, for what Nevin thinks is *real* is that the real is the ideal externalizing itself in the actual. Nevin saw all of creation as a single organism containing two fundamental 'orders of being'. These are the eternal and the spatiotemporal.[88] The ideal, in abstraction, is eternal, and the actual, in abstraction, is spatiotemporal. But they do not exist apart from each other. They co-inhere in reality. Early in his career Nevin conceived of the ideal basically in terms borrowed from Christian Platonism. God had ideas about what, for example, animals were, what rocks were, what water was, and so on. These ideas constituted the eternal 'essence' of creation. No single instance of any animal, rock or water droplet matched the idea, though none was fully divorced from it.[89] The former exhibits a 'generic life', which is instantiated in the particular. Nevin's metaphors for explaining this view are almost always organic. For example,

> In the vegetable world, the acorn, cast into the ground and transformed subsequently into the oak of a hundred years, constitutes in one view only a single existence. But in another, it includes the force of a life that is capable of reaching far beyond all such individual limits. For the oak may produce ten thousand other acorns, and thus repeat its own life in a whole forest of trees.[90]

Nevin's philosophy is not mere Platonism, however. A particular kind of Kantian flavour characterizes his thought as well, for the central theme of

---

87.   E. Brooks Holifield lists the counter-cultural character like this: 'It was Christocentric rather than bibliocentric; it elevated the incarnation over the atonement; it celebrated the corporate Christian "life" within the church rather than individual religious experience; it spoke of the organic development in history rather than of the restitution of the primitive church; and it placed the sacraments rather than preaching at the forefront of Christian devotion.' Holifield, *Theology in America*, 467.

88.   Though this theme runs through virtually all of Nevin's writings, a concise statement of its application to theological anthropology can be found in *The Mystical Presence*, 187–92.

89.   Nevin's Platonism was mediated through the great English archbishop Robert Leighton.

90.   Nevin, *Mystical Presence*, 151–2.

the ideal becoming real in the actual is the basis of Nevin's epistemology. Most thinkers in the United States of Nevin's generation were staunch empiricists. They viewed the mind essentially as a *tabula rasa* upon which was imprinted sensory data from the physical world which was then organized and interpreted according to the customs of experience and language. Nevin lambastes this view, asserting that 'the general character of this bastard philosophy is that it affects to measure all things, both on earth and in heaven, by the categories of the common abstract understanding, as it stands related to the world of time and sense'.[91] Empiricism, in Nevin's view, prohibited talk about God, since the structures said to be in the mind would be unable to comprehend anything eternal or spiritual. Instead, Nevin adopted Kant's language of the active role of the subject in the process of knowing, that what is known is the phenomenon of the ideal in the actual. Where Nevin differs from Kant is that for Nevin, the categories through which such phenomena are experienced (like quantity, quantity, identity, etc.) were not simply heurisms or noetic constructs but rather exist extramentally. Nevin thought that the mind was adapted to knowledge of the ideal in the actual just as the eye is adapted to the reception of light. It is built in such a way that perception is possible, but this must be actively sought by the subject.

Though Nevin was an accomplished speculative thinker, this ontology is not based on an abstraction. Instead, the concreteness of the Incarnation is the foundation for all of Nevin's philosophical thinking. What we have in the Incarnation is an instance of the eternal nature of God in the second person of the Trinity instantiating itself into the actual in the person of Jesus of Nazareth, such that the resulting co-inherence is the real god-human. The organic life of God and the generic life of humanity were thus merged. Nevin can therefore say 'The incarnation is the FACT of all facts, that may be said to authenticate all truth in the world besides. The first miracle, and the only miracle, we may say, of Christianity, is the new creation in which it starts. All else is but the natural product and expression of the life thus introduced into the world.'[92] This quotation evidences a further aspect of Idealism in Nevin's thought, which is its rich idea of history. Salvation in the Princeton orthodoxy in which Nevin was formed was accomplished by the timeless decrees of God. In their system, the Incarnation was only important as a kind of necessary precondition for the execution of the *triplex munus* of Jesus Christ.[93] For Nevin the simple fact of the Incarnation, not the hint it gives toward the will of God exhibited in an eternal decree, is determinative. The rest of Jesus' work – his ministry, death, resurrection and ascension – were part of the redemptive process, too, 'but all this only as the proper

91.   Nevin, *Human Freedom and a Plea for Philosophy* (Mercersburg: Rice, 1850), 42–3.
92.   Nevin, *The Mystical Presence*, 209, emphasis his. I should note that, while I do not discuss it here, the dominant metaphor in which Nevin's treatment of the Incarnation is usually couched is the recapitulation effected by Christ the 'Second Adam'.
93.   The classic statement of this is Charles Hodge, *Systematic Theology*, 3 vols (London: Clarke, 1960), 1:198ff.

and necessary result of the first mystery itself, the entrance of the divine word in a living way into the sphere of our fallen humanity'.[94] This conceptuality, borrowed and adapted from R. I. Wilberforce[95] and particularly from the German Lutheran theologian Isaak Augustus Dorner,[96] could make Nevin sound like a dyed-in-the-wool Hegelian. But this is not the case. Hegel's God was an impersonal principle, except as it used human personality to work itself out in history; Nevin's God was thoroughly personal. In Hegel it is the Spirit which becomes incarnate in individual humans; in Nevin it is the Logos which becomes incarnate in Jesus Christ (though this certainly has a derivative effect on other humans). Humanity in Hegel was a kind of moment in the development of the Spirit, eventually to be *aufgehoben* into its own inner life; Nevin insisted that humanity and God remained distinct.[97] Though his appropriation of Idealist thought was thus far from wholesale, Nevin could still write, a bit tongue-in-cheek:

> We honor German learning and thought, and stand largely indebted to them for such views as we have come to have of man and the world, of Christianity and the Bible. We are not of that class who pique themselves on being good philosophers, because they have never read a line of Kant and have not the remotest conception of what was dreamed of by Fichte and Schelling; or who consider themselves good and safe theologians, because their dogmatic slumbers have never been for a moment disturbed by Schleiermacher and the dangerous school of Tübingen.[98]

Nevin and the Ideal, Related Self

Before concluding with an appraisal of the meaning of Nevin's thought for the current project, it will be beneficial to look in some more detail at the specifics of Nevin's conception of the self, based as it is in his version of Idealism. Since Nevin wrote so incredibly broadly on this topic,[99] I have

94.   Nevin, 'Wilberforce on the Incarnation', in *Mercersburg Review* 2 (1850): 172.
95.   Robert I. Wilberforce, *The Doctrine of the Incarnation of Our Lord Jesus Christ in Its Relation to Mankind and to the Church* (London: Murray, 1849).
96.   Isaak A. Dorner, *Entwicklungsgeschichte der Lehre von der Person Christi von den ältesten Zeiten bis auf die neueste dargestellt*, 2 vols (Berlin, Schlawitz, 1851–3). Nevin was generally very favourable towards Dorner; his divergences are collected in Nevin, 'Answer to Professor Dorner', *Mercersburg Review* 15 (1868): 532–646.
97.   Cf. the fuller comparison in Holifield, *Theology in America*, 470–76.
98.   Nevin, 'Our Relations to Germany', in *Mercersburg Review* 14 (1867): 629–30.
99.   Other examples of essays on this same theme are Nevin, 'Our Union with Christ', *Weekly Messenger of the German Reformed Church* 13 (Feb. 1848), 'True and False Protestantism', in *Mercersburg Review* 1 (1849): 83–104, 'The New Creation in Christ', in *Mercersburg Review* 2 (1850): 1–12, 'Man's True Destiny', in *Mercersburg Review* 5 (1853): 492–520, 'Natural and Supernatural', in *Mercersburg Review* 11 (1859): 176–210, 'The Wonderful Nature of Man', in *Mercersburg Review* 11 (1859): 317–37, 'Nature and Grace', in *Mercersburg Review* 19 (1872): 485–509, 'Christianity and Humanity', in *Mercersburg Review* 20 (1873): 469–86, and 'Biblical Anthropology', in *Reformed Quarterly Review* 24 (1877): 330–65.

chosen to select one essay that is representative of his themes and is applicable to the notion of the self-in-relation as an antidote to an individualistic notion of sin.[100] The essay contains characteristic formulations of human freedom and responsibility, the law, personal identity or selfhood, human consciousness and the will. The result is a sketch of how the self is rooted in its relations to that which is not the self, such that sin must be reconceived not as individualistic, but as a distortion of these life-giving relationships.

Nevin begins by applying his idealistic ontology to humans. Predictably, but clearly, Nevin writes:

> Every man [sic] comprehends in himself a life which is at once both single and general, the life of his own person, separately considered, and the life at the same time of the race to which he belongs. He is *a man*; the universal conception of humanity as it enters into him, as it enters into all other men: while he is, besides, *this* or *that* man, as distinguished from all others by his particular position in the human world.[101]

The general and the particular are joined together in intimate connection, so that one cannot understand the one without the other. Each person's existence is not secured in their own being, but rather by participating in the common life of all. A longer passage on this theme warrants citation.

> The relation between the general and the particular [in humanity] ... is not one of outward conjunction simply; as though the man were, in the first place, complete in and of himself, and were then brought to stand in certain connections with other men, previously complete in the same way. His completeness as an individual involves of itself his comprehension in a life more general than his own. The first can have no place apart from the second. The two forms of existence are not the same in themselves, but they are indissolubly joined together, as constituent elements of one and the same living fact in the person of every man.[102]

'Personality', or as we would call it, human selfhood, is thus conceived as the dynamic inter-relation of these two poles, the individual and the generic. In the rest of creation, in animals, vegetables and minerals, the union of these poles is necessary. Since humans are free and conscious, however, they must choose to unite their individual natures to the generic nature. This is done in two ways, first by the growth in union with Christ by participating in the mystical union effected in the church and in the sacraments, and more generally simply by relating to the other individuals of the generic life, i.e. other people. Thus the self is made in the union of the individual (including attendant concepts like 'will', 'intellect' and 'emotion') with the generic (including the paired attendant concepts of 'the law', 'reason' and 'love').

---

100. Nevin, 'Human Freedom', in *Mercersburg Review* 2 (1850): 97–116, reprinted in James Hasting Nichols, ed., *The Mercersburg Theology* (New York: Oxford University Press, 1966), 286–306. References are to the pagination of the Nichols anthology.
101. Nevin, 'Human Freedom', 288.
102. Ibid.

This union had to be effected, Nevin maintained, at least in part by intelligent, conscious action on the part of the individual.[103] The individual, conscious of its own individuality, 'must receive into itself the general life to which it of right belongs, so as to be filled with it and ruled by it at every point. Then we have a proper human existence.'[104] 'Proper existence' is thus determinatively linked to obedience to the generic law. One is free *and* obedient when one has successfully integrated oneself into the generic life of humanity, and consented to the internal law that governs it. Whereas Hodge thought of the law as authored by God and Finney thought of the law as binding on God,[105] Nevin asserts that the law 'has its being only in God and from God, not, however, as something different from the divine mind itself. It is the necessary form of God's infinitely wise and holy will, as exercised in the creation and support of the actual universe, considered both as nature and spirit.'[106] The law is not God, but does not exist apart from God, either. Instead, the law comes into human consciousness through sociality. When one is united with the rest of the generic human life, one is 'connected' to the law which governs it and which is its principle. Or as Nevin puts it, 'it belongs to the conception of individual life universally that it should be in itself a center of the manifold activities by which it makes itself known'.[107] Human selves are most themselves when their relations with those around them (in their 'manifold activities') align with the law of the generic life, which pits humans in rightly ordered life-giving relationships. 'The subject is not simply an individual center, but knows and seeks itself under this character [the character of being related].'[108] This means, further, that the law takes visible and determinate forms. Nevin suggests three forms, or contexts in which the law is operative and in which the 'proper existence' of the human self is fashioned. These are the church, the family and the state.

Here, then, we have the final piece of the relationality puzzle for Nevin, as well as the final reason, and in a way the most important one, for why sin must not be conceived of individualistically. The individual's sense of self is forged in these three contexts, the church, the family and the state, and it is by social relations within these three realms that we come to understand and, hopefully, assent to the reality of the universal law, the contravention of which is sin. Were it not for the relations, there could not be a self, and no self could know the law, and the concept of sin would be meaningless.

> As no single man is the human race, but only a part of it, having the truth of his being in the organic relations by which he is comprehended, through the family, church and state, in the whole, so the law … can never come near to any man in the way of an

103. Grace, in addition to human action, surely figures into this project of forging selfhood, but Nevin equivocates on how it is to be interpreted.
104. 'Human Freedom', 290.
105. On this, cf. Hewitt, *Regeneration and Morality*, 109 and 182n.75.
106. 'Human Freedom', 295–6.
107. Ibid., 291.
108. Ibid.

absolutely singular and exclusive revelation. It can reach him really only by passing *through* the organic system.[109]

Though he does not cite him, I think Nevin has Finney in mind when putting the matter this way. For the logical conclusion of the apprehension of the law through social relationships is that

> if we suppose the single will to be ... something complete by itself, and then think of the law as existing in the same separate way, each including in itself the claims which belong to it, the two components must necessarily contradict each other [the former as subjective, internal, and individual, the latter as objective, external and universal], and cannot be brought into such form to any true reconciliation.[110]

This has the incredible effect of making liberty, in Finney's sense, sin, in Finney's sense! For the individual will, if it be truly particular, cannot know of the universal or generic, and therefore cannot act in accord with it. When it acts, it acts freely, but cannot act rightly. Therefore, when it acts, it sins. Finney's position is therefore wholly self-defeating. Finney's idea of the law 'is slavish in its very nature. The liberty which the subject may still pretend to assert for himself becomes necessarily licentiousness and sin, while on the other hand any obedience he may seem to yield to the law, as being thus forced and external, can have no reality of worth in the view of the law itself.'[111]

Sin is better understood, as the foregoing has meticulously pointed out, as a rupture in the social relationships in and through which the self is made real. Nevin summarizes his position by saying that sin is essentially a frustration of our ability 'to bring our common human life into its proper form – a problem whose solution runs through the entire social constitution, from the beginning of time to its end. The family, the state, and the church are all comprehended alike in the service of this great design.'[112]

Conclusion

In the end Nevin and the Mercersburg theology wound up going essentially unheard in the larger theological conversation. Their message was simply too counter-cultural to have a lasting effect. Nevin and Schaff made the Incarnation the centrepiece of soteriology; conventional antebellum Protestant theology reserved that spot for substitutionary atonement. Jesus Christ was their focus, as opposed to the Bible. The experience of the community was emphasized, not the individual. The sacraments were indispensable for Schaff and Nevin, whereas they were basically irrelevant

109. Ibid., 296.
110. Ibid., 297.
111. Ibid.
112. Ibid., 306.

for a system focused nearly exclusively on preaching. They were theologically engaged with German Idealism; the rest of the theological landscape, when philosophical, looked more like the British Isles. What one might think would be the natural allies to Mercersburg, the Catholics, high-church Episcopalians and Lutherans, were unresponsive at best. And yet one cannot help but think that Nevin has something genuinely worthwhile to offer the current theological discussion. I have proposed that looking at a different aspect of Nevin's system, one heretofore completely ignored in scholarly analysis, we can better appropriate Nevin's key insights.

The appropriation cannot, of course, be wholesale. Nevin failed to see all kinds of systemic distortions, and would not necessarily have named them as sinful even if he saw them, such as sexism. One of the unfortunate bases of his objection to Finney was, incidentally, that the revivalists accorded a greater role in their worship to women than had previously been the norm.[113] While Nevin spoke out against slavery in his earlier writings, he did not do this as well as he could have, as even he later admitted. Still more problems frustrate the adduction of Nevin's thoughts on sin. He is one of the first and most prominent theologians of the modern era to develop a notion of the self-in-relation. But the concept remains sketched, not filled in. The God relation is primary to such a degree that the social relations seem derivative, and sometimes dispensable. The arenas for interpersonal social relations are named as church, public (meaning, usually, the state – Nevin has been read as a particular kind of nationalist[114]) and family, but that is not intended to be an exhaustive list. Relationships outside of these bounds must surely obtain. Any human self has a relation to his or her body, to his or her history, to his or her future, and so on. The problems which beset theological proposals conceived in the thought-world of German Idealism generally apply to Nevin's work. The meaning of 'the church' is left intentionally vague, so one does not know exactly what one exists 'in relation to' with that *relatum*. Nevin is so 'churchly' a theologian that he seems hardly to have thought of human existence outside of Christianity. The plurality and ambiguity of questions of selfhood today require more careful conception and elucidation of theories of both general human selfhood and its specifically Christian form, should such be said to exist. This is hard work, and there is much left to do. Yet in such an undertaking, it simply cannot be denied that the scholar searching for answers to the self-implicating questions of the self-in-relation and the nature of sin will find a friend, not a foe, in the fascinating work of John W. Nevin.

---

113. In fact, under Finney's presidency Oberlin became one of the first co-educational colleges in the country, and was notable in admitting black students very early in the nineteenth century.

114. Cf. Richard E. Wentz, *John Williamson Nevin: American Theologian* (Oxford: Oxford University Press, 1997), esp. 98–111, and idem, 'Nevin and American Nationalism', in *Reformed Confessionalism in Nineteenth Century America*, 23–42.

Part II

Twentieth-Century Application

Now that we have looked in detail at the representative views of our two types of sin, Albrecht Ritschl's structural sin type and John Nevin's relational self type, we are ready to begin using this twofold typology to chart the course taken by twentieth-century liberation theologians in thinking about social sin. The following three chapters summarize and assess representative views from three different forms of liberation theology. Chapter 4 discusses the development of notions of social sin in Latin American liberation theology. The findings from Chapter 2 on Ritschl's view of sin are helpful in orienting ourselves in this landscape, as nearly all the thinkers conceive of social sin as essentially structural oppression. Many of the problems besetting Ritschl's thought crop up in Latin America, and many of the reasons given for the necessity of rejecting individualistic doctrines of sin are repeated.

Chapter 5 treats representative views drawn from carefully selected feminist and womanist authors. Here the groundwork laid in our nineteenth-century explorations is particularly helpful, for feminist and womanist theology actually use either the structural sin type or the relational self model. In almost no cases are both of these types used creatively together in any developed way. Again, the representative strengths and weaknesses exposed in the foregoing chapters illuminate our assessment and aid in our critical re-appropriation of these doctrines.

Finally, Chapter 6 explores the contours of doctrines of social sin in Asia. As I explain, this is simply too large a topic to be covered in a single chapter, and I have significant reservations about the explanatory power of 'Asia' as a meaningful theological descriptor. Therefore the topic of Korean *Minjung* theology is taken up in more detail, in order to gain an entrée into distinctively Asian modes of thinking on sin, including its inter-religious dimension, the experience of political exploitation, and the twin nemeses of domestic empire and foreign globalization. Here, too, the typology developed in Part I is helpful in drawing into deeper relief the promise and difficulty of contemporary doctrines of social sin. We begin the next stage of our map-making, then, in Peru.

Chapter 4

Individual and Social Sin
in Selected Latin American Theologies

Introduction

On 25 July 1968 a European-educated Peruvian theologian delivered a short lecture to a few Catholic priests and interested laypeople who had gathered together for a conference in Chimbote, Peru, on the disputed social role of the Catholic church in Latin America. Preceding by only a few weeks the epoch-marking Medellín conference of Latin American Catholic bishops (CELAM), the talk was entitled 'Toward a Theology of Liberation', and the theologian was of course Gustavo Gutiérrez.[1] The theological movement spawned in that context (and, to a large extent, by Gutiérrez himself) can hardly be assessed, so influential has it been, and engagement with its primary themes and methods is becoming increasingly important. Developments in the doctrine of sin are not, probably, the most important contribution of Latin American liberation theology, but they certainly rank among the key insights of that school of thought. Their contributions in this area are so important, in fact, that I am convinced that any future doctrine of sin must heed the warnings of Latin American liberation theologians. This engagement of traditional Western Christian views with Latin America will only become increasingly important as Christianity becomes more and more a phenomenon of the Southern Hemisphere.

Generalizing too widely can cause problems when analysing a relatively new collection of themes and methods, but some broad conclusions about the doctrine of sin in Latin American theology can at this point safely be drawn. By way of preview, at least three particular features have emerged. As a rule, Latin American theologians counsel against excessive individualism in articulations of sin. They refuse an arbitrary decoupling of reflection on sin and the Christian vocation to alleviate, where possible, its effects. Finally, their contributions in hermeneutics, especially biblical exegesis, help to disallow the eisegesis of what Krister Stendahl famously calls the 'introspective conscience of the West' into biblical texts on sin.[2] The doctrine

---

1.　Gustavo Gutiérrez, 'Toward a Theology of Liberation', trans. Jeffrey Klaiber, SJ, in Alfred Hennelly, SJ, ed., *Liberation History: A Documentary History* (Maryknoll, NY: Orbis Books, 1990), 62–76.

2.　Krister Stendahl, 'The Apostle Paul and the Introspective Conscience of the West', *Harvard Theological Review* 56 (1963): 199–215.

of sin that has emerged from the Latin American context therefore draws from the best of the tradition it forcefully criticizes, while stamping its own particular imprint upon it. Latin American theology thus represents the first major group of theologies we will be analysing according to our two-pronged typology of rejections of individualism. There has not been, to my knowledge, a great deal of significant reflection on the nature and status of the self in Latin American liberation thought.[3] But there has been a near embarrassment of riches in reflection on the other kind of rejection of individualism – structural and systemic sin. Thus while proceeding through the following analyses of Latin American views on systemic and structural sin, we will do well to keep in mind both the successes and failures of our nineteenth-century exemplar of this type, Albrecht Ritschl and his critique of Schleiermacher.

In this chapter, on the doctrine of sin in Latin American liberation theology, I accordingly seek to do three things. First, I present a broad overview of the major developments in the last forty years (1965–2005) in Latin American hamartiology. Doing this adequately will require the careful examination of a cross-section of representative views from Roman Catholic and Protestant theologians, and from a geographically diverse sample, including in this case Cuba, Mexico, Peru, Uruguay, Brazil and Argentina. I do not mean to imply that the authors considered herein exhaust the available views on sin in Latin American liberation theology.[4] However, the sample pool is large enough, and the views examined are consistent enough, that general conclusions, such as the three previewed above, can reasonably be drawn. Second, I highlight the criticisms of traditional doctrines of sin by Latin American theologians, noting their general validity. Third and finally, I push for greater clarity in their constructive counterproposals by pointing out potential inconsistencies in their formulation and theological problems in their conclusions.

Methodological Caveat

While writing critically in the area of Latin American theology, I have encountered a kind of paradox. A Scylla and a Charybdis threaten my engagement with this school of thought. On the one hand, since I write from a perspective of relative affluence and privilege in North America from the middle of the old Northern European philosophical tradition, I

3.   Ignacio Ellacuria's work in this area is so noteworthy because it is such an exception.

4.   Notably absent, for example, is any reference to the recent and growing literature on Pentecostalism. Charismatic churches are the fastest growing churches in the hemisphere, and while they produce relatively little in the way of 'scholarly' theology, their views on sin and grace represent a major portion of their characteristic beliefs. Numerous studies on this emerging phenomenon are available; one good one is Hannah W. Stewart-Gambino and Edward L. Cleary, eds, *Power, Politics and Pentecostals in Latin America* (Boulder, CO: Westview Press, 1997).

risk appearing presumptuous when criticizing the views of Hispanic and Latino/a theologians. Such theologians, often with good reason, assert that it is precisely the critical view of white European and Anglo-American people of privilege that is the problem with, not the solution for, a doctrine of sin. In that case, appreciative silence following careful listening seems like a more appropriate response than criticism. On the other hand, however, not bothering to enter into dialogue with Latin American theology risks a certain condescension. The most important new books and the most interesting new ideas should be the ones discussed in all theological circles. Disallowing dialogue with liberation theology for fear of presumption implies that the ideas of liberation theologians do not quite favourably compare with the really important works of our time. While I have tried to keep the dangers of both threats squarely in mind, I am convinced that the best way to honour scholarly work is to subject it to as thorough a critique as possible. I have learned immeasurably about the doctrine of sin from liberation theologians, and precisely for this reason (and not in spite of it!) I feel compelled *both* to assess the manifest strengths and attempt to expose the sometimes hidden weaknesses of their positions. This is best done not from the chauvinistic vantage point of some sort of doctrinal watchdog, but rather from that of an appreciative student eager to take this new approach as seriously as possible.

Gustavo Gutiérrez: Criticism of Individual Sin

What was Gutiérrez after in his 'inaugural' lecture on the theology of liberation? More specifically, what did he have in mind with respect to the doctrine of sin? Two factors are at work here, and in the corpus of theological work Gutiérrez produced in the ensuing decades. First, there is a devastating critique of dominant trends in Western theology and doctrine. And second, he presents an alternative view of the concept of sin, seeking to remain in continuity with the biblical message of sin and grace even as he criticizes its occasional deformation in historical formulation and practice. Let us begin with the first of those, his critique of Western theologies of sin.

Gutiérrez' seminal lecture ends with a fascinating juxtaposition of two texts, one from Karl Marx and the other from deutero-Isaiah,[5] regarding the religiously mandated structure of society. According to Marx,

> The social principles of Christianity explain all the viciousness of oppressors as a just punishment either for original sin or other sins, or as trials that the Lord, in infinite wisdom, inflicts on those the Lord has redeemed. The social principles of Christianity preach cowardice, self-hatred, servility, submission, humility – in a word, all the characteristics of a scoundrel.[6]

5.   Or as it is sometimes called, Trito-Isaiah, though my own basically canonical reading resists such pie-slicing.
6.   Gutiérrez, 'Toward a Theology of Liberation', 76. The text cited can be found in the *Marx-Engels Gesamtausgabe* I.6, (Berlin: Dietz Verlag, 1972), 278.

Christianity, according to Marx, has become the religion of the oppressor, and the notion of sin has been his tool for keeping the masses in their quiet submission. Sins are acts of disobedience *against*, not acts of the wrongful exertion *of*, power, on his view. In Marx's thought sins are the discrete acts of the lower classes which upset the stable social structure (usually considered to be divinely ordained), and Sin is their collective name.

Gutiérrez contrasts this view with Isaiah 65, part of which reads 'Behold, I create Jerusalem rejoicing, and her people a joy. I will rejoice in Jerusalem, and be glad in my people; ... They shall build houses and inhabit them; they shall plant vineyards and eat their fruit. They shall not build and another inhabit; they shall not plant and another eat; my chosen shall long enjoy the work of their hands.' For Isaiah, Gutiérrez thinks, exactly the reverse of Marx's position is true of sin. Sin is the sin of the powerful over the powerless. It is sin for one people to be forced to build the houses and plant the crops that another people occupy and eat.[7]

Who is right, in Gutiérrez' mind? The answer is, both are right, but in different ways. Isaiah points to the will of God for God's people, that power be shared among the people and that justice for all be done. This is a normative scriptural claim about the nature of social arrangements. Marx points to the actual practices of a culture putatively based on the ideals of those scriptures, and rightly names them as the gross perversions that they are. This is a descriptive sociological claim about the nature of social arrangements.

In Gutiérrez' earlier writings, from the early essay we are here discussing through his *Theology of Liberation*, he is profoundly critical of the kinds of worldviews whose attitudes towards sin warrant Marx' censure. Those worldviews envision sin as nearly wholly a personal phenomenon, devoid of any social dimension, apart from possibly negative social effects of individual sin. Gutiérrez thinks this is completely wrong. On the contrary, according to Gutiérrez' critique, 'Sin, the breach with God, is not something that occurs only within some intimate sanctuary of the heart. It *always* moves into interpersonal relationships, and hence is the ultimate root of all injustice and oppression – as well as of the social confrontations and conflicts of concrete history.'[8] Put another way, Gutiérrez is saying that sin must always have two dimensions; it entails analytically a break with God, and synthetically a breach with other persons. This overlaps with his insistence that sin is always *both* personal and social in nature. Put most simply, Gutiérrez thinks that sin is not simply a matter of the sinner before God. Whatever must be named as

---

7.   Deutero-Isaiah was of course written during the Exile, so the reference is likely to the practice of the Babylonians forcing the Israelites into labour. The restoration of Jerusalem, and the re-establishment there of the God of Israel's chosen social structure, is the book's great theme. Cf. Klaus Baltzer, *Deutero-Jesaja: Kommentar zum Alten Testament* (Gütersloh: Gütersloher Verlagshaus, 1999), 23–32.

8. Gutiérrez, *The Power of the Poor in History*, trans. Robert B. Barr (Maryknoll, NY: Orbis, 1983), 147.

sin will never be an act divorced from its harmful effects in the world. Sinful situations, structures or social arrangements can never adequately be named as sinful without reference to their root cause in the acts of sinful individuals, but they are nonetheless not reducible to those individual acts, nor are they accordingly any less 'real' or 'sinful' because they are derivative.

The history of Western theologians ignoring the second, social dimension of sin is a long one. Gutiérrez notes that 'There was a period ... when the predominant type of theology neglected the social dimension of sin. In recent decades a growing awareness of the social problem has brought a return to the true perspective with its profound biblical roots; in addition Medellín brought it to mind when it spoke of a sinful situation.'[9] One of the criticisms I will be making of liberation theology later in this chapter is that the zeal with which this deficiency in traditional formulations of sin has been attacked has caused the pendulum to swing far, far to the other side. Latin American liberation theologians often emphasize the social aspect of sin so strongly that the role of the individual is eclipsed. This is perhaps understandable, for as Gutiérrez rightly claims, 'The emphasis on the social dimension of sin [in liberation theology] is due to the fact that this dimension was so little present to Christian consciousness at that time [the time of the Medellín and Puebla conferences].'[10]

This shift is not an arbitrary decision rooted in the decision to criticize dominant theology, but rather 'the emphasis is thus placed chiefly because this perspective, based on the faith, enables us to understand better what has happened and what is still happening in Latin America'.[11] Here we can clearly see the imprint of Gutiérrez' theological method, stated most succinctly as 'critical reflection on praxis'.[12] The practice of dealing with the social effects of sin in Latin America confounded efforts to make sense of the lived experience of the poor. The poor of Gutiérrez' congregation in Lima were little served by the notions of sin Gutiérrez had studied in Europe. The anxiety of the individual over the myriad choices available to him or her, sexual indiscretion, a temptations toward absolutizing the self – these conceptions of sin could make no sense of the dominant factor in Gutiérrez' ministry: institutionalized poverty. Something deeper was needed.

These, then, are the roots of Gutiérrez' criticism of privatized, individualistic notions of sin. He agrees with Marx that too much of Christian theology has placed the blame for sin squarely on the oppressed, and identified resistance to social arrangements with sin itself. He exposes the clean break between individual acts of sin and their experience and proliferation in the social sphere as the chimera that it is. He points out the near impossibility of an

9.   Gutiérrez, *The Truth Shall Make You Free: Confrontations*, trans. Matthew J. O'Connell (Maryknoll, NY: Orbis, 1990), 136.

10.   Ibid., 138.

11.   Ibid.

12.   Gutiérrez, *A Theology of Liberation*, trans. Sister Caridad Inda and John Eagleson (Maryknoll, NY: Orbis, 1973), 3–12.

act that was sinful (because it was a breach of friendship with God) that did not also have social consequences. Doctrines of sin which ignore this fact are, on Gutiérrez' view, fundamentally impoverished and can even become violently oppressive.

Gutiérrez: Proposed Corrective of Tradition

Now that the criticism has been articulated, let us turn to the more constructive aspects of the doctrine of sin which is to replace the deficient, individualistic one. Gutiérrez was one of the major leaders at the two major CELAM conferences mentioned above and one of the texts emerging from the Puebla conference of Latin American Bishops in 1979 contains a clue to Gutiérrez' proposed correction: 'Sinfulness on the personal level, the break with God that debases the human being, is always *mirrored* on the level of interpersonal relations in a corresponding egotism, haughtiness, ambition, and envy.' Further, 'These traits produce injustice, domination, violence at every level, and conflicts between individuals, groups, social classes, and peoples. They also produce corruption, hedonism, aggravated sexuality, and superficiality in mutual relations.'[13] This passage marks a kind of transitional stage in the development of a characteristically Latin American doctrine of sin. The social dimension of sin is seen here not as something qualitatively different from sin at its personal level. Haughtiness and arrogance at the level of the individual is mirrored as egotism and domination at the social level. The cumulative effect of acts of violence by sinful individuals is its mirror image, a violent social system. Commenting on this passage, Gutiérrez writes, 'All this is a description of a situation of sin, a notion that, as we have already mentioned, was central in Medellín and which Puebla here takes up again with greater force and insistence.'[14]

For Gutiérrez, the link between personal and social expressions of sin is therefore *causal*. Personal sins cause situations which must be named as sinful. Consider this lengthy quotation from *A Theology of Liberation*:

> Sin – a breach of friendship with God and others – is according to the Bible the ultimate cause of poverty, injustice, and the oppression in which persons live. In describing sin as the ultimate cause we do not in any way negate the structural reasons and the objective determinants leading to these situations. It does, however, emphasize the fact that things do not happen by chance and that behind an unjust structure there is a personal or collective will responsible – a willingness to reject God and neighbor. It suggests, likewise, that a social transformation, no matter how radical it may be, does not automatically achieve the suppression of all evils.[15]

13. Paragraph 328, emphasis added.
14. Gutiérrez, 'Freedom as Gift and Task at Puebla', in James B. Nickoloff, ed., *Gustavo Gutiérrez: Essential Writings* (Minneapolis: Fortress Press, 1996), 158.
15. Gutiérrez, *A Theology of Liberation*, 24.

One is tempted to see a kind of dialectic of sin at work in passages like this. Such a view would see the sinful acts of individuals as the causes of sinful situations or structures, with those sinful situations or structures then acting back on the sinner in such a way as to perpetuate the sin. But this is not Gutiérrez' position. The structures of sin are not, in Gutiérrez' view, accorded agential power. To call them 'sinful' is not to say that they sin, for Gutiérrez insists on the derivative nature of sinful structures. Structures cannot act. Structures are not morally evaluable. While Gutiérrez wants to expand the notion of sin from its previously privatized and individualistic myopia, he is extremely careful to maintain the critical link between sin as the act of persons and the structures which bear the sinful effects of those acts.

Since this is a critical distinction, perhaps some more citations from Gutiérrez will show his caution on this matter. For example, he writes, 'Sin is a rejection of the gift of God's love. The rejection is a personal, free act. It is a refusal to accept God as Father and to love others as the Lord loved us. Only the action of God can heal human beings at the root of the egotism that prevents them from going out of themselves.'[16] Or again, 'The importance of the social consequences of sin does not mean forgetting that sin is always the result of a personal, free act.'[17] Sin is primarily understood as an act against God, and derivatively as a failure to love one's neighbour. Because sin is the first, it is also the second, not vice versa.[18] However, love of God and love of neighbour are intertwined, for as Gutiérrez writes, 'There is no love for God without love for one's brothers and sisters, particularly those who are most poor, and this means ... a commitment on the level of social structures, "with all the consequences that will entail on the plane of temporal realities."'[19] Recall that for Gutiérrez, as for many other liberation theologians, human liberation unfolds according to a three-layered scheme, involving political, personal and religious liberation.[20] The oppressed must first be freed from the unjust social structures which dominate their lives. Following this, there must be a kind of personal transformation 'by which we live with a kind

16.   Gutiérrez, *Truth Shall Make You Free*, 137–8.

17.   Ibid., 139.

18.   The revised version of *A Theology of Liberation* contains a fascinating footnote to this effect. Gutiérrez writes, 'Sin is a rejection of friendship with God, and *in consequence*, with other human beings. It is a personal free act by which we refuse to accept the gift of God's love.' 226 n.101. This is not included in the original version of the book, and could be evidence that Gutiérrez tries to distance himself from the massive shift occurring later in some liberation theologies, where sin is against God only in view of its violation of neighbour or creation. For more on what is at stake in this distinction, cf. Gutiérrez, *We Drink from Our Own Wells: The Spiritual Journey of a People*, trans. Matthew J. O'Connell (Maryknoll, NY: Orbis, 1984), 96–9.

19.   Gutiérrez, *The Power of the Poor*, 146. The text he cites is from Puebla § 327.

20.   Gutiérrez and other liberationists often credit Pope Paul VI's encyclical *Populorum Progressio* for this insight.

of profound inner freedom in the face of every kind of servitude'.[21] Finally, there must be a liberation before God from sin. Each level of liberation is intimately connected with each of the other two, so it makes little sense to say that one could have liberation in the religious sphere (and therefore a restoration of love for and friendship with God) without a corresponding liberation in one's interpersonal relations.

Gutiérrez has sometimes been accused of espousing an overly rosy optimism concerning the possibilities for the creation of utopia on earth. This is probably due to the fact that human effort towards liberation on the first two levels, the political and the personal, is both possible and mandated in Gutiérrez' theology. Against his detractors Gutiérrez writes, 'In my own approach to theology, sin occupies a central place ... Because sin is radical evil, it can only be conquered by the grace of God and the radical liberation that the Lord bestows. The relationship between grace and sin is played out in the inmost depths of the human person.'[22] Each of the levels of liberation is effected, finally, by God's gratuitous love; but liberation on the religious level is exclusively God's domain.

A slightly different way of putting this could be in terms of the central motif of Latin American liberation theology, the Kingdom of God. As the Kingdom of God operates on both the individual and collective or social levels, with both immanent and transcendent dimensions, sin, too, must be viewed simultaneously in its personal and social aspects.

> Not only is the growth of the Kingdom not reduced to temporal progress; because the word is accepted in faith, we see that the fundamental obstacle to the Kingdom, which is sin, is also the root of all misery and injustice; we see that the very meaning of the growth of the Kingdom is also the ultimate precondition for a just society and a new humanity.[23]

This implies that Gutiérrez adopts a position that we have been advocating throughout this book, namely that sin is best known in its overcoming, and that a redemption which has social effects must accordingly address a situation which is not exclusively individual. On this Gutiérrez writes,

> Because sin is a personal, intrahistorical reality, a part of the daily events of human life, it is also, and above all, an obstacle to life's reaching the fullness we call salvation. Sin is regarded as a social, historical fact, the absence of fellowship and love in relationships among persons, a breach of friendship with God and with other persons, and therefore, an interior, personal fracture.[24]

The restoration of friendship with God and other persons heals both the interior, personal fracture of sin and its communal effects.

---

21.   Gutiérrez, *A Theology of Liberation*, xxxviii.
22.   Gutiérrez, *The Truth Shall Make You Free*, 139.
23.   Gutiérrez, *A Theology of Liberation*, 103.
24.   Ibid., 102–103.

Summation: Gutiérrez and the Individual/Social Distinction

Gutiérrez has been, in my view, extremely successful in his attempt to interpret the Latin American experience from the perspective of biblical faith. His work with the poor and his theological writings bear witness to the reality of sin that is simply unable to be articulated in the hyper-individualistic, privatized hamartiological idiom he inherited from late Western theology. His critique of the doctrine of sin is penetrating and persuasive, and his constructive counterproposal has been widely influential. Most importantly, by adopting a view which sees the social dimensions of sin as caused by personal sin, while not being fully reducible to those personal sins, Gutiérrez is able to maintain moral culpability for sin at the individual level. In my view, only two substantive critiques of Gutiérrez' view on sin have merit. The first is that the sociological analysis he adopts to articulate his vision risks rigidifying the oppressor/oppressed distinction too firmly. His doctrine of sin does indeed depend on the power analysis that locates sin in the oppressor. If this strategy eventuates in wholly identifying the powerful with sinners and the oppressed as the wholly innocent sinned against, he has lost the dynamic tension in his threefold view of liberation. Rather than seeing liberation as the dynamic overcoming of sin by grace *within* each person, it becomes merely a new arrangement *among* people. This is not Gutiérrez' intent, since he wishes to maintain a unity-in-distinction among all three levels of liberation. But, as many critics have pointed out, Gutiérrez' rhetoric of oppressor vs oppressed can sometimes seem more like the parsing of a population than the naming of a universal phenomenon.[25]

The second critique concerns the agential status of the structures which Gutiérrez describes as sinful 'in a derivative way'. Gutiérrez went out of his way to insist that the structures do not act. They are sinful only because they are the product of sin, and are consequently a breach with God. They are not the producers of sin; only sinners produce sin. Yet as we shall soon see, this caution was quickly lost in the subsequent generations of Latin American theologians, and was almost immediately obscured in the European and American commentators on and appropriators of liberation theology. To get at what this shift entailed, to see how sinful social structures meant first 'products of sin' then 'producer of sin', let us take a brief detour into the

---

25.   Cf., for example, Michael Sievernich, *Schuld und Sünde in der Theologie der Gegenwart* (Frankfurt: Knecht, 1982), 265–8 for an assessment of the German-language reaction to this distinction. *Mujerista* theology developed partially due to the realization that the sin of sexism was often hidden under claims to innocence by 'oppressed' Latin American men. One of the most articulate, even if sometimes intransigent, critics of the rigidification of the oppressor/oppressed distinction is Schubert Ogden. Cf. his *Faith and Freedom: Toward a Theology of Liberation* (Nashville: Abingdon, 1979), and his 'The Concept of a Theology of Liberation: Must a Christian Theology Today Be So Conceived?' in Brian Mahan and L. Dale Richesin, eds., *The Challenge of Liberation Theology: A First World Response* (Maryknoll, NY: Orbis, 1981), 127–40.

reception of Gutiérrez' and his compatriots' liberation theology in Europe, particularly in the Roman *Curia*.

The Vatican Response

It is well known that this first wave of liberation theology, of which Gutiérrez was typical, garnered an extremely icy reception in the Vatican. Even though a lecture by Pope John Paul II had opened the second meeting of CELAM in 1979 (which had been read as tacit permission to proceed along the lines liberation theology had begun, if not as complete acceptance of liberation teaching), many Latin American liberation theologians were in persistent fear of reproach or censure by the Vatican, and their fears were heightened when Leonardo Boff (whose views on sin are discussed below) was silenced for a year in 1985, and again in 1991.

The International Theological Commission (ITC) was established in 1969 to assist the Vatican's Congregation for the Doctrine of the Faith (CDF). It was to act as a consultant and *peritus* to the CDF. The Commission comprised experts in fields as varied as liturgy, biblical exegesis and systematic theology. In September 1977 at the Vatican's request the commission prepared a document entitled 'Declaration on Human Development and Christian Salvation', in order to provide a general outline for how traditional social teaching of the Catholic church met the new Latin American perspective. The text evinces a general sympathy for the great themes of liberation theology. However, its authors were careful in addressing the perceived shift in the approach to the doctrine of sin emerging from Latin America. The ITC's views on sin in liberation theology are summarized in this telling passage:

> We may dispute how legitimate it is to speak of 'institutional sin' or of 'sinful structures', since the Bible speaks of sin in the first instance in terms of an explicit, personal decision that stems from human freedom. But it is unquestionable that by the power of sin injury and injustice can penetrate social and political institutions. This is why, as we have pointed out, even situations and structures that are unjust have to be reformed.[26]

There is thus a cautious embrace of liberationist formulations of sin. The structures which perpetuate oppression are at least named 'unjust' and there is a sense that the continued existence of these structures are linked with individual sin, though the exact connection is not made explicit. The rest of the document reflects the ITC's ambivalent position towards Latin American liberation theology. They admitted that 'all of us should listen to the cries of our brothers and sisters, all those all over the world who are

---

26.   International Theological Commission, 'Declaration on Human Development and Christian Salvation) in Alfred T. Hennelly, SJ, ed., *Liberation Theology: A Documentary History* (Maryknoll: Orbis, 1990), 213.

treated with injustice, are oppressed by tribulations, suffer from poverty, are distressed by hunger'. Yet they urged extreme caution in linking the status of these conditions with sin and their overcoming with human action, which could contradict the hard-won unity of church doctrine. 'What has been laboriously achieved [doctrinal unity] must not be facilely jeopardized. This is particularly the case with all issues touching the relationship between human development and salvation.'[27]

The lukewarm attitude of the ITC turned cold in the response of the CDF. Two official documents were later issued by the Vatican regarding Latin American liberation theology. The first is the famous 'Instruction on Certain Aspects of the "Theology of Liberation"', in 1984.[28] This document, authored by the then prefect of the CDF, Cardinal Ratzinger, was extremely critical of much of the theology coming from Latin America, though no theologians were explicitly named. The second document, 'Instruction on Christian Freedom and Liberation', was issued nearly two years later in 1986.[29] This was a much more irenic document which praised warmly and chastised only gently liberation theologians. The praise came for liberation theology's worthwhile emphases on social understandings of the Christian faith, the conviction that salvation is 'integral' – relating to the whole person, not just the soul, and on their preferential option for the poor.[30]

Yet the Vatican's praise for liberation theology was not restricted only to LC. There are actually two major admissions regarding the worth of liberation theology in the otherwise excoriating LN. The first affirmation of liberation theology comes in the form of a general appreciation for the theme of liberation. This was included near the beginning of the document at the demand of John Paul II, over Cardinal Ratzinger's objections.[31] One such example of this general appreciation is 'The aspiration for liberation, as the term suggests, repeats a theme fundamental to the Old and New Testaments. In itself, the expression "theology of liberation" is a thoroughly valid term: it designates a theological reflection centered on the biblical theme of liberation and freedom, and on the urgency of its practical realization.'[32] Yet quite surprisingly, the second area where liberation teaching, especially as Gutiérrez had formulated it, was most warmly embraced was on the doctrine of social sin! Recall from above that Gutiérrez had taught that the fundamental liberation was liberation from sin, which was a religious conception of an act of rebellion against God which always had social effects, which were to be

27.   ITC, 'Declaration', 218.
28.   Hereafter cited LN, for its Latin name *Libertatis Nuntius*, with section numbers.
29.   Hereafter cited LC, for its Latin name *Libertatis Conscientia*, with section numbers.
30.   Though they tried unsuccessfully to alter this phrase to read 'a love of preference for the poor'.
31.   Cf. Robert McAfee Brown, 'The Roman Curia and Liberation Theology: The Second (and Final?) Round', in *Christian Century* 103 (1986): 552.
32.   LN, III.4.

called sinful in a derivative but genuine sense. This teaching is nearly exactly mirrored by Ratzinger's pen. For example, Ratzinger begins, 'New Testament revelation teaches us that sin is the greatest evil, since it strikes humankind in the heart of its personality. The first liberation, to which all others must make reference, is that from sin.'[33] Yet this sin has social effects which must also be addressed. One prime example of the sinful effects of human sin is the perpetration of horrors on the innocent, paradigmatically so in the case of Jesus. 'Universal love and preference for the poor distinguish the message of the divine reign that both purifies human history and transcends it. Sin, which is the refusal to accept this message, brings Jesus to the cross; the cross is the result of the resistance of those who refuse to accept the unmerited and demanding gift of God's love.'[34] LN shows more sensitivity to the subtleties of the concept of liberation than did some other opponents, who mistook social transformation as a precondition for the forgiveness of sins. This was not Gutiérrez' view. He thought that God's forgiveness simply had to have social effects when it was rightly understood. Those effects occurred when people responded to God's forgiveness in the appropriate way; that is, social renewal took place for Gutiérrez when the forgiveness given in the inbreaking of the Kingdom of God was understood aright. This is actually quite close to the situation as Ritschl described it, who saw the Kingdom of God, as I showed in Chapter 2, as both gift and task. LN proceeds,

> Unquestionably, it is to stress the radical character of the deliverance brought by Christ and offered to all, be they free or slaves, that the New Testament does not requires some change in the political or social condition as a prerequisite for entrance into this freedom. However, the Letter to Philemon shows that the new freedom procured by the grace of Christ should necessarily have effects on the social level.[35]

Though Ratzinger may have thought he was contradicting Gutiérrez and the rest of the first-generation theologians of liberation, he was actually agreeing with them when he writes 'Consequently, the full ambit of sin, whose first effect is to introduce disorder into the relationship between God and humankind, cannot be restricted to "social sin." The truth is that only a correct doctrine of sin will permit us to insist on the gravity of its social effects.'[36] This does not mean that the structures are not sinful. Ratzinger continues to argue that one cannot 'localize evil principally or uniquely in bad social, political or economic "structures" as though all other evils came from them so that the creation of the "new person" would depend on the establishment of different economic and socio-political structures'.[37] In a

33.   LN, IV.12.
34.   Gutiérrez, *On Job: God-Talk and the Suffering of the Innocent*, trans. Matthew J. O'Connell (Maryknoll: Orbis, 1987), 99.
35.   LN, IV.13.
36.   LN, IV.14.
37.   LN, IV.15.

way, on this point Ratzinger actually goes farther than Gutiérrez had gone. Gutiérrez did not think structures could cause sin or evil, or that they could even be said to act at all. He thought that they were sinful because their endurance was against God and that they mirrored the perpetration of sin in individuals. But yet it is unequivocally clear in LN that 'there are structures which are evil and *which cause evil* and which we must have the courage to change'.[38] The structures can actively *cause* evil. They are not primarily agents; they are first and foremost the outcome of individual deeds.

> Structures, whether they are good or bad, are the result of human actions, and so are consequences more than causes. The root of evil, then, lies in free and responsible persons who have to be converted by the grace of Jesus Christ in order to live and act as new creatures in the love of neighbor and in the effective search for justice, self-control, and the exercise of virtue.[39]

When Ratzinger is critical of the liberation theologians of sin, his objections come on grounds that seem nearly irrelevant to the Latin American context, such as inordinate pride or a tendency towards atheism. 'Many of our contemporaries must first rediscover a sense of sin. In man's desire for freedom there is hidden the temptation to deny his own nature. Insofar as he wishes to desire everything and to be able to do everything and thus forget that he is finite and a created being, he claims to be a god.'[40] Atheism is clearly far more a European problem than it is an issue in Latin America. But yet he writes,

> Dependence of the creature upon the Creator, and the dependence of the moral conscience upon the divine law, are regarded by him as an intolerable slavery. Thus he sees atheism as the true foam of emancipation and of man's liberation, whereas religion or even the recognition of a moral law constitute forms of alienation. Man then wishes to make independent decisions about what is good and what is evil, or decisions about values; and in a single step he rejects both the idea of God and the idea of sin. It is through the audacity of sin that he claims to become adult and free, and he claims this emancipation not only for himself but for the whole of humanity.[41]

Though our decisions about 'what is good or what is evil, or decisions about values' must not be made without reference to the prior action of God, still we must act forcefully in implementing so much as we are able structures of human interaction which accord with God's will. On this, Ratzinger writes,

> It remains true however that structures established for people's good are of themselves incapable of securing and guaranteeing that good. The corruption which

38. LN, IV.15, emphasis mine.
39. LN, IV.15.
40. LN, II.37.
41. LN II.41.

in certain countries affects the leaders and the State bureaucracy, and which destroys all honest social life, is a proof of this. Moral integrity is a necessary condition for the health of society. It is therefore necessary to work simultaneously for the conversion of hearts and for the improvement of structures.[42]

Thus we are seeing the roots of what will become an extremely complicated problem in Latin American theology. There is a consensus among the CELAM bishops and the theologians, like Gutiérrez, who worked with them, and even among traditional opponents of liberation theology, that the structures of social interaction overseeing life in Latin America were profoundly distorted, and must be named somehow as 'sinful'. Yet the specifics of how this was to be so conceived escaped consensus. Though Gutiérrez had been so careful to name sin primarily as a matter before an individual and God with sinful social effects, less careful thinkers began to invest these social effects, these sinful social structures, with agential power. Above we saw Ratzinger's writing to this effect.[43] There is also Archbishop Oscar Romero, who often opined on the narrow definition of sin that ignored the non-individualistic dimensions. He once wrote 'It is not a matter of sheer routine that I insist once again on the existence in our country of the structures of sin. They are sin because *they produce* the fruits of sin: the death of Salvadorans – the swift death brought by repression or the long, drawn out, but no less real, death from structural oppression.'[44] Writing slightly later, but summarizing his understanding of the teaching of Puebla and Gutiérrez on sin, Jose Ignacio González Faus writes, 'When human beings sin, they create structures of sin, which in their turn, *make human beings sin*.'[45]

42. LN, V.75
43. To be fair, I should point out that LC softened the point made in LN regarding the sinfulness of social structures and whether they could act. For example, 'the sin at the root of unjust situations is, in the proper and primordial sense, a voluntary act that has its source in the freedom of individuals. Only in a derived and secondary sense is it applicable to structures, and only in this sense can one speak of "social sin."' LC, V.75. Not everyone was happy with this 'retreat', however. For example, Alfred Hennelly wrote, 'I believe there is a major weakness in this chapter with regard to its treatment of another central motif of liberation theology, and that is the concept of "social sin." Is it not clear, as in the case of apartheid in South Africa, that though the structures were the creation of individual sinful acts and are continued in existence by individual human acts, nevertheless the oppression and suffering they inflict upon human persons for generations upon generations is immeasurably greater than any individual act of sin? ... I find it impossible to understand why such "social sin" cannot be called sin in a very true and extremely immediate sense.' Alfred T. Hennelly, SJ, 'The Red-Hot Issue: Liberation Theology', in *America* 157 (May 24, 1986): 427.
44. Oscar Romero, 'The Political Dimension of the Faith from the Perspective of the Option for the Poor', in *Voice of the Voiceless: The Four Pastoral Letters and Other Statements*, trans. Michael Walsh (Maryknoll: Orbis, 1985), 184, my emphasis. The occasion for Romero's essay was the conferral of an honorary doctorate at Louvain in February 1980. He was murdered six weeks later.
45. Faus, in John Sobrino and Ignacio Ellacuria, eds., *Systematic Theology: Perspectives from Liberation Theology* (Maryknoll: Orbis Press, 1995), 198, emphasis

We are thus faced with a serious problem. In very loosely idiomatic English usage, structures are sometimes accorded agential status. However, closer semantic and analytical examination reveals the truth that action requires intention and consciousness, and that therefore impersonal structures cannot act.[46] They cannot produce sin. Social structures are simply the names given to facts regarding certain human states of affairs. Road systems are 'structures of transportation' constructed by humans which simultaneously enable and constrain human behaviour (such as driving). When these systems are bad, as in the case of most of Boston, humans do the wrong things, like cause traffic accidents. But it is the humans who do those things. Humans alone can act in a way such that the action can be called sinful. Thus to aver, as so many inheritors of Gutiérrez' thought have done, that the structures really sin seems enormously problematic. Subsequent sections of this chapter seek to show that the roots for this shift in thinking about sinful social structures lie in several areas. There is, in Juan Luis Segundo's and Leonardo Boff's thought, such a close connection between a person's actions and his or her 'state' that sin is essentially hypostatized when the person is in a sinful situation. Juan Alfaro and Aldo Etchegoyen will argue that from a biblical perspective, identifying sin with willing was never really appropriate in the first place. Justo González and Jose Comblin argue that it is the social sin which is primary, and the individual sin which is to be seen as derivative of its social location. Yet in all these various ways, the danger of exculpation looms large. The intent of Latin American theologians in opening up the horizons upon which sin was analysed, away from its individualistic distortion, is admirable. However, the role of the individual in sin is invariably eclipsed, the structure accorded agency, and the attendant problems left essentially unsolved. Let us now begin this wide-ranging journey through some less-

in original. It is worth pointing out that Faus actually misquotes John Paul II's encyclical *Sollicitudio Rei Socialis* in support of his position. Faus says that the encyclical urged liberation from 'sin and the structures which produce it.' ibid., 199. The actual text urges liberation from 'sin and the structures produced by sin as it multiplies and spreads.' *Sollicitudio Rei Socialis*, VII.46.

46.   Pointing out this fact is a major contribution of analytic philosophy. My allegiances on this point lie with both Elizabeth Anscombe and especially Donald Davidson, both of whom insist that in order for an agent to perform an action, the action must be *intentional*. Intention is a function of intelligence, or of the mind. Since a corporate structure lacks intellect and intention apart from its constituent parts, it really does not make sense to speak in any strict way about the action of a structure of human relation, even though people often do speak idiomatically of structures acting. The most important works on this matter are Donald Davidson, *Essays on Actions and Events* (Oxford: Clarendon, 1980), G. E. M. Anscombe, *Intention* (Oxford: Basil Blackwell, 1979) and John Searle, *Intentionality: An Essay in the Philosophy of Mind* (Cambridge: Cambridge University Press, 1983). The appropriation of these insights into a relational model of selfhood can be found in 'An Agentless Semantics of Action' and 'From Action to the Agent' in Paul Ricoeur's masterpiece *Oneself as Another*, trans. Kathleen Blamey (Chicago: University of Chicago Press, 1992), 56–112.

known terrain of Latin American liberation theology, beginning with the fascinating work of Segundo.

Segundo and the Hypostatization of Social into Individual Sin

The Uruguayan Jesuit theologian Juan Luis Segundo belongs with Gustavo Gutiérrez to the first wave of Latin American liberation theology. By the time of his death in 1996, Segundo had written dozens of books and hundreds of articles on liberation theology. Segundo represents a kind of transitional phase from theology based primarily on imported European thought-forms done in the Latin American context, to a truly indigenous Latin American theology done in accordance with its own exigencies and by its own methods. He is perhaps best known for his searching and influential methodological treatise *The Liberation of Theology*, in which Segundo argues for a reinterpretation of the hermeneutical circle in order to grant the experience of poverty a larger role in theological discourse.[47] No topic has escaped comment from Segundo's (often critical) pen, and the doctrine of sin is no exception. The second volume of a five-volume series considered a landmark of liberation theology is devoted to rethinking the concepts of grace and sin into each other from the dual perspectives of Freudian psychology and liberation exegesis.[48] The final volume of that series, *Evolution and Guilt*, is a creative synthesis of the nascent liberation emphasis on the structures of social sin and the concept of evolution, especially, though not exclusively, as formulated in the evolutionary thought of Pierre Teilhard de Chardin. I shall deal with these two main works in reverse order, beginning with *Evolution and Guilt*.

In *Evolution and Guilt*, Segundo identifies sin with resistance to the evolution of higher forms of order. Human experience is analytically temporal, and that presupposes change in the way humans relate to each other. It is God's will, argues Segundo, that those changes lead one ever nearer to 'true humanity'. Sin is thus the obstruction of this ever-continuing process of hominization. Put more specifically, sin is resistance to better social and political arrangements.[49] Evolution in general, Segundo thinks, takes place on two different 'vectors'. One is destructive, the other constructive. One the one hand, the second law of thermodynamics holds that the amount of order in any closed system decreases through time. Even though energy is

---

47.   Juan Luis Segundo SJ, *The Liberation of Theology*, trans. John Drury (Maryknoll: Orbis Books, 1976), esp. chapter 2.

48.   Segundo, *Grace and the Human Situation*, trans. John Drury (Maryknoll: Orbis Books, 1980). The series is called *A Theology for Artisans of a New Humanity*.

49.   From a decidedly non-liberationist perspective, Karl Schmitz-Moorman makes essentially the same point that sin is resistance, though the higher forms of order are biological and social, not political, in nature. Cf. his *Die Erbsünde: Überholte Vorstellung – bleibende Glaube* (Olten, Freiburg im Breisgau: Walter, 1969).

conserved in all physical processes, the 'order' of that energy will decrease due to the inevitable degradation of energy forms. The simplest, least usable form of energy is heat, which increases as dissipative, evolutionary processes move forward. Disorder is therefore a necessary consequence of evolution through time. On the other hand, episodic and localized *increases* in order are contingent consequences of evolution, as well. Evolution can create pockets of extraordinarily highly ordered energy. Segundo's adduction of Teilhard's evolutionary scheme largely lacks the anthropocentrism that marks the French palaeontologist's work,[50] but perhaps the evolution of humankind is the best example of this theme. The human brain, to take just one instance, is the most complicated, highly ordered physical object on earth. It is the product of extensive evolutionary processes, during which the energy involved in its production was conserved, but highly ordered forms of energy were localized in the brain, and the heat created was wasted and dissipated. In the evolution of physical objects and processes, then, we see a dialectical interaction of positive and negative vectors, of constructive and destructive forces.

Much the same is true, Segundo thinks, of sin and redemption in the course of the drama of human history. This drama is placed in the context of the doctrine of creation. Segundo insists that we must take an evolutionary approach to creation. The subject matter of creation is not evolutionary, for 'this evolutionary outlook is not the "content" of the Christian message ... [but] such an outlook is *the key* to Christianity. In other words the whole Christian message – and particularly the relationship between sin and redemption – should be viewed from that angle of vision.'[51]

Segundo's position does not involve an overly optimistic 'accumulative, a-critical, straight line evolutionary process' in creation,[52] but rather a dialectical process comprising two opposing dynamics which, 'though they point in different directions, these two vectors – or tendencies, or forces – are indispensable and complementary, *each in its own way*'.[53] The interplay of sin and grace in creation mirrors, by analogy, the two vectors present in the evolution of the physical world by physical processes. The positive force of the evolution of creation is 'love, grace, life, and God's gift'.[54] The negative force is 'egotism, sin, and enslavement to the world and the flesh'.[55]

Sin is thus a necessary, even constitutive, part of being human, for it belongs to the low-level structure of human evolution. One facet of sin is

50.   Cf., for example, Pierre Teilhard de Chardin, *The Phenomenon of Man*, trans. Bernard Wall (New York: Harper, 1959), esp. 163–80, and T. M. Schoof, OP, *A Survey of Catholic Theology: 1800–1970*, trans. N. D. Smith (New York: Paulist, 1970), 115–18.

51.   Juan Luis Segundo, *Evolution and Guilt*, trans. John Drury (Maryknoll, NY: Orbis, 1974), 59.

52.   Ibid., 64.

53.   Ibid., 129, italics in original.

54.   Ibid., 126.

55.   Ibid., 127.

egotism, an excessive valuation of the self by the self. While this is a kind of 'negative energy', it also can contribute positively to the sorts of things we value in society. Many biographers have concluded that Martin Luther King, Jr, to take one example, was profoundly egotistical (to say nothing of being sexist).[56] He believed in himself and in his message and in his unique situation in history so much, that he could be quite blind to the needs of those around him. And yet one cannot help but see the seeds of some of the incredible successes at social reform in that, frankly, egocentric mindset. Over the course of time, sin is basically destructive and negative, but not therefore *absolutely* evil. 'Sin is a condition that subdues and enslaves me against my own will', even though 'it is a part of my being, the most basic and low-level part if not the most profound and authentic part. It sustains me and yet at the same time prevents me from being the human person I desire to be.'[57]

Although sin is a necessary component of the structures of human development, it is not the profoundest component. Segundo places grace there. Grace is the positive vector of evolution. It is the love that overcomes selfishness and greed. Grace takes the self which is secured by egotism – by the innate tendency of each person to *be* their own person and to care for themselves – and brings it to self-giving and other-securing love.[58] Although this dynamic is most easily visible on the level of the individual, it should not be therefore restricted to this level. Grace is not 'exclusively a liberative dynamism that allows us to gradually gain control over the inertia of our individual nature'.[59] Grace names that gift of God which overcomes the gap between intent and effect, between life in the kingdom on earth and life in the Kingdom of God. Segundo thinks that the requirements of human existence-in-development (evolution's two vectors) imply that we will not have the power to enact the good which we know we should do; there is a 'moral gap' between is and ought, between knowledge of the good and its effective pursuit. This is a social reality. Grace makes the pursuit of the social good possible and more effective by helping individuals work in consort to live in social structures which are maximally loving and minimally exploitative.[60]

56.   For a provocative constructive argument about King's personality, as well as a reliable collection and refutation of 'sanitized' views of King, see the controversial book by Michael Eric Dyson, *I May Not Get There With You: The True Martin Luther King, Jr.* (New York: Touchstone, 2001). I should also note that this is my example, not Segundo's.

57.   Segundo, *Evolution and Guilt*, 73.

58.   Segundo, *Grace and the Human Condition*, 14–28. In my opinion, Segundo's use of Freud's categories obscures rather than elucidates an otherwise basically valid point here.

59.   Ibid., 37.

60.   Segundo rejects the *exitus-reditus* format of a similar view in traditional Christian theology. As Frances Stefano points out, this view of grace-in-history implies that 'grace is not a gradually unfolding plan set on a future goal', but an 'adventure in gratuitous living' in the present. Its *telos* does not consist in someplace to 'go' (or return) other than the

As Segundo stresses, with the help of grace, '*Everything*, in the strictest and most absolute sense of the word, depends on whether or not we do approach such a society.'[61]

Segundo's work is hard to compare with others' in Latin America. His use of Teilhard's evolutionary categories for 'hominization' and Freud's psychological analysis of sin are, as far as I know, without significant parallel in liberation theology. Yet there are some resemblances between his conclusions and the work of others. His statement that sin belongs explicitly to the 'lower levels' of human being due to the structures in which that person exists does bears a strong congruence to some other Latin American theologians, especially the next figure we will discuss, Leonardo Boff. This 'hypostatization' of sin is certainly one contributing factor in the problem outlined above, namely the attribution of sinful agency to social structures (since simply existing in the structures *makes* one sin, in Segundo's thought), as well as risks collapsing finitude and sin into one another. Yet there is also in this line of thinking the deepest respect for the gravity of human sin, and a recognition of the clear fact that when the structures ordering human interactions are more and more oppressive, the sins stemming from them can be increasingly wicked. For another way of viewing this complex dynamic, let us now turn to the work of Leonardo Boff.

Leonardo Boff and Structures of Oppression

Leonardo Boff, an erstwhile Franciscan priest who lives and works with the poor in Brazil, is passionate about two things: the gospel and his people. He has been unwilling to make one compromise for the other.[62] Educated in South America and then Europe (where Ratzinger and Kloppenburg were his *Doktorväter*), Boff overstepped the bounds of appropriate theology in his writings on the church, according to the Vatican.[63] While most of the liberation theologians who ran afoul of Vatican teaching were charged with an over-reliance on Marxism, Boff was seen to accord too great a role in church life to the power of the Holy Spirit.[64] This is noteworthy, because

present universe but in something valuable and worthwhile to *do* in the universe right now'. 'The Evolutionary Categories of Juan Luis Segundo's Theology of Grace', in *Horizons* 19 (1992): 27–8.

61.   Segundo, *Evolution and Guilt*, 111.

62.   Boff appropriates the ancient Christian slogan 'theologia ante et retro oculata' to describe his view of looking back on past formulations of the gospel, and looking forward at the situation in front of him. Cf. his 'Two Eyes of Theology', in *Faith on the Edge*, trans. Robert B. Barr (San Francisco: Harper, 1989), 111–18.

63.   The Portuguese subtitle of one of his main books on the church is 'Essays in Militant Ecclesiology'. The book is translated as *Church, Charism and Power: Liberation Theology and the Institutional Church*, trans. John Drury (Maryknoll: Crossroad, 1985).

64.   Cf. the official CDF reproach of Boff, 'Notification Sent to Fr. Leonardo Boff regarding Errors in His Book *Church: Charism and Power*', in *Liberation Theology: A Documentary History*, 430.

some of the early resistance in many Roman Catholic circles to the notion of structural sin was due to the perception that this was simply a new way of naming what the Marxists had called class struggle.[65] If Boff was to be rejected, it would have to be on other grounds.

Sin is known in its overcoming as well as in its commission. The experience of grace can tell us as much or more about our radical need for grace as it does about the nature of the grace-giver. Though this is a widely held position by the thinkers considered in this book, perhaps no one is more explicit than Boff that this is the case. The idea of grace is logically dependent (and sometimes even parasitic) upon a prior conception of sin. 'Redemption to' is always necessarily also 'redemption from'. Boff's work on the concept of grace in Latin American liberation theologies unmasks the predominantly social and structural understandings of sin emerging from his context. Boff is tireless and subtle in his critique of the individualistic and spiritualistic distortion of Jesus' proclamation of social and material grace. Two of Boff's best books are actually devoted to each of these aspects of the distortion of sin and grace. In his marvellous devotional book *Way of the Cross – Way of Justice*[66] Boff takes a traditional Catholic practice of devotion for the individual, namely, meditations on the stations of the cross, and transforms it into a communal meditation on the implications of Jesus' path down the *Via Dolorosa* for life and the suffering in it of the present day. Boff tries to overcome the spiritualist distortion of grace in his book *The Lord's Prayer: The Prayer of Integral Liberation.*[67] There he looks at the petitions of the Lord's prayer and exposes how easily the prayer has become decoupled in Christian history from its very pragmatic consequences. 'Daily bread' became a metaphor for the spiritual nourishment of the church. 'Forgive our debts' became a cipher for the general forgiveness of sins instead of a particular concern for those forced to go into debt to stay alive.

Yet the clearest exposition Boff gives of his views on grace and sin comes in his early book *Liberating Grace*. In this work Boff describes sin and grace in terms of the individual in society, and more specifically in terms of what he calls the 'fundamental project of a human being'. This is Boff's way of situating the self in society. There is a certain orientation of both self and culture. A person can be abidingly combative, or consistently irenic. A culture can be continuously militant, or reliably peace-loving. These two aspects are closely connected, and both people and cultures form habits orienting themselves towards the execution of their projects. As Boff puts it, 'The fundamental project of a human person is intimately bound up with the fundamental project of the culture in which he or she lives.'[68] Given

65.   Gregory Baum, 'Structures of Sin', in idem and Robert Ellsberg, eds, *The Logic of Solidarity: Commentaries on Pope John Paul II's Encyclical 'On Social Concern'* (Maryknoll, Orbis, 1989), 110–26.

66.   Trans. John Drury (Maryknoll: Orbis, 1980).

67.   Trans. Theodore Morrow (Melbourne: Dove Communications, 1983).

68.   Leonardo Boff, *Liberating Grace*, trans. John Drury (Maryknoll: Orbis, 1988), 141.

this fact, the habitual grace that will aid in the completion of these projects must be correspondingly social in character.[69] Boff doubts the ability of non-liberationist perspectives to guarantee such a social framework for grace, and thinks that either one side or the other has been stressed too much. Either the self is not seen as situated in a culture, or the culture is described without reference to the concrete characteristics of people who compose it. The former of these troubles him most. He writes, 'The traditional Catholic conception, for all its good points, is excessively individualistic. Even when dealing with sin, conversion, and the earthly commitments of Christians, it considers them from a highly individualistic standpoint.'[70]

Since the fundamental projects of a person and the culture in which that person finds herself are so closely linked, Boff proposes that the relationship between the sin of an individual and extrapersonal, social sin falls under the rubric of a 'fundamental option'.[71] This fundamental option, understood positively or negatively, involves the ability of the person to say a fundamental 'yes' or 'no' to God. In traditional Roman Catholic moral theology, the vocabulary of 'fundamental option' has often been used in discussing the distinction between mortal and venial actual sins. In order for a sin to be mortal, three factors must obtain. The matter must be severe, the will of the sinner must be fully engaged and consenting, and the sinner must know fully the evil to be caused by the sin.[72] Boff argues that this distinction is operating with excessively individualistic assumptions and needs to be re-thought in terms that include a social, extrapersonal dimension of sin.

This is why. Human choice, according to Boff and many other Catholic liberation theologians, is contextual, and varies according to the possible choices set before the agent in his or her social setting.[73] Now, when the

69.   Habitual grace is 'the permanent disposition to live and act in keeping with God's call'. *Catechism of the Catholic Church*, 2000.

70.   Boff, *Liberating Grace*, 141.

71.   Boff, *Liberating Grace*, 124–33. For an appreciative and fuller exploration of this problematic in Boff's theology, cf. also Mark O'Keefe, OSB, 'Social Sin and Fundamental Option', in Clayton N. Jefford, ed., *Christian Freedom* (New York: Peter Lang, 1993), 131–43.

72.   Cf., among others, the exhortation from John Paul II, *Reconciliatio et Paenitentia*, 17.12, which reads, 'mortal sin is sin whose object is grave matter and which is also committed with full knowledge and deliberate consent'. For further on the distinction, cf. *Catechism of the Catholic Church*, § 1855.

73.   Many liberation theologians owe explicit (and sometimes implicit) debts to Piet Schoonenberg's concept of 'situated freedom' when making this point. Cf. especially his *The Sin of the World: A Theological View*, trans. J. Donceel (Notre Dame, IN: Notre Dame University Press, 1965). A further resource has been Rahner's distinction between transcendental, unthematized freedom (which is where the fundamental option resides) and the categorical, conscious varieties of freedom wherein one's fundamental orientation becomes concrete, for good or ill. Cf. his *Foundations of Christian Faith*, trans. William van Dych (New York: Crossroad, 1978), 90–115. Or for a more extensive look at this distinction, Rahner, *Theological Investigations* 6:178–96. In both the cases of Rahner and Schoonenberg, the influence of Heidegger's notion of finite freedom is never far in the background.

social system around a moral agent, in which she is embroiled, sets before her options for her choosing that are essentially sinful, it comes as no surprise that personal sin results. When the fundamental option of the culture around him, so to speak, is sinful, agents in the culture appropriate that sinfulness. Thus two conditions for the perpetration of mortal sins are not met, on Boff's view, in a context of social sin. The moral agent cannot fully consent to his act, since his will has been excessively conditioned by the social context, and he cannot reasonably be expected to know the full evil effects of his act, so impaired is his moral imagination by the situation of sinfulness. Sympathetically commenting on Boff's position, Mark O'Keefe writes, 'When the social world hides or skews values and fails to aid the development of authentic freedom, the fundamental option is necessarily affected. Social sin affects the ability of the person to know and choose value. Thus it hinders the person's ability to know the creator and the transcendent ground of value.'[74]

This is terribly important for Boff. The salvation of the individual person can be seen as a function of the righteousness of the structures in which he is located. As he puts it,

> The social dimension of the human being is ontologically rooted in the very core of the human being as a person. It does not arise after the individual dimension. It is not merely the sum of various juxtaposed individuals who happen to form a community of society. It is not a mere byproduct that is reducible to a more basic reality. Ontologically speaking, we may say that the social dimension is fundamental ... It is a structural reality that helps constitute the human person. Either a person is social or is not a person at all.[75]

This is the challenge that Boff sets for himself and for others. Grace has been so conceived in an individualistic way without reference to the social context in which each individual exists, that we are stuck now in trying to think of a way for grace to be appropriately social. Unless the fundamental project of a culture is properly oriented to God, 'If a theology is to be meaningful to people today, particularly in Latin America, then it must indicate how grace is revealed in its social, liberative dimension and how it criticizes and unmasks those in power.'[76]

The risks associated with Segundo's position, described above, apply to Boff's doctrines of sin and grace as well. While Boff does not directly ascribe agency to inanimate structures and arrangement of persons, he identifies *so closely* the orientation of a person with the orientation of the culture that it becomes hard to see how sin could be anything but hypostatized in inhabitants of a sinful society. This seems to me to be the most pressing objection to Boff's claims, though he has met much more resistance on other grounds. For example, Boff has been read as evincing a kind of fatalistic

74.   O'Keefe, 'Social Sin and Fundamental Option', 141.
75.   Boff, *Liberating Grace*, 141–2.
76.   Ibid., 29.

determinism. When sinful social structures are in place, personal sin must necessarily result, and there's nothing we can do about it.

This is related to the criticism that he hypostatizes sin, but is levelled more on the basis of an allergy to determinism than a desire to defend the abiding goodness of human nature. Yet there is perhaps a subtler critique of Boff's views, as well, in addition to the hypostatization motif. Boff employs a phenomenological method to describe the interpersonal encounter of grace in history. This is behind his insistence that both sin and grace are known in the context of being among other people.[77] Yet it is at least unclear, and may even not be possible to explain, how such a phenomenology would describe an 'encounter' with a structure, which Boff's arguments require. What would an encounter with a social structure be?[78] By what means would one be able to ascertain that the 'fundamental project' of a social structure was sinful? Obviously it would have sinful effects, such as institutionalized poverty, widespread sickness, the destruction of the natural environment, and so on. But encountering these means encountering other subjects.[79] I confess that I do not have any idea what the phenomenology of actually meeting a 'structure' would be. Here again we see both the strengths and weaknesses of Latin American theologies of sin; in their vigorous pursuit of a doctrine of sin that takes seriously the broad experience of human misery that is not easily localizable in the sinful will of an individual, they resort to notions of 'structural sin' which are, upon closer examination, not entirely coherent.

We have thus far, however, seen only two representatives of this tendency in Latin American doctrines of sin, Leonardo Boff and Juan Luis Segundo. Let us cast our net wider to see whether other theologians' emphases on the social dimensions of sin also lead to these problems. To that end, in the rest of this chapter I offer something less than a full survey of views on this matter, but something more than concatenated quotations from representative authors. The theologians whose views I discuss here have touched on sin to varying degrees in their writings, yet all of them, in my opinion, exhibit the same strengths and potential weaknesses in their presentations. Structures and social arrangements are rightly named as sinful, but the warrants for this claim and explanations offered for why this is so are less than wholly convincing. We will here consider another Latin American Catholic theologian, Juan Alfaro, and two Latin American Protestant theologians, Justo González and Aldo Etchegoyen, and then we

77. Ibid., 100–103, for example.
78. All of Boff's supposed examples of the experience of grace in meeting a 'structure' are really just contexts for meeting other subjects, which defeats the purpose of a doctrine of social sin. For example, he says that a criminal can encounter the law code, and then for some reason his sentence is for less than the time prescribed by the law. This is experienced as 'grace'. But what Boff really means is that the criminal encounters a gracious judge in this situation. *Liberating Grace*, 95.
79. Much of Boff's intersubjective analysis relies on categories drawn from Martin Buber's dialogic philosophy, which allows 'nature' actually to be a subject, not just an object.

will conclude this chapter by looking at a representative American advocate of Latin American notions of sin, Rebecca Chopp. In all of these cases I have distilled their writings on sin down to their rejection of individualism and, when offered, their proposed alternatives.

A Latin American Miscellany: Alfaro, Etchegoyen, González

Juan Alfaro is a Spanish-born Catholic New Testament scholar who has lived and worked for three decades on the US–Mexico border. His writings on sin try to make sense of the experiences of the poor with whom he lives, especially those harmed in immigration issues and the poor. His reason for the rejection of individualism in doctrines of sin is quite simple: it is unbiblical. The dominant methodologies employed in theology today attempt at ever sharper demarcation of concepts and a tighter articulation of ideas. This stands in marked contrast to Alfaro's opinion of the worldviews of the biblical authors. Rather than delimit precisely the content named by words like 'sin', Alfaro asserts,

> They did not attempt to clarify ideas and notions, thus circumscribing them and limiting them, but rather they expanded the ideas by giving more of their aspects and concrete manifestations and effects. Thus, if we look into the idea of sin in the Bible, we find a wide range of terms which give us a rather general notion, and not the precise clear notion we desire.[80]

Alfaro goes on to say that this methodological disconnect between biblical authorship and dominant dogmatic theology has consequences for the *content* of the doctrine of sin. The biblical authors, according to Alfaro, discussed sin in terms of a constellation of concepts like 'transgression, disobedience, rebellion, evil, lawlessness, iniquity, abomination, debt, crime, death, flesh, error, folly, trespass, slavery, straying, wickedness, lying and deceit'.[81] Given Alfaro's exegetical stance, it comes as no surprise that he would want to expand the dominant theological doctrines of sin to encompass more than what he feels is the excessive focus on individual moral sins. 'The biblical authors speak of spiritual realities with allusive and cautious words, for they are more intent on showing the concrete circumstances and experiences in which sin and salvation reveal themselves through this history and life of man [sic].'[82] Thus a biblically grounded doctrine of sin would, in Alfaro's opinion, simply not feel beholden to any kind of focus on the individual will, nor should it even necessarily be concerned with attendant concepts like responsibility. 'Sin' in the Bible simply names something that is not as

80. Juan Alfaro, *Christian Liberation and Sin* (San Antonio: Mexican American Cultural Center, 1975), 13.
81. Ibid.
82. Ibid.

God would have it. When we encounter any such thing, 'It is from those concrete experiences that we can now draw a general idea of what they [the biblical authors] may have meant and also, what their words might mean for our world of today.'[83] Though Alfaro has not developed an extensive answer for how sin and liberation translate from the Bible to the current day, he does give some hints. For example, he reads the Exodus story of the plagues (Ex. 7:1–12:42) as a three-tiered example of confrontation with the structures of evil and a corresponding liberation from them. The first three plagues (water to blood, frogs and gnats) focus on the theological level. Moses takes the position of a god, with Aaron as his prophet, and he meets and opposes Pharaoh and his prophets, the 'court magicians'.[84] The purpose of this confrontation is to determine on whose side the God of Israel stands. Plagues 4–7 (flies, livestock disease, boils and storms) show the political aspect of liberation. Moses and Pharaoh are here conceived as political leaders negotiating the structures of governance, and the plagues affect Pharaoh's ability to govern. The final three plagues (locusts, darkness, death of firstborn) open up the socio-economic level of liberation. Pharaoh's people complain here about the devastating economic effects of the plagues, and before the killing of the firstborn sons of the Egyptians (which decimated the economy), Alfaro notes that 'the climax of the socio-economic confrontation comes when every Israelite is ordered to borrow objects of gold and silver from every Egyptian so as to leave them penniless. The rich are left empty while the poor go away enriched.'[85] Sin, therefore, names in Alfaro's thought the entire spectrum of 'wrongs' in this situation – the political usurpation of Israel by Egypt, the idolatry of Pharaoh claiming divine status, and the socio-economic exploitation of the Israelites. Alfaro's point is clear: how can reference to any one theory of 'individual' sinfulness account for all of these dimensions?

Aldo Etchegoyen is a Methodist theologian living in Argentina who has asked similarly hard questions. As bishop for the district of Buenos Aires he was confronted daily with the material poverty of the people with whose spiritual care he was entrusted. Like Alfaro, Gutiérrez, Boff and others, he found that he simply could not understand their plight in terms of the individualistic idiom he had inherited from his Methodist background. He asks instead, 'What is happening in our continent because of the structures of oppression?'[86] For Etchegoyen the primary example of the structures of sin is the ever-increasing economic dependence of poor Latin Americans,

83. Ibid.

84. Alfaro, 'God Protects and Liberates the Poor', in *Option for the Poor: Challenge to the Rich Countries*, ed. Virgilio Elizondo and Leonardo Boff (Edinburgh: T & T Clark, 1986), 30–31.

85. Ibid., 31.

86. Aldo Etchegoyen, 'Theology of Sin and Structures of Oppression', in Dow Kirkpatrick, ed., *Faith Born in the Struggle for Life: A Rereading of Protestant Faith in Latin America Today* (Grand Rapids: Eerdmans, 1988), 156.

especially the indigenous peoples forcibly converted to Christianity, on foreign finance. Their debt grows, and their ability to meet subsistence levels of earnings wanes accordingly. Etchegoyen points out how hard it is to find individuals who are personally at fault for this situation. Contracts were legally signed, money was freely lent, and so on. But the injustice that stems from this financial structure far outpaces the sum of the series of acts which created it. Individual 'blame' is not sufficient to account for the sin of the situation. He writes, 'The structures of power are, in the final instance, the cause of the great problems which our continent faces today.'[87] What is more, there is a kind of snowball effect to contend with when facing up to the structures of oppression. When individuals are at fault for sin, the recourse seems clear enough, even if not always possible. The sin is to be named as such, the sinner identified, and either punishment or mercy to be meted out. But what, Etchegoyen asks, are we to do when the structures themselves are sinful? Changing policies and social arrangements is an obvious first step, but policies newly put in place may not necessarily be any better than the old ones. No structure, no matter how just or efficient, can heal past wounds nor promise not to harm society again. 'The structures of oppression deepen, strengthen, and coordinate their action.' There is no escape apparent, since 'the present situation of the poor of the world is linked to the process which the modern world has been following since the thirteenth century'.[88] Since Christianity is essentially a social, not solitary, phenomenon, in Etchegoyen's view, Latin America must be cautious in its dealings with other regions. As he digs into his Methodist heritage, Etchegoyen notes that it was the sociality of mission and evangelization that brought Methodism to Argentina, from England through America. For that he is grateful. However, from the same regions came 'the forces of money, military instruction, control of news, domination of the laws of commerce … All this converted our societies into structures of oppression and domination.'[89] Etchegoyen stops short of offering anything like a roadmap out of these structures of sin, but he, like Alfaro, is clear that no individualistic remedy can cure an ill so thoroughly social.

Another Methodist, the theologian and historian of Christianity Justo González, is one of the most prolific writers of Latin American theology. He has authored more than fifty books and hundreds of scholarly articles. He has increasingly turned his attention to the problem of sin recently, and his conclusions support my thesis that there is a groundswell of attention being paid to the social, extrapersonal dimensions of sin in contemporary Latin American liberation theology. González mercilessly criticizes what he views as the still-regnant theme of white North American theology, which he views as excessively individualistic and overly preoccupied with an analysis

---

87.   Ibid., 157. He is citing a document from the Latin American Council of Churches, for which no source is given. The sentiment is surely also his own, however.

88.   Ibid., 162

89.   Ibid., 165.

of the morality of discrete acts. The concept of sin as alienation, which has dominated much of the history of theology, centres on the individual.

> Alienation is mostly understood in its psychological dimensions, having to do with how one relates to oneself and others. One is inwardly alienated if one is not at one with one's identity. One is alienated from others if there is a rupture in relationship or communication. One is alienated from God if one does not know or does not accept God's love.[90]

But this conception of sin as alienation does not do justice to the fuller experience of sin uncovered and named by liberation theologies. Understanding alienation in purely, or even predominantly, psychological terms 'can be seen and criticized as one more step in the internalization and individualization of sin. And these in turn are two of the main reasons why it is so difficult for Christians today to speak of sin in terms that are pertinent to the many forms in which alienation is experienced.'[91]

This tendency towards internalizing and individualizing sin led, from the early church fathers through the medieval period to Luther, to an 'atomization of reality into a series of individuals, and the further atomization of the individual into a series of acts'.[92] This coheres with aspects of liberation theology besides its explicit formulations of sin. If the situation into which we have fallen such that we need God's liberating redemption to extricate us from it is basically an interior, private issue, then why would there be any social dimension to the redemption? González, like Alfaro before him, finds this view to be completely unbiblical.

> The God of the Bible is concerned with the misuse of property at least as much as with the misuse of sex. Yet we hear very little in the church about the misuse of property ... This selective preaching and teaching is not mere coincidence. It is because we have learned to interpret 'sin'. like so many other elements in biblical doctrine, in a manner that is less offensive to the powerful.[93]

This is another way of saying that the doctrine of sin has become private so that sins may continue to appear in their public form as righteousness.

This is why we must have not only psychological analysis of the individual but also concrete social analysis of systems. González writes,

> If sin is an individual matter, and the best way to analyze reality is as a series of disconnected decisions, the sin of the powerful is no different than the sin of the powerless. In each case, sin consists in making the wrong choice, and has little to

---

90.   Justo L. González, 'The Alienation of Alienation', in Andrew Sung Park and Susan L. Nelson, eds, *The Other Side of Sin: Woundedness from the Perspective of the Sinned-Against* (Albany: SUNY Press, 2001), 61.

91.   Ibid.

92.   Ibid., 62.

93.   Justo L. González, *Mañana: Christian Theology from a Hispanic Perspective* (Nashville: Abingdon, 1990), 135–6.

do with the complex web of human relations in which the powerful exploit the powerless.[94]

This is yet another way of saying that sin has become privatized, and done so in such a way that everyone appears equally sinful. When sins are located in the will of the sinner, then since all human wills are basically the same, all sins will basically be the same, too. As a corollary, intentionality becomes the critical criterion by which actions are to be judged sinful or not sinful. Peter Abelard famously insisted that if an archer aimed his arrow at a deer but missed and killed a man, he was not guilty of murder. If he had intended to hit the man, he of course would be guilty.[95] González, among many other Latin American liberation theologians, points out how myopic this view can be. When sin resides only in the will of the putative sinner, virtually all social dimensions of sin are cast aside. González hauntingly asks,

> Is sin so limited to the will and the intention that it is impossible to sin unknowingly or unwillingly? Were the atrocities of the Spanish conquistadores not sinful, because they thought they were serving Christ? Was the taking of land from the native inhabitants of North America not sinful, because those who did it thought they were serving God? Are the consequences of neoliberal capitalism in Central America or in the Philippines not sinful, because investors in richer countries are not aware of those consequences?[96]

As a church historian, Gonzalez knows that this was not always the case. 'In the early church, the confession of sins was both public and specific.' When this changed (staying specific but becoming private in the Roman Catholic church and staying public but becoming general in the Protestant churches, 'the result was that sin came to be seen increasingly as having to do mostly with an individual's relationship to God'.[97] What is more, when a Christian's main experience of sin comes in the form of the penitential system, it is little wonder that no attention is paid to the extrapersonal character of sin. One is called upon to recollect certain acts one has committed (or omitted), with little recourse to extenuating collective or social factors. González writes, 'In the penitential system, one does not focus on the structural dimensions of sin, nor even on one's own sinfulness, but rather on disconnected acts of sin.'[98] This blindness to the big picture has a personal side in González' life. He recalls that when he was growing up in Cuba, women held all kinds of positions of power in the church. He was so used to this that by the time he migrated to the United States, he found the discussions about the

94.   Ibid.
95.   Peter Abelard, *Ethica seu scito teipsum* XIV.4. For the influence of Abelard on this point, cf. P. L. Williams, *The Moral Philosophy of Abelard* (Lanham, MD: University Press of America, 1980).
96.   'Alienation of Alienation', 63.
97.   *Mañana*, 136.
98.   'Alienation of Alienation', 62.

acceptability of certain roles in the church for women to be baffling. Though he at first attributed the enlightenment of his upbringing to the forward-thinking character of the Cuban church, he later reconsidered. What was at work in the Cuban church was not enlightenment, but sin – the sin of racism, to be precise.[99] Women had always, even in male-dominated societies, been allowed to express their femininity by taking care of those in their culture considered to be less than fully human, such as the elderly, children and the sick. González asserts that something like this is true of the Christian missionaries in Cuba; since the 'natives' were less than fully human, women could be allowed leadership roles in their governance. There is thus 'an indissoluble connection between sexism and racism'.[100]

Finally, González makes the point that sin need not be *only* social, but also a sinful personal response to a sinful structure or situation. In a move mirroring what some feminists have said about sin, sin can be the passive acquiescence to oppression. Not standing up to one's oppressors can be sin. The gospel is an imperative as well as an indicative; the Christian message demands justice among and without its adherents. Oppressors sin by inflicting injustice, and the oppressed sin by accepting it.[101]

Conclusion: Chopp and the Reception of Latin American Views on Sin

In taking the first steps to rethink a doctrine of sin that was not restricted to the navel-gazing individualism of many traditional formulations, Gustavo Gutiérrez had been insistent that theologians maintain a critical tension between the personal responsibility and corporate guilt for sin. As our foray into other Latin American countries in subsequent decades, viewed from other perspectives, has shown, this critical tension has largely been eclipsed. The emphasis in sin has been so strongly social in nature that sufficient

---

99.   Justo González, 'Searching for a Liberating Anthropology', in *Theology Today* 34 (1978): 386–94.

100.   Ibid., 387.

101.   Justo L. González and Catherine G. González, *Liberation Preaching* (Nashville: Abingdon, 1980), 23. This kind of rhetoric brings up a point I have opted to omit from this chapter, but it is important enough at least to mention. Clearly some kind of activism is implied in the liberationist's call to the oppressed to stop accepting their oppression. But there are widely diverging views regarding the acceptability of violence for attaining those goals. In his book *Doing Theology in a Revolutionary Situation* (Philadelphia: Fortress Press, 1975), Jose Miguez Bonino argued for the *sui generis* status of the situation in Latin America, implying that revolution there would be uniquely permissible, if not mandated, by Christianity. On the other hand, one Latin American bishop (now Cardinal Dario Castríllon Hoyos) was asked by a reporter after Puebla what he thought about the revolutionary strands present in some liberation theologies. He replied, 'When I see a church with a machine gun, I cannot see the crucified Christ in that church. We can never use hate as a system of change. The core of being a church is love.' *National Catholic Reporter*, 20 June 2000. Hoyos is no liberationist, to be sure, but this comment particularly captures the sentiment of other Latin American liberation theologians.

care has not been given either to the individual's role in sin or to the actual content of what it means for a structure or system to be *sinful*. This social emphasis, which I regard as a case of the pendulum of sin swinging too far to the social side, is clearest not in Latin American liberationists' own writings, but in their appropriation by others. By way of closing this chapter, and beginning to segue to the next chapter, which will be a discussion of feminist and womanist critiques of individualism in sin, let us look very briefly at one of the most prominent advocates of liberation theology and its conceptions of sin. This is the Methodist scholar Rebecca S. Chopp.

Chopp concludes one summary of the major developments in Latin American theology by stressing its distinctiveness on sin. Recall that whereas for Gutiérrez and the theologians at Puebla and Medellín the sins of individual persons had been the primary focus and sinful social structures the derivative but genuinely sinful outcome, Chopp changes the emphasis to just the opposite.

> Sin ... in liberation theology is reflected on not merely through individual moral acts or existential separation and despair, but *primarily* in terms of social structures. Sin results in suffering, whose burden is carried, time and time again, by the poor of history. Sin is radical distortion, not of some private relation with God, but of all reality, especially of the historical-political world that God gives us to live in.[102]

When Chopp does speak more directly about the sin of individuals, she too, like most of the other authors we have examined in this chapter, emphasized the situatedness of the self, the plasticity of the self to its sinful environment, and the fallaciousness of former doctrines of sin which were centred on the individual. For example, Chopp writes,

> Sin both constitutes and is expressed through the historical structures of oppression; it is the whole of creation, both natural and social, groaning in travail. This is not to exclude the notion of sin as the willful act of an individual turning away from God; it is, rather, to make sense of human ride, hubris, and concupiscence in relation to all of God's creation. Sin is inclusive of alienation, and alienation must be understood through social categories.[103]

While she thus appears to be appreciative of the roots of sin in the individual along the lines that Segundo, Gutiérrez and others saw them (greed, egotism, etc.), Chopp is far more critical than the liberationists that these have a genuine place in a constructive doctrine of social sin:

> Traditionally, sin has been understood as the fallenness of all creation, the inability to be or do what God intended – caused, of course, by the willful turning away from God. Sin has been primarily understood as personal: the dark night of the soul, the agony of the individual in doubt, fear or confusion, and the struggle for control

---

102. Rebecca Chopp, 'Latin American Liberation Theology', in *The Modern Theologians*, ed. David F. Ford (Oxford: Blackwell, 1997), 413, emphasis added.

103. Rebecca Chopp, *The Praxis of Suffering: An Interpretation of Liberation and Political Theologies* (Maryknoll, NY: Orbis, 1986), 24–5.

over appetites and desires. It should be no surprise that liberation theology is critical of the privatism and individualism that results when sin is interpreted in personal terms; for liberation theologians sin must be understood as the distortion of human existence in its political nature, its intersubjective character, and its anticipatory orientation toward the future.[104]

I do not intend to pit Chopp against CELAM or against Gutiérrez in an attempt to prove that they were right and that Chopp and the popularizers of liberationist formulations of sin are wrong. In fact, I do not think that this is the case. But to see the trajectory along which these revolutionary thoughts of Gutiérrez have travelled is to see both some of the strengths and weaknesses of Latin American thought. As I showed in Chapter 2, Albrecht Ritschl went miles in the service of rethinking sin on less individualistic grounds, and made a genuine achievement in considering sin from a structural point of view. Yet he could never even have imagined writing something as beautiful as these haunting words of Chopp:

> Sin results in suffering, the suffering of creation groaning in travail, the suffering of children without any hope. Sin manifests and embraces suffering, the suffering of lost identity, the suffering of freedom without a future, and the suffering of a future without freedom. Sin extracts its price as the victimization of the poor, the suffering of the tortured, the dispossession of the homeless. These are the victims of sin not because of moral inferiority or human depravity, but because they bear the brunt and carry the special burden of the *world's sin*. In the retrieval of this symbol, sin's arena is human praxis and its primary realization is massive global injustice.[105]

As haunting and, frankly, as *true* as this perspective is, we flirt with calamity to embrace it uncritically. In the context of a rhetorical flourish, the world can sin, a structure can sin, a system can sin. But this simply cannot blind us to the incontestable fact that on the everyday level on which we all lead our lives, sin also comes to us in less grandiose ways. We see the wickedness of real people – *individual people* – doing wickedness, ranging from the spectacularly evil to the pathetically trivial, and everything in between. When we are most honest with ourselves, we see that the story of sin is our story, too. We are fools to think that our sin could ever be ours alone – that it does not harm, implicate and stem from others – and therefore we simply must assert the strongly social character of sin. On this the Latin American liberationists teach us much. But we can also learn from their excesses and remind ourselves that if social sin is to be properly conceived and theologically explicated, it is nonetheless the social sin of social individual sinners. With this caveat in mind as we consider the prospects for just such a future formulation of social sin, we now turn to our second example of doctrines of social sin in the last five decades, namely the exploding literature on sin from feminist and womanist theologians.

104. Ibid., 128.
105. Ibid., my emphasis.

Chapter 5

INDIVIDUAL AND SOCIAL SIN
IN SELECTED FEMINIST THEOLOGIES

Introduction to Feminist Theologies of Sin

The origins of feminist theologies of sin are difficult to name, as everything hinges on what one intends by the phrase 'feminist theology'. If what is meant by this is an articulated concept of some aspect of religious life, in this case of human nature and sin, written by a Christian woman from a view which seems in some fashion uniquely to speak to women's experience of that aspect of religious life and thought, then feminist doctrines of sin go back at least to the fascinating 'parable of the eager servant' written by Julian of Norwich in the fourteenth century.[1] But then again, women have been writing and reflecting on their experiences of sin and suffering much further back than this. Hildegard of Bingen[2] and Mechthild of Magdeburg[3] in the high middle ages wrote movingly and fascinatingly of their images of redemption (and sin) born of their mystical experiences. And before this comes a whole host of women ascetics, mystics and lay thinkers whose experiences of God and of sin took a shape which should not be ignored.[4] Yet when scholars think of feminist theology, something else is usually in mind. Feminist theology generally, and in this book, exclusively, is related instead to the rather more self-conscious effort to identify, root out, and replace sexist constructions in the materials and forms of theology with non-sexist ones.

The origins of this self-consciously 'feminist theology', as opposed simply to theology written by women, lie in the much more proximate past. With respect to sin, this past is usually nominally dated to 1960, and the now famous publication of Valerie Saiving's seminal article exposing the flagrant androcentrism of Reinhold Niebuhr's doctrine of sin.[5] Saiving took the

---

1.   Julian of Norwich, *Revelations of Divine Love*, trans. Elizabeth Spearing (London, Penguin, 1998).
2.   Especially the *Scivias* and *The Book of Divine Works*.
3.   Especially in *The Flowing Light of Godhead*, trans. Christiane Mesch Galvani (New York: Garland, 1991).
4.   For the best full-scale history of these figures and movements, cf. Rosemary Radford Ruether, *Women and Redemption: A Theological History* (Minneapolis: Fortress Press, 1998).
5.   Valerie Saiving, 'The Human Situation: A Feminine View', *Journal of Religion* 40 (1960): 100–12. Saiving also deconstructs Anders Nygren's anthropology in this essay. I find her objections to Niebuhr far more compelling.

position that Niebuhr's insistence on the central role of *superbia* (pride) in sinning was simply the universalization of male experience to cover all human experience of sin. Saiving noted that excessive pride born of the life of near-constant self-transcendent activity was hardly the defining experience for women. She responded with an account towards what a doctrine of sin might look like based on more equitable gendered experience. Judith Plaskow,[6] Susan Nelson Dunfee,[7] Daphne Hampson[8] and many others subsequently engaged in similar projects. Their insights were profound, but will not be discussed in this chapter, for they focus on formulating ways of speaking about *individual* sin which speak to women's experience. This is most certainly a legitimate and even necessary theological enterprise. This approach has had a long life; many feminist theologians are still engaged in such an agenda.[9] But this book is not primarily interested in evaluating new versions of ways to theologically describe the sins of individuals.[10] Many, many feminists have instead gone in some directions that bear directly on the topic of this book, however, and we will need to look at some of them in depth.

The concept of sin is one that has special purchase in feminist theology, because it is probably the one doctrine more than any other (excepting, perhaps, a male-centred Christology) that has served to legitimize and perpetuate the oppression of women. This has taken so many forms that I cannot name them all. A partial list would have to include, for example, the fact that women's bodies were seen to be inherently closer to 'nature' and therefore more sinful. Eve has been blamed for all the effects of 'The Fall'. When sinless human action (as defined by men) depended heavily on the control of the will by reason, instead of by the passions, men could accuse women of being less rational (partly because sexism helped men prevent

---

6.   Judith Plaskow, *Sex, Sin and Grace: Women's Experience and the Theologies of Reinhold Niebuhr and Paul Tillich* (Lanham: University Press of America, 1980).

7.   Susan Nelson Dunfee, 'The Sin of Hiding', *Soundings* 65 (1982): 316–27.

8.   Daphne Hampson, 'Reinhold Niebuhr on Sin: A Critique', in *Reinhold Niebuhr and the Issues of Our Time*, ed. Richard Harries (London: Mowbray, 1986), and idem, 'Luther on the Self: A Feminist Critique', in *Feminist Theology: A Reader* (Louisville: Westminster John Knox, 1990), 215–25. The appellation 'Christian' is now inappropriate for Hampson, but 'theologian' may well not be.

9.   Cf., for example, Linda Mercadante, *Victims and Sinners: Spiritual Roots of Addiction and Recovery* (Louisville: Westminster John Knox, 1996) and Angela West, *Deadly Innocence: Feminist Theology and the Mythology of Sin* (London: Cassell, 1995).

10.   I also have significant reservations to projects of naming particular women's sins. Depending on how it is done, this strategy risks replacing the false universal of men's experience in traditional sexist theologies with any of a number of forms of gendered essentialism. I view the work of Dunfee, Saiving, et al. as a perhaps necessary stage in the development of a feminist Christian theology, but I hope we can move towards more inclusive concepts in the Christian description of the human condition which are nonetheless cognizant of the risks of false universals. For theologians this involves noting one's particularity but speaking boldly out of it, too.

women from being educated) and therefore more sinful. And the list goes on and on.

Structural Sin in Feminist and Womanist Theologies

Yet, perhaps somewhat ironically, it is precisely in the locus of theological anthropology and sin that I find the most fascinating work in contemporary constructive feminist theology. Very early on in feminist theology, women were seeing that the whole way of going about sin-talk was inappropriate to biblical concepts of sin, to the best of the history of theology, and, most importantly, to the realities of women's experiences of sin in the modern world. That experience highlighted, for example, the interconnectedness of life, the stunning power of what seemed to be coldly impersonal structures arranging human relationships and interactions, and the socially and linguistically constructed worlds which at once welcomed and trapped women in patterns of sin.[11] The literature emerging (or better, exploding) from this new way of conceiving sin is simply enormous. Entering into this territory can be extremely daunting, but I have found, and I intend to show, that the two types of ways to construe sin in non-individualistic ways are an excellent way to categorize, understand, and assess this burgeoning and profoundly important literature.

Mary Potter Engel

Our first figure is Mary Potter Engel. Her work represents a helpful jumping-off point both because of the size of her writings on sin (which is basically one essay – though it is cited in nearly *every* major work of feminist theology on sin) and because her treatment of sin is a microcosm of the transition from feminist approaches to sin which tried to make, first, the specific point that the sin of individual women may be different from

---

11.   On this last category, which will not be discussed in detail in this chapter, Mary McClintock Fulkerson has made some fascinating contributions. Cf. especially *Changing the Subject: Women's Discourses and Feminist Theology* (Minneapolis: Fortress, 1994), 'Sexism as Original Sin: Developing a Theacentric Discourse', in *Journal of the American Academy of Religion* 59 (1991): 653–75 and 'Contesting the Gendered Subject: A Feminist Account of the *Imago Dei*', in Rebecca S. Chopp and Sheila Grave Devaney, eds, *Horizons in Feminist Theology: Identity, Tradition and Norms* (Minneapolis: Fortress, 1997), 99–115. Fulkerson's work is relevant to a concept of social sin, since she locates sin within the oppressive forms and means of discourse of a linguistic community (following primarily poststructuralist thought in this matter). Her work is omitted from this discussion not because it is not significant, but because it lies somewhat outside the bounds of my topic, which is to correlate doctrines of social sin according to the categories of structural sin or the relational self. Depending on how she is read, Fulkerson's work fits into both or neither, and determining that would simply take up too much space.

the sin of individual men, to the second, more general point that sin as a whole looked different – especially that it looked more *social* – when viewed through women's eyes.[12] Her view of sin and evil also blends aspects of the two types of ways of avoiding individualism in sin, though she has more in common with the structural sin type than she does with the relational self type.[13]

Conceptually, Engel pairs sin with evil. The two combined constitute wickedness. Evil is systemic, and sin 'refers to those free, discrete acts of responsible individuals that create or reinforce these structures of oppression'.[14] The two are mutually intensifying. Sin does not 'cause' evil, nor evil sin, but the two reinforce each other. Systems of evil breed sinners who then build up extant systems of evil. Theologically speaking, evil has two sides, lament and blame. Evil as lament allows us to side with the victim of evil (in Engel's context, this usually means the victim of abuse) and in solidarity with her give voice to the experience of oppression. On the other hand, 'evil as blame redirects attention to the structures that have power over her and for which she is not solely, ultimately, or directly responsible'.[15] Potter thinks this kind of formulation is preferable to a reinterpretation of original sin, which she thinks inevitably places blame excessively on the victims, and insufficiently on the perpetrators, of violence and oppression. Engel goes on to reinterpret traditional notions of sin from the perspective of the victims of abuse and violence. For example, Engel recasts 'sin as disobedience' into the mould of 'sin as a betrayal of trust'. Victims of domestic violence are not told they are sinful for 'disobeying' their violent abusers; they are told that the abusers are sinful for betraying the trust implicit and explicit in, say, the marriage contract.[16] 'Sin as concupiscence' is similarly recast from the perspective of the victim along the lines of 'our distorted relationship to weakness, vulnerability, and dependence'.[17] Whereas the problem of desire and dependence takes shape in abusive men as the concupiscent desire for more power over a dependent other, the same dynamic can lead to an over-subjection to men in women. In both cases, there is a contempt for vulnerability and interdependence. Engel thus names this as 'the lack of consent to the dependence and fragility of our lives'.[18]

---

12. Mary Potter Engel, 'Evil, Sin, and the Violation of the Vulnerable', in *Lift Every Voice: Constructing Christian Theologies from the Underside*, idem and Susan Brooks Thistlethwaite, eds, (San Francisco: Harper, 1990), 152–64.

13. Inclusion in this section need not imply, for Engel or the other figures listed here, that the author so grouped does not have a relational view of the self. In fact when pressed, they would, I think, agree that human selves are to be conceived in the relationships which contribute to their development. However, the point I am making is that in the criticisms of individualism that these women share, the relational self does not function as the criterion for judgement; social structures of sin and evil fit that role.

14. Ibid., 155.

15. Ibid.

16. Ibid., 157–8.

17. Ibid., 162.

18. Ibid., 163.

The basic shapes of the feminist expressions of the structural sin type of critique of individualism in sin are thus starting to come into view. The 'sins' of women are at least talked about differently, and may be different altogether from the sins of men. This happens particularly by noting the kinds of contexts in which this sin occurs, and that means an analysis of the structures of evil which reinforce such sin. I will refrain from making an extended critique of the success or failure of these approaches until the end of this chapter, but at least something should be said at this point about Engel's programmatic suggestions. The recasting of individual sins of disobedience, concupiscence, pride and anger seem to me extremely valuable pastoral approaches to speaking with victims of abuse in theological terms. However, regarding its status as a piece of systematic theology, I am less sure of its adequacy. Engel admits that 'I find it important to point out that evil and sin, though inseparable, are to be stressed differently in varying contexts. When one is speaking of perpetrators, sin, individual responsibility, and accountability should be stressed ... When one is speaking of and to victims, evil should be stressed.'[19] Engel asserts this because she wants to 'avoid blaming the victim and giving the impression that perpetrators (largely men) and victims (largely women) are co-responsible or equally sinful'.[20] While this may certainly be true of the particular sins of violence and abuse, I wonder about its adequacy as something like a full doctrine of sin. The interplay between victim and perpetrator is so much less obvious in the everyday world in which we find ourselves than it is in the horrible situations in which the victim of abuse and violence finds herself.[21] Broad experience frustrates most attempts at the clear delineation of perpetrator and victim. Miroslav Volf, for example, has levelled an extraordinary critique against the kind of neat division of the world into victim and perpetrator, oppressor and oppressed to which Engel's thought could lead. Growing up in war-ravaged Croatia, Volf found that every side in the battle could legitimately construe themselves as victim and the other as sinful aggressor.[22] Cannot this kind of facile opposition between rigidified groups of sinners and sinned against be *somehow* transcended in our thinking about sin? We must withhold judgement on this, however, until examining many more thinkers whose scope of sin is more appropriately broad and whose writings are accordingly more wide-ranging.

19.   Ibid., 156.
20.   Ibid.
21.   Though Engel's point, and the point of countless other feminists is well taken and extremely important, the situation is anything but obvious to the victim trapped in it at the time.
22.   Miroslav Volf, *Exclusion and Embrace: A Theological Exploration of Identity, Otherness, and Reconciliation* (Nashville: Abingdon, 1996).

Elisabeth Schüssler Fiorenza

Elisabeth Schüssler Fiorenza certainly fits the bill in both of those respects; the breadth of both the scope her thinking encompasses and the writings which witness to it is quite remarkable. Schüssler Fiorenza is a pioneer in the field of feminist interpretation and criticism of the Bible. Her book *In Memory of Her: A Feminist Theological Reconstruction of Christian Origins* is already a classic of theology constructed in close conversation with biblical hermeneutics.[23] In that work Schüssler Fiorenza synthesized traditional tools of New Testament study with a brand of feminist hermeneutics of suspicion in order to interrogate key New Testament texts, as well as texts from the early history of the church. The general pattern of hermeneutics she follows can be summarized as 'suspicion, proclamation, remembrance, and creative actualization'.[24] She unearthed a picture of a community that was more hospitable to women than had earlier been imagined. Many scholars had asserted that the early Christian outlook on women moved towards equality, but that this shift was a symptom of an imminent Pauline eschatology which made little of *difference* in general (neither Greek nor Jew, male nor female, etc.). Schüssler Fiorenza moved past this, however, arguing that there was actually content in the proclamation of Jesus that asserted the full equality of women. Evidence of this was the central roles accorded to women in Jesus' ministry as well as in the early church, in addition to the explicit words of Jesus, and particularly to the scenes in the gospels of the woman who anoints Jesus, whose story should be told where the gospel is proclaimed, 'in memory of her' (Mark 14:9 and parallels).[25] To this end, Schüssler Fiorenza began to discuss sexism as a distortion of the structure of society proclaimed by Jesus to be in accord with God, and therefore as something like 'structural sin'.[26]

23.   (New York: Crossroad, 1983).

24.   Schüssler Fiorenza, *Bread, Not Stone – The Challenge of Feminist Biblical Interpretation* (Boston: Beacon, 1984).

25.   Relevant biblical texts cited by Schüssler Fiorenza would include the fact that women were the first witnesses of the resurrection, that women remained loyal to Jesus during his arrest and trial, and the extreme importance of women as the first followers of Jesus to bring his gospel to a predominantly Gentile audience.

26.   Lucia Scherzberg, in her excellent book *Sünde und Gnade in der Feministischen Theologie* (Mainz: Grünewald, 1991), titles her chapter on Schüssler Fiorenza 'Sexism as Structural Sin and the Discipleship of Equals as the Location of the Experience of God', 76–90. However, nowhere in the chapter, and nowhere in Schüssler Fiorenza's writings can I find an actual equation of the religious category of *sin* with the structures of domination and oppression which Schüssler Fiorenza discusses everywhere. It is beyond doubt that Schüssler Fiorenza finds these structures to be appalling and unequivocally *wrong*, but it is not obvious that they are wrong because they are sinful. This is a theological category which at least brings God into the description of the structure, even if the structure is not said to be against God alone. It is still worth discussing Schüssler Fiorenza's contribution, because an author writing from a more explicitly theological position could easily incorporate Schüssler Fiorenza's condemnation of patriarchy or *kyriarchy* into a framework of sin.

But Schüssler Fiorenza has written much more than this, besides, and some of her work is relevant for the current project, as it exhibits a certain amount of continuity with the structural sin type of avoiding individualism in doctrines of sin as well as moving toward the relationality type usually more characteristic of feminist Christian theology. Schüssler Fiorenza uses the word *kyriarchy* to refer to the top-down power structures of domination and subordination effective in the social and political life in the family and the state.[27] *Kyriarchy* is based on the idea that the lord, the father and the master are superior to the subject, family and slave. It is this fact of governance, or the very existence of such a structure, which then leads to androcentrism. Androcentrism is, in Schüssler Fiorenza's eyes, one of the rhetorical constructs of an already sexist community which serves to legitimate the authority of that community.[28]

Schüssler Fiorenza's reconstruction of the early Christian community which sprang up in the wake of the Jesus movement shows a marked difference from the 'kyriocentric'[29] view apparent in simplistic readings of the later writings of the New Testament. Schüssler Fiorenza's main metaphor for describing her reconstructed vision is the *ekklesia*. The *ekklesia* as a social concept means a structure of organizing human interpersonal interactions devoid of any hierarchy, patriarchy, *kyriarchy*, and so on. It is utterly egalitarian in all its social (i.e., economic, judicial, educational, etc.) manifestations. But more than an intellectual concept, the *ekklesia* functions for Schüssler Fiorenza as an eminently practical location of social interaction that is not a distortion of Jesus' message and historical praxis. '[E]*kklesia* comes through the agency of the Spirit to visible, tangible expression in and through the gathering of God's people around the table, eating together, a meal, breaking the bread, and sharing the cup in memory of Christ's passion and resurrection'. This implies, further, 'eating together, sharing together, drinking together, talking with each other, receiving each other, experiencing God's presence through each other, and in doing so, proclaiming the gospel as God's alternative vision for everyone, especially for those who are poor, outcast, and battered'.[30] This could be read as a way of talking about sin and its overcoming. *Kyriarchy* is what is wrong, and *ekklesia* helps overcome it. But precisely here Schüssler Fiorenza's role as a New Testament scholar shows its shortcomings; a theological

---

27.   Elisabeth Schüssler Fiorenza, *But She Said: Feminist Practices of Biblical Interpretation* (Boston: Beacon Press, 1992) contains the fullest (and first) discussion of *kyriarchy*. For a shorter discussion, cf. 'The Ties that Bind: Domestic Violence against Women', in Mary John Manzanan, et al., eds, *Women Resisting Violence: Spirituality for Life* (Maryknoll: Orbis, 1996), 42–6.

28.   This is not the dominant position in feminist theology; most feminists reverse the order of causality between rhetorical construct and social system, or else view them as mutually implicating. Cf. Schüssler Fiorenza, *In Memory of Her*, xix.

29.   This is Schüssler Fiorenza's later word to describe the interpenetrating nature of *kyriarchy* and androcentrism.

30.   Schüssler Fiorenza, *In Memory of Her*, 345–6.

appropriation of her writings simply must inquire into the question of just why it is that *kyriarchy* is wrong. The warrant for her claim, when one is present at all, amounts to a common-sense understanding of human flourishing. It is practically self-evident to her that this kind of structure harms women and so is to be avoided and indeed abolished. Schüssler Fiorenza, to my knowledge, only uses the term 'structural sin' a handful of times in her writings and never invests it with much real content.[31] While it may in fact be self-evident that *kyriarchy* is to be opposed on the grounds that it is oppressive to women, most feminist systematic theologians have gone a significant step further than this and argued that such oppressive social structures are properly sinful because they are against God as well as women.[32] We should note that this does not by any means constitute a failure in Schüssler Fiorenza's work; on the contrary, it evinces a carefulness on her part not to stray inappropriately from her chosen vocation as a New Testament exegete. However, we will in the following pages need to look more carefully at more explicitly theological interpretations of the human social condition, even as it was necessary briefly to explicate the biblical basis for that description in Schüssler Fiorenza's work.

Ivone Gebara

Although she holds earned doctorates in both philosophy and theology, one theologian who has taken the actual experience of women with utter seriousness is the Brazilian thinker Ivone Gebara. Gebara, like Schüssler Fiorenza, focuses on the eminently practical understandings of religious life in her writing. Just as Schüssler Fiorenza reflects on what it must have been like to be a woman in the early *ekklesia* of the Jesus movement, Gebara's major work on evil and suffering, *Out of the Depths*, is unabashedly concrete and hands-on when it comes to what is elsewhere more theoretically called sin.[33] Yet this mature work could only develop, as did Schüssler Fiorenza's, after an arduous process of evolution in Latin American feminist theology. In an interview from 1993, Gebara traced three stages of this evolution.[34]

---

31.   Schüssler Fiorenza, 'Das Schweigen brechen sichtbar werden', in *Concilium* 21 (1985): 388–9, *In Memory of Her*, 347, and 'Emanzipation aus der Bibel: Gegen patriarchalisches Christentum', in *Evangelisches Kommentar* 16 (1983): 195–6.

32.   Not many feminists have made what seems to me to be the obvious corollary point here; patriarchy and domination is harmful for, and diminishes the flourishing of, men, too, though certainly in different ways than it does for women. The reasons for this omission are certainly understandable. But the point that in sinful social structures, *no one wins* is important enough to make more forcefully.

33.   Ivone Gebara, *Out of the Depths: Women's Experience of Evil and Salvation*, trans. Ann Patrick Ware (Minneapolis: Fortress, 2002).

34.   Published in *Readings in Ecology and Feminist Theology* ed. Mary Heather MacKinnon and Moni McIntyre (Kansas City: Sheed and Ward, 1995), 208–13.

The first stage accompanied the translation of seminal texts from 'first world' secular feminists and feminist liberation theologians. Gebara and her colleagues began to name their oppression, located it in misuses of the Bible, and sought role models and 'usable material' in less overtly patriarchal texts.[35] The second phase witnessed a 'feminization' of latent theological concepts. This amounted to a kind of addition to the dominant models of doing theology of women's experiences. It did not, on the whole, change the way theology was conceived and practised. But the third stage, in which Gebara now locates herself, is characterized by a thorough re-thinking of the method, content and task of Christian theology.[36] This signifies a deep rupture with the way theology has traditionally been done, and makes Gebara's inclusion in this chapter both necessary and difficult.[37]

Gebara encounters in women's experience of evil a confusing mixture of evil's transcendence and immanence.[38] Evil is at once a grand overarching concept within which reflective people interpret their lives, and yet it is also much more familiar and immediate. It is, briefly, exceedingly domestic. Gebara employs a strict phenomenological method, explicitly indebted to Paul Ricoeur and implicitly to Edmund Husserl, to bracket out consideration of the overarching concept of Evil temporarily, the better to remain concrete in her analysis of evils.[39] In this way, evil can be seen as something as simple as the horrifying reality experienced by women whom Gebara knows are forced to say: 'Today I was lucky. There was a lot of trash in the streets.' Gebara laments that 'Collecting trash confers the power to eat: who among the politicians would set the standard so low?'[40] There is also the mundane but daily pain of having soap but not water, or water but no soap.[41] Gebara is pointing out that in Latin American women's experience, evil is not so

35.   Ibid., 209.
36.   Ibid., 211.
37.   The strategy of selecting individual theologians works less well for Latin American women theologians, who tend to view theology as an extremely communal practice. A list of other women whose views are relevant here would have to include the *mujerista* theology of Ada Maria Isai-Diaz; cf. her *En la Lucha: Elaborating a* Mujerista *Theology* (Minneapolis: Fortress, 1993), 166–84 for her account of the interlocking structures of sin which oppress women, conceived along similar lines as Gebara's. Elsa Tamez locates roots of oppression in the Christian claims to exclusive access to the source of liberation and redemption; cf. her *Bible of the Oppressed*, trans. Matthew J. O'Connell (Maryknoll: Orbis, 1982), and specifically with reference to sin and redemption, *The Amnesty of Grace: Justification by Faith from a Latin American Perspective*, trans. Sharon Ringe (Nashville: Abingdon, 1993). Maria Pilar Aquino also discusses some of the communal or corporate facets of redemption, but does not discuss in great detail the roots of sin in social structures. *Our Cry for Life*, trans. Dinah Livingstone (Maryknoll: Orbis, 1993). I do think that all of these perspectives are similar enough to each other that discussing Gebara more in depth rather than three or four superficially is the best strategy.
38.   Gebara, *Out of the Depths*, 57.
39.   Ibid., 11 and 56.
40.   Ibid., 42.
41.   Ibid.

much *interpreted* as it is immediately and immanently experienced by a them. Thus Gebara wants us to focus not on a kind of cosmic account of Evil, but on the very domestic, palpable and mundane *evils* which all people, particularly women, experience every day.[42]

This last statement hints at the structural dimensions of human evil. There is something about the way the question of evil and sin has been posed by male theologians and philosophers that has, in turn, actually *contributed to* and *exacerbated* the evils which women experience. Dominant theology has relied overmuch on binary categories which understand men as created good and women as incarnate fallen evil.[43] Following Rosemary Radford Ruether's thought, Gebara maintains that this denigration of women as embodied evil manifests itself not only in acts of sin committed against women, but also the denigration of the natural environment. In fact, in another work Gebara explicitly explores the links between a growing ecological awareness and the liberation (particularly, but not only) of women.[44]

Gebara is aware that her emphasis on women's experience of evil could make it appear that she is blind to the sins women commit. She quotes the haunting passage from Zygmunt Bauman, who writes, 'As a rule, victims are not ethically superior to their victimizers; what makes them seem morally better, and makes credible their claim to this effect, is the fact that – being weaker – they have had less opportunity to commit cruelty.'[45] Gebara thus asserts that she can 'detect in some way, directly or indirectly, that they [women who experience evil] have also themselves committed immoral acts'.[46] Since women in Latin America are rarely allowed into the kinds of positions of power where they could contribute to the creation of systems of domination, in their own way they acquiesce to them and further their sinful ends. The youngest daughter of some Mexican families, for example, is not allowed to marry in order that she be free to care for her parents in their old age. The mother is often viciously cruel in enforcing this 'structure of evil' that harms her daughter.[47] Mothers tell their daughters not to be like the 'prostitutes, single mothers, black and indigenous women, and lesbians' present in their communities.[48] The power of evil makes itself known most when those who suffer most from it make it stronger by remaining in it. Yet Gebara's reflections on evil are also deeply rooted in the hope born of the equally domestic, equally concrete experiences of salvation of the

---

42.   Ibid., 14.
43.   Ibid., 4.
44.   Ivone Gebara, *Longing for Running Water: Ecofeminism and Liberation*, trans. David Molineaux (Minneapolis: Fortress, 1999).
45.   Zygmunt Bauman, *Postmodern Ethics* (Oxford: Blackwell, 1993), 227–8, quoted in Gebara, *Out of the Depths*, 95.
46.   Gebara, *Out of the Depths*, 96.
47.   Ibid., 98.
48.   Ibid., 99.

women among whom she lives,[49] as well as hope in what she elsewhere calls 'women's collective power'.[50]

Gebara's work represents a powerful effort to engage the roots of the experience of evil (dualisms, binary oppositions, the identity of women with 'nature' and the denigration of both) and the concrete phenomenology of that experience. She seems not to fall victim to the potential weaknesses which beset the sinful structures type of response to individualism; unlike Engel, Gebara is extremely careful not to imply women's innocence nor divide too neatly oppressor from oppressed. She has a developed notion of God and God's Trinitarian dealings with and will for humanity, such that naming structures as sinful has religious as well as moral and ethical power.[51] Yet the real question remains, for Gebara, what would happen if she were to remove the self-imposed eidetic brackets of her feminist phenomenology of evil? I do grant that she thinks ontologies of evil are inevitably sexist, and therefore to be avoided; but this commitment of hers does not necessarily disallow a more careful look at *sin* than she has so far offered. It is clear that individual acts of wilful sin contribute to the existence of the structures which shape experience, and that this experience is rightly called evil. But what is it about humans that make us prone both to constructing and complying with structures that perpetuate evil? Gebara is clear on and critical of the methods that will not help bring us to this understanding, but we may have to await more work from her before we can know a more conclusive answer. Navigating this dynamic between asserting the sinful status of structures of oppression and maintaining relative silence about its individual sources and wilful perpetuation is truly a challenging course. Let us now turn to another group of women who have thought hard about the extrapersonal nature of structures of evil.

Womanist Theologies

The designator 'womanist' derives from Pulitzer Prize winning novelist Alice Walker's notion of 'womanish'. To be womanish is to be the opposite of girlish. According to Walker, acting womanish means 'wanting to know more and in greater depth than is good for one; outrageous, audacious, courageous and willful behavior', but also 'responsible, in

---

49.   For some moving examples of these, cf. *Out of the Depths*, 121–32. I should also note here that 'relatedness' figures heavily into her notion of salvation, though her emphasis on structures of sin and evil warrants her inclusion under that type of critique of individualism.

50.   Ivone Gebara, 'Option for the Poor as an Option for Poor Women', in Elisabeth Schüssler Fiorenza, ed., *The Power of Naming: A Concilium Reader in Feminist Liberation Theology* (Maryknoll: Orbis, 1996), 145.

51.   Ivone Gebara, 'The Trinity and Human Experience: An Ecofeminist Approach', in Rosemary Radford Ruether, ed., *Women Healing Earth: Third World Women on Ecology, Feminism and Religion* (Maryknoll: Orbis, 1996), 13–23.

charge, serious'.[52] This notion has been richly put into the service of black women's experiences of oppression in the now-established but still-emerging school of thought called womanist theology. Many of the major voices in womanist theology have made contributions to concepts of sin, particularly to the interplay between social and individual sin. Most of these contributions can be fitted into the 'structural sin' type, though they, like many other emerging schools of thought, resist clean classification. But racism is at the very least not easily reducible to individual conscious acts by individuals who are racist, though this obviously happens. Womanist theologians tend to think of sin primarily in terms of the structures of society which perpetuate racism and sexism, particularly the ways in which they reinforce each other. Coupled with emphasis on the structures of sin we find in womanist theology an interesting appeal to non-doctrinal sources of wisdom on sin and its overcoming which is then put to use in something like doctrines of sin. We will look briefly at three representative womanist theologians, Jacquelyn Grant, Delores Williams and Emilie Townes, and see their unique perspective on the structures of sin.

Jacquelyn Grant

Jacquelyn Grant was perhaps the first explicitly theological writer in the womanist movement. Her major work, *White Women's Christ and Black Women's Jesus*, detailed the class assumptions and sometimes overtly racist formulations of white feminist Christology.[53] In that book she begins with the idea that black women's experience, particularly their encounter with racism, sexism and classism, made them uniquely qualified to understand the person of Jesus and his work in overcoming sin, which is, for Grant, essentially the three systems of oppression just named.[54] Grant's work in exposing the racist and sexist assumptions of other theologies, perhaps somewhat ironically the particular theologies of white feminists and male black liberationists, goes back nearly thirty years. Already in the late 1970s Grant had pointed out that 'where racism is rejected, sexism has been embraced. Where classism has been called into question, racism and sexism have been tolerated. And where sexism is repudiated, racism and classism are often ignored.'[55] She concludes that this implies a genuine crisis in liberation theology, for 'in order for liberation theology to be faithful to

---

52.   Cited in Delores Williams, 'Womanist Theology: Black Women's Voices', in *Yearning to Breathe Free: Liberation Theology in the U.S.*, ed. Linda Rennie Forcey, et al., (Maryknoll: Orbis, 1990), 62.

53.   (Atlanta: Scholar's Press, 1989).

54.   Ibid., 146.

55.   Jacquelyn Grant, 'Black Theology and the Black Woman', in Gayraud S. Wilmore and James H. Cone, eds, *Black Theology: A Documentary History, 1966–1979* (Maryknoll: Orbis, 1979), 418.

itself it must hear the critique coming to it from the perspective of the Black woman – perhaps the most oppressed of all the oppressed'.[56] Her cry was not unheard, as many of the leading black theologians eventually broke their silence on male oppression of women in the black community.[57]

To be more specific than that sin, in Grant's thought, is the interlocking systems of racism, classism and sexism is fairly difficult.[58] This is partially due to the fact that she thinks of human misery and fallenness in different terms, such as 'troubling' or 'servanthood'.[59] In a telling (though vague) passage, Grant writes, 'Human beings have been overcome by their own weaknesses and limitations. This old humanity/old creation is the old order that is characterized by personal, political, and social sins, all of which have become translated into socio-political hierarchies for which the primary goal is domination of the strong over the weak.'[60] These preliminary remarks are helpful at getting at the womanist challenge to contemporary doctrines of sin, but remain too general for us to follow them much further. Fortunately other womanists have taken up Grant's mantle and pressed the issue more.

Delores Williams

Delores Williams, a Presbyterian lay woman who taught for a number of years at Union Seminary in New York City, was another of the first African-American women to reflect systematically on sin. She first took a historical approach at how sin had in fact been viewed throughout the black experience in America, first by looking at slave spirituals, then in the autobiographical writings of former slaves, and finally in the still incipient black theology of liberation, particularly James Cone's theology. She came to the conclusion that the dominant theme in those concepts of sin (articulated with varying degrees of thoroughness and self-consciousness) hardly ever even *mentioned* individual sin.[61] Sin was perhaps tangentially related to 'the trouble and burdens the slaves had to bear'[62] or could refer to

56.   Ibid., 419.
57.   For one example, cf. James H. Cone, 'Black Theology and the Black Church: Where Do We Go from Here?' in *Cross Currents* 13 (1977), 147–56.
58.   For a bit more of Grant's thought on this, cf. Jacquelyn Grant, 'Womanist Theology: Black Women's Experience as a Source for Doing Theology, with Special Reference to Christology', in *Journal of the Interdenominational Theology Center* 13 (1985): 199–201.
59.   Jacquelyn Grant, 'The Sin of Servanthood: And the Deliverance of Discipleship', in Emilie Townes, ed., *A Troubling in My Soul: Womanist Perspectives on Evil and Suffering* (Maryknoll: Orbis, 1993), 199–218.
60.   Grant, 'The Sin of Servanthood', 202.
61.   Delores S. Williams, 'A Womanist Perspective on Sin', in Emilie Townes, ed., *A Troubling in My Soul: Womanist Perspectives on Evil and Suffering* (Maryknoll: Orbis, 1993), 137.
62.   Ibid., 133.

the need for a general purging of the whole world or the slave community of its afflictions in a universal way.[63] Perhaps most interesting for our project is the notion in many narratives of slaves and ex-slaves' lives, sin is clearly demarcated from the individual's actions. Consider this somewhat lengthy conclusion of Williams:

> In the spiritual songs and the autobiographies there are intimations of two kinds of moral action incorporated into the Black understanding of transgression. One can be termed 'wrongdoing', which (in some autobiographies) may refer to specific acts like stealing for which the ex-slave does not feel responsible. Rather, the responsibility is put upon the oppressor whose conduct creates the condition making stealing necessary on the part of the slave. And then there is that transgression that involves collective social evil far more serious in its consequence than acts of wrongdoing; this social evil occurs when one dominant group exerts its power in a way that brutalizes another group with less power ... The result of social sin was consignment to hell.[64]

One of the commonest forms this social sin took for black women was the denigration of their worth by sexualization. They were told that they were by nature sexually promiscuous and therefore 'less than human'.[65] That this is wrong is so clear that Williams asserts, 'In the construction of a womanist notion of sin informed by the Black community's and Black theology's belief in social sin, it is quite legitimate to identify devaluation of Black women's humanity and the "defilement" of their bodies as the social sin American patriarchy and demonarchy have committed against Black women and their children.'[66]

Not only in her more historical investigations into the record of the experiences from which Womanist theology is 'sourced' does Williams emphasize the social, structural aspects of sin, but also in her own constructive work. Williams' major work is her book *Sisters in the Wilderness*.[67] There she retells the story of Sarah, Hagar and Abraham mostly from the perspective of Hagar, Sarah's Egyptian slave and concubine for Abraham, who is cast out into the wilderness with her son Ishmael.[68] The 'white' Sarah made the 'African' Hagar her slave, and Abraham made her his surrogate – this experience is quintessentially the experience of women of African descent in America. Slave women were very often the concubines for their male masters, and lived in fear of being cast out or

63.   Ibid., 134.
64.   Ibid., 138.
65.   Ibid., 140–43.
66.   Ibid., 144. 'Demonarchy' is defined as 'the oppression that white American social institutions, directed by both white men and white women, exert on the lives of Black women'. For more, cf. Delores Williams, 'The Color of Feminism: Or Speaking the Black Woman's Tongue', in *Journal of Religious Thought* 43 (1986): 42–58.
67.   Delores Williams, *Sisters in the Wilderness: The Challenge of Womanist God-Talk* (Maryknoll: Orbis, 1993).
68.   Ibid., 15–33.

killed for 'impertinence'.[69] Black women in recent years have been alienated from many of the white leaders of the feminism movement, who tried to universalize a generic 'women's experience' that was not properly analysed according to economic and particularly racial lines. The result has been a relegation of the 'underside of the underside' (poor black women) all the way to the edges of society.[70] While interweaving the stories of American women of African descent and Hagar, Williams is also recasting the concept of sin into structural categories. She describes the interlocking nature of classism, sexism and racism. Her critiques of male black liberation theology are some of the most incisive. Williams points out how hard many black male liberationists labour to show that God is unqualifiedly a liberator. Williams thinks this preconception blinds them to the more ambiguous reality that God liberates some while leaving others to liberate themselves, as well as the wrenching fact that the liberation of one group in the Bible is almost always the enslavement or oppression of another. Williams is perhaps most clear on this point when showing how an exclusive identification of the black community with Israel being led out of Egypt to the promised land makes them forget about the subsequent slaughter and displacement of the Canaanites.[71] Thus the paradigm for Williams cannot be total liberation and fulfilment *or* the Exodus, but rather the wilderness. God met Hagar in the wilderness, and God meets black women in the wilderness into which they have been cast today, as well, where sheer survival and then 'quality of life' become the primary concerns.[72]

Like many of the theologians we have seen who advocate seeing sin as structural, Williams likewise envisions a structural redemption. She writes, 'I contend that the need for social salvation ... presents a necessary and serious challenge to all Black Christians.'[73] But this redemption is not to be sought anywhere but here and now. For Williams, as for many womanist theologians, eschatology is the enemy of social change, debilitating our drive for justice and wholeness in the present life.[74] Williams wants us to 'leave heaven and "otherworldly" pursuits to the business and judgment of God. There is only the material world in which to work out a plan of salvation for Black people and the Black community'.[75] Her vision of social salvation is informed by what she calls a 'Black common sense', which is 'the collective knowledge, wisdom and action Black people have used as they have tried

---

69.   Ibid., 62–71.
70.   Ibid., 144.
71.   Ibid., 92.
72.   Ibid., 110–19.
73.   Delores Williams, 'Straight Talk, Plain Talk: Womanist Words about Salvation in a Social Context', in Emilie Townes, ed., *Embracing the Spirit: Womanist Perspectives on Hope, Salvation and Transformation* (Maryknoll: Orbis, 1997), 98.
74.   Though there are of course many exceptions to this. Letty Russell, as well as some other indebted to Jürgen Moltmann's theology of hope, come immediately to mind. Cf. her *Human Liberation in a Feminist Perspective: A Theology* (Louisville: Westminster, 1974), 27ff.
75.   Williams, 'Straight Talk', 98.

to survive, to develop a productive quality of life and to be liberated from oppressive social, religious, political, economic and legal systems'.[76] This liberation can be achieved here and now by the good work of cooperative communities. Williams advocates a richer appreciation of the 'heroes and sheroes' of Black history,[77] emphasizes the 'can do' nature of social renewal, over against those whose defeatism frustrates genuinely possible change,[78] and a shift from what she sees to be an excessive emotionalism in Black churches toward more thoughtful and critical thinking and corporate planning.[79] This combination can serve as a 'map for a journey to salvation in the here and now'.[80] Denominational infighting as well as multi-religious concerns should be subjugated to this task. Williams empathizes with a recent African-American Presbyterian document which pushed for social renewal of Black children and communities, as opposed to trying to be 'heard by others', which Williams takes to mean 'heard by oppressive White and Black denominational structures'.[81] Indeed, Williams' views of the breadth of the church and the depth of the need for this-worldly redemption from sinful social structures combine in her view that 'along with the original distinguishing marks of apostolicity, catholicity, unity and holiness, the church needs to add another mark, namely, opposition to all forms of violence against humans, nature, the environment, and the land'.[82]

I find Williams to be a fascinating conversation partner and a very able guide through the terrain of black women's experiences. Her rich thought provides what may become a solid basis for a more developed concept of what the phenomenon in the world is which is helpfully named as 'sin'. Yet I find myself critical at several points in her writings. Primarily, I wonder what to make of the 'evil forces in society' which Williams names as the source of the oppression of black women.[83] She has been more than clear that she is unhappy with traditional use of concepts like 'demons' or 'devils', noting how quickly this can turn into a strategy of exclusion and domination (naming another as a devil frees one from having to treat her or him as a human being). Yet Williams will also say things like 'Growing up in an African-American community in the urban South in the late forties and fifties, I learned early to recognize the forces bent on conquering black women's power to resist and rise above obstacles.'[84] A force implies

76.   Ibid., 99.
77.   Ibid., 105–10.
78.   Ibid., 110–14.
79.   Ibid., 115–17.
80.   Ibid., 117.
81.   Ibid., 118.
82.   Ibid. I have been unable to find in her work an explanation of the distinction between nature, the environment and the land.
83.   Williams, *Sisters in the Wilderness*, x.
84.   Ibid. Yet here she doesn't really refer to 'forces' as such, but people, such as white men who rape black women with impunity and individual lynchings of black men. One gathers Williams means something more by 'force of evil' than 'racist and sexist person' but the relationship is not clear.

action. Can a structure act? Does an ideology act? Or does she mean that there were certain people who acted in certain ways that ended up being incredibly oppressive toward black women? If the latter is true (and I think it is, basically), we don't really have a significant step forward in understanding social sin. What we would have would be social factors for helping us to understand an individual's sin.

The second objection I raise against Williams' work is its seemingly Pelagian character. I link this with her dismissal of eschatology as a possible source of social renewal. Williams equates eschatology with pie-in-the-sky quietism. If that is what the Christian view of the last things is, then Williams knows it will not lead to what she wants, which is social renewal. But is seeking divine help really just a symptom of an unwillingness to work hard enough to fix the structures of sin here and now? Or is it the case that our sin runs so deep, our eyes have been blinded so severely that we need a better guide than our neighbours and ourselves can provide? On this last point, I find Townes to be a helpful complement to Williams. Let us now turn to her work for a brief look at one final vision of a womanist contribution to sin.

Emilie Townes

Emilie Townes tends to speak more in terms of suffering than sin. But the two are related concepts for Townes: the oppressed suffer from the sins of the oppressors. Yet unlike Williams' injunctions for the oppressed to 'get it together' to stop the cycles of oppression, Townes more often includes explicit references to a third party – God. Townes thinks that God denounces suffering and its causes. Therefore, 'A womanist ethic [of suffering] must be dedicated to eliminating suffering on the grounds that its removal is *God's redemptive purpose*'.[85] Townes asserts, without denigrating the necessity and effectiveness of liberative human action, 'God has taken suffering out of the world through the resurrection of Jesus. Because God loves humanity, God gives all peoples the opportunity to embrace the victory of the resurrection.'[86] That action of God calls for a response, which should take the form of envisioning new horizons of human structures rid of the sins which cause suffering.[87]

Townes' essay 'The Doctor Ain't Taking No Sticks' is a thought-provoking and allusive meditation on the nature of corporate sin and suffering. While it offers little in the way of theory behind the causes for human suffering,

85. Emilie Townes, 'Living in the New Jerusalem: The Rhetoric and Movement of Liberation in the House of Evil', in *Troubling in My Soul*, 84, emphasis mine.

86. Ibid., 85.

87. For more on the specifics of such envisioning from the womanist perspective, cf. Emilie Townes, *Womanist Justice, Womanist Ethics* (Atlanta: Scholars Press, 1993), 173–212.

particularly racism, the essay does represent a more pressing concern than 'explanation' for womanist theology: coping. Townes suggests that the rite of lament, notably found in its communal form in the book of Joel, can powerfully embody the kind of communal wholeness that names as sinful evil-inducing social structures. Townes is here principally concerned with the 'structures of health and health care'.[88] (Townes is primarily a theological ethicist.) She compellingly shows that the discrepancies in access to health care between blacks and whites, the differing levels of risk for contracting serious diseases, and the factors contributing to drug and alcohol abuse are systemic distortions which cannot helpfully be reduced to the sinful actions of individual agents. However, in contrast with Williams' semi-Pelagian approach to the overcoming of these sinful social structures, Townes asserts that 'we need help/ we can't do this ministry alone/ we can't witness to the world in isolation/ we can't fight off the hordes of wickedness and hatred with a big stick/ we can't do this by ourselves anymore, Lord/ we need some help./ No, we need some divine help.'[89] Townes views 'hope that is birthed from lament' as the most powerful source for the transformation of sinful social structures – more powerful, even, than our most well-intentioned actions undertaken without reference to the God who gives hope.[90]

Reformation Re-engaged

As I demonstrated in Chapter 2, Albrecht Ritschl was able to mine the rich *depositum fidei* to find some critical insights he then could use to censure the dominant mood of theology of his time.[91] He found especially fertile soil for this in the sixteenth-century Protestant Reformation. Ritschl tended not to use their particular formulations of sin, per se, though Luther's twin concepts of faith as trust and sin as mistrust did come into play. Instead, he rethought and re-emphasized Luther's notion of Christian vocation and recovered the simultaneously immanent and eschatological view of the kingdom of God. Further, in Chapter 3 I showed that John Nevin utilized the emerging sophisticated view of history in mid-nineteenth-century America to recover a sense of how thoroughly communitarian and anti-individualistic Reformed thought and practice had been, and wrote what remains the greatest extant piece of American Calvin scholarship in partial service to that end. Perhaps surprisingly, some feminists are using some of these same strategies to reform the doctrine of sin in the present day. I examine the

88.   Emilie Townes, 'The Doctor Ain't Taking No Sticks', in idem, ed., *Embracing the Spirit*, 184.

89.   Ibid., 182. Many of Townes' essays contain verse, as the one just cited.

90.   Ibid., 191.

91.   It is a wonderful irony of history that the neo-Reformation or neo-Orthodox theologians tried to do the same thing to censure Ritschl and Ritschlians, thinking that Ritschl had not already done so.

work of two such thinkers, the Reformed theologian Serene Jones and the Lutheran theologian Deanna Thompson. Both of these thinkers have cast a simultaneously critical and appreciative eye to the theology of the sixteenth century in an attempt to glean the riches of that tradition, while vocally rejecting and leaving behind its more objectionable components. This may be somewhat surprising, given that Luther and Calvin are often vilified and then dismissed in feminist theology, when they are discussed at all. Though Thompson and Jones are not by any means the only feminists who engage in a more charitable way with the work of Calvin and Luther (or who find within the ambiguous Christian theological tradition as a whole the necessary critiques and material properly to reshape Christian thought and life)[92] they do seem to me to be the ones who have seen the possibilities of Reformation theology specifically in the area of sin.

Serene Jones

In her first book, *Calvin and the Rhetoric of Piety*,[93] Serene Jones kept her feminist commitments in the background, but as her body of work continues to unfold we can see some of her later preoccupations in nascent form. One of these key insights is the close connection between form and matter in theological discourse, and the attendant power of language to shape corporate and individual understandings of the self. Though she ended up developing this interest along the lines of 'dramatic script' or 'story', Jones showed in the first book Calvin's mastery of French and Latin oratory styles and how this enabled him to 'have the ear of all of Europe' when he stood to speak.[94] In the same way that rhetoricians and theologians can benefit mutually from mutual engagement with the other's work, Jones thinks, so too can feminist theology and feminist theory learn from one another. That conversation has usually been less of a dialogue and more of a monologue, with secular feminist theory speaking and the theologians listening. But Jones is confident that classical Christian theology, freed at least partially from its sexist presumptions and articulations, can speak meaningfully to secular feminist theory.[95] While to tell that whole story would be well beyond our scope here, several of these areas of mutual enrichment have relevance for a feminist theological approach to the doctrine of sin. In fact,

92.   Elizabeth Johnson, .n *She Who Is* (New York: Crossroad, 1992) provides one clear example of this kind of approach.

93.   (Louisville: Westminster John Knox, 1995). An even more thorough analysis of this subject matter, albeit with less emphasis on the relevance of rhetoric for theology, is Olivier Millet's *Calvin et la dynamique de la parole: Etude de la rhetorique reformee* (Genève: Editions Slatkine, 1992).

94.   Jones, *Calvin and the Rhetoric of Piety*, 11.

95.   On this, especially, cf. the illuminating essay 'Companionable Wisdoms: What Insights Might Feminist Theorists Gather from Feminist Theologians?' in *Blackwell Companion to Postmodern Theology* (Oxford: Blackwell, 2001), 294–308.

as Jones asserts, '[N]o single topic in Christian theology has more resonance with feminist theory than the much disdained topic of sin. Feminist theory is based on the belief that oppression of women is profoundly *wrong*, that the world is not as it should be, and that the brokenness we experience cuts deep into our social fabric and has done so for a long time.'[96]

One example of the ways feminist theory can be enriched by theology is the eminently practical concerns of the latter. Feminist theory can be seen as too much an ivory tower preoccupation, carried on by the elite and well-educated, and by those who can afford to spend time on such intellectual matters. This can, in a way, perpetuate the very stratifications and hierarchies secular feminists are trying to undo. Jones reflects on the practical issues emerging from feminist theological reflection on ecclesiology, and groups her reflections on the church under the heading of 'bounded openness'.[97] The trick of an ecclesiology informed by feminist principles, Jones contends, is to keep a healthy balance between normativity (i.e., adhering to a certain set of standards) and criticism (i.e., continually calling into question such standards), between boundedness and openness. 'As a community of sinners, the church is required to constantly practice, with respect to its own identity, a posture of humility and self-critique.' Given this need, the church should 'applaud [the tools of postmodernism and feminism's] assistance in keeping the community aware of its confessed tendency toward self-enclosed and prideful perceptions of reality'.[98] Thus the relatively mundane tasks of hospitality and boundary drawing, of mission and self-care are embodied and carried out in a real-life egalitarian community. This, Jones thinks, is something feminist theorists should take seriously.

The main problem with the Reformation formulations of sin is, in Jones' view, not so much their content as their order of exposition. To explain what she means, Jones employs a dramatic legal metaphor. The way Luther and Calvin told the story, a proud and self-righteous man stands before a just judge, and is pronounced guilty by him. Devastated by this judgment, the man does not know what to do. He is racked with despair, shocked that the image he has had of his powerful self has turned out to be a sham. Then the judge intervenes and says to him, 'Even though you have not warranted such treatment, one has spoken for you and has offered to stand in your place of judgment. I find no sin in him, and so I find no sin in you. You are thus made just in my eyes.' This formulation, while admittedly powerful,

---

96. Jones, *Feminist Theory and Christian Theology: Cartographies of Grace* (Minneapolis: Fortress, 2000), 96.

97. This is a recurrent theme in Jones' work. The most extended discussions appear in Serene Jones, and *Feminist Theory and Christian Theology*, 153–76, 'Bounded Openness: Postmodernism, Feminism and the Church Today', in *Interpretation* 55 (2001), 49–59, and 'Graced Practices', in *Practicing Theology*, ed. Dorothy Bass, et al. (Grand Rapids: Eerdmans, 2002), 51–71.

98. Jones, 'Bounded Openness', 58.

rests upon the critical assumption that the one being judged has a very robust view of their own self, and that such a negative judgment would thus come as a complete shock. The resulting experience of justification and sanctification would then be experienced as a reconstruction of the just deconstructed self.

Jones makes the obvious but important point that this is simply not, in general, the experience that most women have. But this datum is not grounds for discarding the Reformation conceptuality. Instead, Jones suggests that we *invert* the dramatic script: the players and the plot are retained, but they are told in a sequence which makes sense of the experience of women. As was mentioned above, women suffer from not having a 'skin' to envelope their being. Institutionalized sexism buttresses the risk that the female self will diffuse into its constituent relationships. Like a cistern with cracks, the water of the self in women can too easily fall out and be lost. Thus, not unlike her Reformed forebear Karl Barth, Jones suggests that the law-gospel sequence be replaced with a gospel-law order. Rather than the just judge pronouncing judgment upon the prideful self, the loving judge pronounces a word of sanctification and justification first, quite apart from any reference to one's need to be justified from something or sanctified for something else. In this way women receive first the self-integrating benefits of divine grace that forge their identity anew, affirm them in their embodiment, and enable them to do the work for which they were created. Jones suggests maintaining Calvin's insistence that the depth of sin goes 'all the way down',[99] but that the traditional word for this extensiveness of sin, total depravity, be replaced with 'the unenveloped self'.[100] One of the ways Calvin had talked about total depravity was with the metaphor of 'despoilment'. While this word could have connotations of impurity or defilement, its more basic meaning was of disintegration – of falling apart. Luce Irigary's image of the feminine self as one which risks falling apart, an image precisely in need of being enveloped, is thus yet another way that Jones can use feminist theory in the service of feminist theological sin-talk.

Once the sanctifying lines of the drama of grace have been pronounced, the woman can hear the message of justification aright. Jones has in mind not a version of 'blaming the victim' as we saw in Chapter 2 with Schleiermacher's view of evil and sin, but rather a release from the corporately imposed prisons of gender essentialism and oppression. She does not view women as perfectly innocent victims of these oppressions, however, as she acknowledges an 'implicated resistance' to shunning such constructions.[101] She likewise warns against an 'arrogant triumphalism' which could be housed in, with and under the culpable construction of one's 'other' simplistically as oppressor.

This is ground-breaking work in several ways. Many feminists have been off-put, to say the least, regarding the constructive possibilities of more

99.   Jones, *Feminist Theory and Christian Theology*, 97–100.
100. Ibid., 120.
101. Ibid., 119.

eschatologically oriented categories like justification and sanctification. After all, has not eschatology been used as a tool of the oppressor – as a way to say, 'Persist in your sufferings, as you will be repaid in the age to come'? Yet contrary to this dominant assumption, Jones sides with Calvin, Barth and Schleiermacher, insisting that sin is seen as such only in the graced context of its opposite. This strategic move pays rich theological dividends, as it is able to be hard-headedly realistic about the gravity of sin without inflicting such harsh sin-talk on the people who need to hear it least. Instead, sin told as a retrospective flash-back in the drama of the imputation of grace becomes, in Jones' skilful rhetorical hands, a way of solidifying and enveloping the hitherto diffuse and vulnerable feminine self.

Jones' work thus represents a creative blending of the two strategies I have been explicating regarding the correction of individualism in doctrines of sin. She assumes, though she does not argue for, the fact that persons are formed in their relationships, and she notes how sin is best understood in light of these relationships. She also regards sin as a transpersonal systemic force. Her rehabilitation of a Calvinist doctrine of original sin is particularly insistent on this point.[102] But the problems which beset those strategies for overcoming individualism in general plague Jones' theology, too. She wants to assert that even women whose agency is crippled by their own and others' sins are still responsible for their actions, because they are putatively 'free'. Were freedom to be understood relationally, this would be acceptable, for the relationality said to constitute the self would then not be undone by reference to an essentialist faculty said to determine responsibility (i.e., free will). But this is not Jones' strategy.[103] What is more, Jones accords a significant place in her conception of sin for 'sinful structures', but does not elaborate on just what these structures can do. Consider the following quotation on this matter:

> [R]ecognition of the pervasive, insidious, and historically persistent forces of destruction at work in the world sits at the heart of the feminist movement. Additionally, feminists contend that women are not only victims of these destructive forces, but perpetrators as well. Feminists also assert that these forces of destruction are structural and hence larger than individual intentions or actions, and yet they still insist that individuals be held responsible for harms done and for goods left undone, for oppressive forces unleashed and then left unchallenged. In other words, when analyzing forces of women's oppression, both persons and structures must be held culpable.[104]

102. On being 'born' into original sin, Jones tells the story of her own daughter's birth. Immediately after she was delivered the baby was taken from the maternity bed, cleaned, and adorned with a 'feminine' pink hat that said, 'It's a girl!' The 'original' sins of gender construction are present at birth. Jones, *Feminist Theory and Christian Theology*, 117.
103. Jones characterizes her position as 'strategic essentialism'. Jones, *Feminist Theory and Christian Theology*, 42–8.
104. Ibid., 96–7.

While in principle I agree with Jones, I simply do not know what it means for a structure to be culpable.[105] This will, as I have repeatedly pointed out, need to be clarified if the extremely useful and insightful theology Jones has articulated will continue to be of worth in excising individualism from the doctrine of sin.

Deanna Thompson

The Lutheran theologian Deanna Thompson has done much the same for Luther's conception of the human condition as Jones has done for Calvin's. One of the most potentially powerful and beautiful areas of Luther's theology is his unrepentantly Christocentric *theologia crucis*. No other aspect of his thought is, however, potentially more dangerous for women, and other oppressed groups as well. The theology of the cross is so powerful that it is dangerous, much like the chemicals used in chemotherapy. When one is sick with cancer, treatment with such chemicals can kill a tumour; if one is not sick and comes into contact with them, they can kill the whole person.[106] Much of Thompson's work has thus been to outline carefully the ways in which Luther's thought's on sin can be helpful to women without being collaterally harmful. Most of this involves taking a careful look at the ways individual women can sin, and so is not directly relevant to the purposes of this book, but Thompson also makes some searching suggestions about Luther, women and social sin.

First, she points out that Luther was critical, perhaps above all else, of the inordinate authority he saw given to the structure of the medieval church.[107] While Luther's later stance squarely on the side of the state against the uprising of the Saxon peasants in 1525 means, for Thompson, that Luther is not unambiguously an opponent of unjust social structures, the fact that he was so fearless in his own personal prosecution of injustice can inspire and inform feminist theologians.[108] Second, Thompson argues

105. In Jones' defense she does articulate a fairly subtle notion of oppression according to both feminist theory and feminist theology, in ibid., 69–93. But while this allows her to name with some specificity what 'structures' or 'cultural forces' are to be resisted, it remains unclear in any precise way how to understand these in her Reformed theological framework of sin. For my part I do not think that they are incompatible, but it would have to be shown in what ways they connect.

106. My example, not Thompson's.

107. Deanna A. Thompson, *Crossing the Divide: Luther, Feminism, and the Cross* (Minneapolis: Fortress, 2004), 74–9.

108. I do not think Thompson is as fair as she should be in considering this profoundly contentious aspect of Reformation history. She calls Luther's position a 'nightmare', in ibid., 56. But she fails to see the point that Peter Blickle and many others have been making persuasively for years, namely that there was not in the late medieval period the kind of consciousness of alternative forms of governing that would have allowed Luther to see any other way around the issue of the peasants. Peter Blickle, *The Revolution of 1525: The German Peasants' War from a New Perspective*, trans. Thomas A. Brady, Jr and

that Luther's message of unconditioned grace is so powerful that it can in fact speak meaningfully to women today. In much the same way as Jones inverted the 'dramatic script' of the Reformers to have sanctification enter first, Thompson labours to show that the gospel need not be only conceived of as the rebuilding of the once-proud self brought to its knees by the wrath of the law.[109] When proclaimed aright, it can also be a message of hope for liberation from the structures of sin which hold people (particularly women) in bondage.[110] Yet more than this, it will also gently reveal the ways that women themselves participate in these structures. Thompson approvingly cites Sally Purvis, who writes,

> One of the most frustrating aspects of being involved in feminist groups is the extent to which ... they mimic the very oppressive structures they seek to overcome. Commitments to cooperate degenerate into attempts to dominate, the common good is lost in cliques, horizontal violence abounds as the powerless attack one another, and the most commonly shared experience can be a sense of betrayal.[111]

Thompson does not see this comment as antifeminist; instead, she thinks it drives home the point that unless individual women are completely honest with themselves about their sin (for which Luther can be painfully helpful) they will not be able to see the depths to which they are implicated in the structures from which they wish to be freed. She concludes, 'Locating sin and its accompanying *Anfechtung* within the female self will allow us to call women to account for their personal sin, as well as for their collusion with sinful structures external to the self.'[112]

Luther's theology of the cross is a kind of double-edged sword on this matter; its emphasis on grace can be heard as a word of hope in the midst of suffering, and that suffering itself is seen less to be redemptive as such, in Luther's account, than it is the sometimes inevitable consequence of real love in a violent world. But, Thompson asks, 'does a cross theology offer adequate resources to resist those structures and perpetrators of violence that inflict unbearable pain on thief victims?'[113] Thompson is more interested in prompting discussion on this question than answering it authoritatively, but she does conclude her discussion of Luther and social sin by saying,

> Luther's [view of sin] is at once a personal and a corporate story ... I propose that the first word a feminist theology of the cross will speak to the wounded,

Erik Midelfort (Baltimore: Johns Hopkins University Press, 1981). Thompson also seems to exculpate the peasants of any wrongdoing; there is no mention in her book about the horrors committed *by* the peasants before Luther wrote even a single word against them.

109. Thompson, *Crossing the Divide*, 139–41.

110. Ibid., 111.

111. Sally B. Purvis, *The Power of the Cross: Foundations for a Christian Feminist Ethic of Community* (Nashville: Abingdon, 1993), 16, quoted in Thompson, *Crossing the Divide*, 110.

112. Thompson, *Crossing the Divide*, 110.

113. Ibid.,113.

the vulnerable the oppressed, is the spirit, the gospel, the word of hope, without losing sight that each life must inevitably undergo the undoing by the letter, the law, of any and all attempts at self-sufficiency before God.[114]

The Relational Type of Social Sin in Feminist Theologies

That brings to a close our exposition of the ways feminist and womanist theologians have tried to articulate a notion of non-individualistic sin by focusing on the social structures which bear that sin and cause the experience of evil. I have voiced my appreciation for many aspects of their constructive proposals as well as raised some concerns about the adequacy and coherence of their positions in the foregoing pages. At the end of this chapter I will summarize these concerns in the form of a several broad but distilled critiques of the concept of social sin as it has been articulated. But before this we must consider the other type of strategy to combat individualistic doctrines of sin. This is the model of the relational self. I covered a large number of different authors (eight) above in the section on structures of sin; I limit myself to two models of the relational self, those of Marjorie Suchocki and Rosemary Radford Ruether. Besides affording us the opportunity to see in depth two models of selfhood which avoid individualism in sin, which is the main benefit of covering only Suchocki and Ruether, there is also far less consensus among feminist theologians who advocate this 'type'. This makes grouping theologians together much harder. Wanting to avoid hasty generalizations, therefore, only Suchocki and Ruether will be examined.[115]

114. Ibid., 115.
115. There are many, many more feminist theologians who would fit this type. Catherine Keller sees feminism's contribution to a view of human wholeness, and sin is consequently 'brokenness'. Catherine Keller, *From a Broken Web: Separation, Sexism and Self* (Boston: Beacon, 1986), 7–46 and 96–154. Carter Heyward has shown the explicit connections between feminism and her understanding of sin as social, economic and spiritual 'isolation'. Heyward, *Saving Jesus from Those Who Are Right* (Minneapolis: Fortress, 1999). She has developed this position out of her earlier works, such as *The Redemption of God: A Theology of Mutual Relation* (Washington, DC: University Press of America, 1982), wherein sin was conceived basically as 'wrong relation', though in that book the concept was woefully underdeveloped. Sallie McFague, Catherine Keller, Rita Nakashima Brock, Carol Christ and numerous others also employ relational thinking in their views of feminism, though they have not thought through relationality and sin to the extent that Ruether and Suchocki have.

Marjorie Suchocki

As a member of the 'process' school of theology and philosophy, Marjorie Suchocki cannot but see relationality at the very core of every reality, not least human personhood. Her work is, therefore, a good starting point for this investigation into the connections between relationality, personal identity and moral culpability. I propose to group salient reflections of Suchocki on relationality into three circles. The outer circle is the most general of these, and consists of a kind of generic application of Whiteheadian metaphysics to the question of the human person. The middle circle, slightly more constrained in scope, construes the relationality of the outermost circle in terms of what must be the case in human relationships such that sin can result from them. Finally, the innermost circle of her reflections on the matter outline certain forms of human relationships, the presence of which allows for full human personhood, and the absence or deformation of which constitute human sin.

In discussing Suchocki's contributions to understanding the Christian doctrine of sin in a relational framework I shall be focusing on two of her main works. *God, Christ, Church*,[116] Suchocki's first book, is an introductory text treating most of the traditional loci of systematic theology from the perspective of Whiteheadian philosophy, but with special attention paid to the doctrine of the human person and sin. Her other important book in theological anthropology, *The Fall to Violence: Original Sin in Relational Theology*,[117] is best understood in the context set by *God, Christ, Church* and the temporal self set out there.

Let us begin with the widest ring of Suchocki's relationality. At the most basic level, Suchocki says, we cannot describe who or what we are without reference to something else outside of ourselves. When asked about one's identity, for example, a common first response is often to name a place of origin which somehow contributes to who the self thinks she or he is. One might also point to an occupation, or one could name a family connection. The point is, at the most basic level, personal identity cannot be described without naming the person in relation to virtually everything outside the person, and the sum of those relationships determines, in part, who the person is.

Those familiar with process philosophy in general will recognize this as the pattern Whitehead follows in his metaphysics. The most basic metaphysical concept is for Whitehead the *actual occasion*. An actual occasion is a transient, fleeting entity, always in the process of becoming. Suchocki summarizes Whitehead on actual occasions by describing them as 'a drop of experience that comes into existence through the creative

---

116. Marjorie Hewitt Suchocki, *God, Christ, Church: A Practical Guide to Process Theology* (New York: Crossroad, 1982).

117. Marjorie Suchocki, *The Fall to Violence: Original Sin in Relational Theology* (New York: Continuum, 1994).

process of concrescence. They are the building blocks that, through an essential interconnectedness, make up the composite world of rocks, trees, and people.'[118] The process of becoming weaves together what Whitehead calls 'prehensions', which are something like feelings, or states of being related to, but often lack the conscious awareness that one actual occasion is prehending another. These elements 'feel' each other, relate to each other spatially, causally, interactively, and so on. Each interaction between actual occasions is an event, and from that event a new actual occasion occurs. In Whitehead's memorable phrase, 'The many become one, and are increased by one. In their natures, entities are disjunctively "many" in process of passage into conjunctive unity.'[119] Thence novelty arises, complexity increases, and 'concrescence' occurs. Concrescence is the name given to this activity of becoming. It is the integration of various prehensions into an actual entity or actual occasion.[120] The process of the concrescence of prehensions into actual occasions continues indefinitely until such time as a 'satisfaction' takes place. Satisfaction is said to occur when a subject's prehensions are integrated into a concrete unity.

In Whitehead's philosophy, which he called a 'philosophy of organism',[121] all of this is happening primarily at an incredibly small scale. Whitehead was, among other things, an expert in the emerging quantum theory, and many of his philosophical insights were derived from his observations of reality at the sub-atomic level. For Suchocki's anthropology, however, this all takes place at the macro-level. When a person is born, she can be described as an 'actual occasion' who immediately has prehensions of the world around her. As those prehensions are synthesized in the process of concrescence, a new 'actual occasion' emerges, though it is named by those in the outside world as the selfsame actual occasion all along. As more and more prehensions become synthesized in the person, subjectivity emerges from the relational world. In contrast to idealist philosophers like Kant, for whom the already extant subject (especially her mind) 'produces' the world around her, Whitehead and Suchocki conceive of the world as 'producing' the subject by means of these processes.

This, then, is the broadest circle of relationality germane to Suchocki's anthropology. The second circle, included and implied in the first but slightly more specific and constrained in scope, is the relationship of the self to time. The self, says Suchocki, is related intimately to her past, future and present, and it is from a complex of these relations that sin is said to emerge. Suchocki writes, 'The past, which was originally an objective reality into

118. Suchocki, *God, Christ, Church*, 257.
119. Alfred North Whitehead, *Process and Reality*, ed. David Ray Griffin and Donald W. Sherburne (New York: Free Press, 1978), 21.
120. The difference between an actual occasion and an actual entity is only that God is an actual entity, and never an actual occasion, because God is non-temporal in God's primordial nature, whereas actual occasions are by definition temporal.
121. Whitehead, *Process and Reality*, 151, and passim.

which one was thrown without one's consent, enters into one's subjective reality. When that past works against positive relationships that enrich the person, then that past is demonic.'[122] The chances for the existence of nourishing interpersonal relationships are diminished by the facticity of their obscuration in the past. Obviously, this amounts to a version of original sin. While the past does not determine the future in Suchocki's anthropology, it does constrain what will be possible in the immediate future. 'There is always a wedge of novelty [in the process model] that entails a degree of freedom and responsibility. The degree may be great or small, and the very reason for naming [the powers of the past] is because they leave but small room for freedom. But they cannot annihilate it completely.'[123]

Another key aspect of one's relationship to the past comes in the form of the social institutions and structures which condition one's selfhood. In an extended analysis of Walter Rauschenbusch and Reinhold Niebuhr on the nature of unjust institutions, Suchocki points out that 'individuals raised within such societies internalize the unjust norms, thus supporting them and ensuring their perpetuation. Since it is the individual *self*-consciousness that is so formed, it becomes constitutive of the self, and difficult to transcend ... Original sin simply creates sinners.'[124] The past builds a wall around us, separating us from life-giving relationships with God and others. 'Sin imprisons one in a particular form of the past. By choosing to become a bearer of the demonic, one allows that past to become the determiner of one's reality.'[125]

The temporally relational self is also intimately linked to the future. 'There is also the imprisoning power of sin that comes, not from being overly bound by the past, but through fear of the future as death.'[126] Borrowing a bit from existentialist philosophy, Suchocki notes that the fact of one's own impending death prompts a feeling of anxiety. 'Knowledge [of one's death] brings the death of the future in to the present, annihilating the beauty of the present with the fear of that which is not yet.'[127] The death of others to whom we are related breaks in upon us as well, since those relationships are internal to who we are, and so we cannot fully 'survive' their deaths.

The innermost ring, more focused still than Whiteheadian relationality and general temporality, are the three relations that constitute human personal identity, and the distortion of which constitutes human sin. These three relations are *memory*, *empathy* and *imagination*. There is a kind of correlation between these three and temporality (memory with the past, empathy with the present, and imagination with the future), but each

---

122. Suchocki, *God, Christ, Church*, 17.
123. Ibid.
124. Suchocki, *The Fall to Violence*, 126, italics hers.
125. Suchocki, *God, Christ, Church*, 18.
126. Ibid., 20.
127. Ibid., 21.

relation is more than just temporal. Suchocki thinks that the self can be described as existing in three phases. There is a 'receptive phase' wherein the realities preceding the self converge, an 'integrative phase' wherein the emerging subject creatively unifies those convergences, and a 'projective phase' wherein the properly integrated subject joins the rest of the universe in the creation of ever more novel realities.[128] The self experiences the receptive phase in her memory. Past realities are called to mind. She thinks about the way things were, how she used to be, what she used to do.[129] But this is not enough, for rarely will old ways of being and acting perfectly map onto how the self should make sense of the present time. This requires empathy. By empathy she means not merely an emotion, but is rather the name Suchocki gives to the social character of the self. Empathy is the self's awareness of its surroundings and of the others in it. When the self acts in the world, it anticipates the consequences of its action by taking into account the reality of the other-than-self.[130] Finally, in imagination one transcends the present by envisioning a future not yet real, and by that vision one can participate in the transformation of the present.[131]

When these fundamental relations are obscured, sin results. The failure of memory causes the sin of the perpetuation of injustice. Selves (and groups, for that matter) who do not 'remember well' do not grasp that the violence done in the past produced only pain and suffering. The self sometimes seems to stop at nothing to justify the perpetuation of such ways of being, however, by continually distorting memories and configuring them into a narrative of the legitimization of violence.[132] Empathy is prone to two distortions. When empathy is minimized, the self is absolutized, which is named by the sin of pride. When empathy is maximized, the other to which the self relates is absolutized, which is the sin of hiding or self-abnegation. Finally, a distorted imagination is sinful to the extent that it cannot envision a future which is different from the present, and cannot provide the self with an aim towards which she might exercise her freedom. All three of these relations, memory, empathy and imagination are forms of self-transcendence. Their distortion, sin, is violence. Suchocki calls sin not rebellion against God, but rather violence against all creation, or the perpetuation of ill-being.[133] God is of course affected by sin (in a process world, everything affects everything), but that is seen as a derivative of the primary manifestation of sin in distorted relationships.

Suchocki considers herself quite self-consciously to be a feminist theologian. Many other women have been more vocal and forthright than Suchocki about the ways feminist methodologies and emphases inform their

---

128. Suchocki, *The Fall to Violence*, 55.
129. Ibid., 36–8.
130. Ibid., 39–40.
131. Ibid., 40–42.
132. There are some affinities between Suchocki and Rene Girard on this point.
133. Suchocki, *The Fall to Violence*, 13, 18–19.

theological arguments. But Suchocki thinks she is uniquely placed to discuss feminist theological anthropologies because of the close connection between feminism and process thought. Besides this family resemblance between the two approaches, Suchocki writes, a synthesis of the two approaches can be particularly helpful in expounding the doctrine of sin. Suchocki uses the image of weaving to show how threads from each methodology can be woven together into a unified fabric.[134] Some of the relevant features of feminist theology Suchocki singles out are critiques of 'patriarchal assumptions of pre-established graded orders of being, and the concomitant notion that each grade of being is inferior to all orders above it', as well as the rejection of anthropological dualisms like 'male/female, mind/body and intellect/emotions'.[135] Most importantly, each methodology can serve the critical function of exposing the totalizing effects of traditional theological systems. 'A feminist-process theology, speaking from the rootedness in interrelationship which permeates all of our existence, threatens to put cracks in our cherished certainties concerning the absoluteness of our belief systems.'[136] That can be an uncomfortable experience, but is surely a necessary one, as well.

Suchocki also has specific ideas on how feminist and process thought relate to sin. She presents a cursory history of feminist thoughts on sin, trying to show a major shortcoming which process metaphysics can shore up, and points out a weakness of process thought strengthened by feminist thought. Suchocki traces the characteristic feminist emphasis that pride is predominantly the sin of males through many of the texts (Saiving, Dunfee, Plaskow, Hampson, etc.) cited at the beginning of this chapter. This insight quickly developed into the virtual identification of sin with patriarchy itself, such as in the early works of Mary Daly and others.[137] In Suchocki's view, this shift was a necessary one to account for the reality of the oppression of women, but had the unfortunate side-effect that 'the myth of female innocence as opposed to male evil tugged at the edges of feminist theology'.[138] Two options became available to circumvent this problem. The first was Rosemary Ruether's expansion of the concept of sin to include both the individualistic categories of male and female as well as the always already sinful social systems in which those individuals are located. Suchocki cites approvingly Ruether's insight that 'sin is the misuse of

---

134. This is especially present in her essay 'Weaving the World', *Process Studies* 14 (1985): 76–86.

135. Ibid., 78.

136. Ibid., 85.

137. Suchocki, 'Sin in Feminist and Process Thought', in Terence Fretheim, et al., eds, *God, Evil and Suffering: Essays in Honor of Paul Sponheim* (St Paul: Luther Seminary, 2000), 144. The books by the authors to which she refers are Mary Daly, *The Church and the Second Sex* (Boston: Beacon, 1967), Rosemary Radford Ruether, *Liberation Theology* (New York: Paulist, 1972), and idem, ed., *Religion and Sexism: Images of Woman in the Jewish and Christian Traditions* (New York: Simon and Schuster, 1974).

138. Suchocki, 'Sin in Feminist and Process Thought', 147.

freedom to exploit other humans and the earth and thus to violate the basic relations that sustain life. Life is sustained by biotic relationality, in which the whole attains a plenitude through mutual limits in interdependency.'[139] The second way forward stems, in Suchocki's view, from the work of such feminists as Judith Plaskow[140] and Susan Nelson, who, following Saiving, have noted that there might be particular ways of sinning that are linked to gender constructions and social roles. Far from being overly prideful, women may be tempted to the sin of refusing selfhood, or of having no self-worth at all. If the cure for sin as pride is self-sacrificial love, applying that medicine to the sin of self-less-ness only exacerbates the condition. In a similar vein Nelson's view of sin, reminiscent of Eve's Eden experience, is that of 'hiding'.[141] Salvation would accordingly not consist in denying the prideful self, but in finding it at all. Suchocki summarizes by claiming that 'Plaskow and Nelson followed Saiving by disavowing both myths [the myths that males or females were evil], and Ruether took us the furthest by relating the social effects of evil to original sin.'[142]

Yet Suchocki sees a shortcoming in all of this. 'While feminist thought presupposes the systemic sin of patriarchal sexism, the major treatises on sin deal with the individual.'[143] As should be evident from the foregoing, process thought can, in reverse fashion, sometimes lose sight of the individual by focusing so much on the context into which she is placed. 'To blend process and feminist thought, then, creates the possibility of correcting the underdeveloped notion of individual sin within process thought, and of increasing the understanding of the power of systemic sins in feminist thought.'[144] The result is a powerful restatement of Suchocki's position, outlined above, that sin is 'the violation of well-being ... It is the lessening of the good of the community, and therefore also the lessening of the good of the individual, for the individual is always and inevitably in community. All sin is therefore both individual and social.'[145] When the individual is placed in society, she is not responsible for what she receives from that matrix, but 'one is responsible for what one does with what one has received'.[146]

While I find Suchocki generally convincing on the theoretical consonance between feminism and process thought, her characterization of feminism seems dated at best. It is true that the feminists responding to Reinhold Niebuhr's work on sin largely capitulated to his individualistic categories. However, it seems myopic of Suchocki to focus solely on these thinkers

139. Ruether, *Gaia and God* (San Francisco: Harper, 1992), 141.
140. Judith Plaskow, *Sex, Sin and Grace: Women's Experience and the Theologies of Reinhold Niebuhr and Paul Tillich* (Lanham: University Press of America, 1980).
141. Susan Nelson Dunfee, 'The Sin of Hiding', *Soundings* 65 (1982): 316–27.
142. Suchocki, 'Sin in Feminist and Process Thought', 147.
143. Ibid., 150. Rosemary Ruether is actually cited as a notable exception.
144. Ibid.
145. Ibid., 151.
146. Ibid.

as representatives of the whole movement. Contemporary women writing on the topic of sin are anything but individualistic. Feminism has become global, ecological and political. Those are all social categories. Another process feminist coeval with Suchocki, Catherine Keller, regards feminism as irreducibly social, and uses communal psychological concepts to elucidate her theology of sin as brokenness.[147] Suchocki's caricature of feminism does not mortally wound her argument for sin as violation of well-being, but it does represent a serious shortcoming in her stated goal of applying Whiteheadian metaphysics to the service of women's experience.

It should be clear from the foregoing that at the very least, Suchocki's version of the self has great value in construing selfhood in non-superficially relational ways. Yet I believe she has gone too far. By making the self contingent on a certain arrangement of certain relationships, Suchocki risks inability to account for the presence of a self at all. I think this is not limited to Suchocki's theology, but is true of process metaphysics generally. This shortcoming of Suchocki's anthropology plays out in the problem of the status of the relational self as a moral agent. If, as Suchocki posits, the self is always 'coming to be' or always 'in process', at what point in the self's development has sufficient growth taken place such that one could say the self was now responsible for her actions, be they moral or immoral? Put another way, Suchocki's anthropology seems to have a *teleological* structure. Everything that is comes to be from the processes of concrescence and satisfaction, including the self, which means that the self only exists at the end of those processes. If that is the case, it seems that William Christian's criticism of Whitehead's metaphysics similarly applies to Suchocki's anthropology. In a particularly concise passage, Christian writes,

> If the structure of an actual occasion is teleological, and the realization of its aim is wholly extrinsic to the occasion, then we have a case of there always being jam tomorrow, never jam today. For suppose the satisfaction aimed at in the process A is realized *only* in the entities which succeed A, for example, B. Then the satisfaction of A will be a factor in the process of B. But this latter process aims at the satisfaction of B, which would in turn be realized only in C. Thus it would be true not only that the satisfaction of A is not realized in A, but also that there would be no finite entity in which the satisfaction of A is completely realized. It would follow that there is always becoming, but nothing becomes; there is creativity, but nothing is created; there are relations, but no genuine terms; there is causation, but no cause and no effect.[148]

147. Catherine Keller, *From a Broken Web*, 7–46 and 96–154.

148. William A. Christian, *An Interpretation of Whitehead's Metaphysics* (New Haven: Yale University Press, 1959), 22, italics his. I should note, however, that while he raises this as a potential objection to the logic of concrescence, he concludes that it does not make the theory internally inconsistent. Cf. ibid., 42–7. I believe that the objection does significantly vitiate process-based anthropologies, though perhaps not process metaphysics in general.

Suchocki has a response to this sort of critique, but unfortunately in developing it she has to unsay what she helpfully said about the relational basis of selfhood, for she emphasizes the necessity of the *faculty* of freedom when discussing moral culpability. Suchocki is forced into an argument for the presence of freedom in the moral agent without being able to offer an account of its origins or features. In discussing the power of the past to affect human choice in the present, I quoted above Suchocki's claim that 'The power is greater than the individual, since it comes with the weight of a past that cannot be avoided. But in the process model there is always a wedge of novelty that entails a degree of freedom and responsibility. The degree may be great or small, but [the past] cannot annihilate it completely.'[149] But where does this freedom come from? The simple fact that it is 'entailed' by the logic of process metaphysics does not testify to its actuality. In a chapter on 'Guilt and Freedom' in *The Fall to Violence*, it is as though Suchocki has to take back much of what she says about the relational self in the rest of the book, for she knows that it wars against personal responsibility. She says that it is only 'given this freedom [that] there is an established basis for responsibility for one's actions'.[150] But she surely has a peculiar version of this content. In what is usually the stock example of determinists, Suchocki compares the self to a rock.

> Even a rock is composed of electrons and atoms and molecules that in themselves have a response-ability relative to their past and to their environs. The rock changes, yielding to erosion and radioactive decay. The rock does not have freedom in a human sense, but in its very constitution, it has a response-ability that represents a miniscule indeterminism on a chain that includes, at its other end, what we call human freedom.[151]

But by 'freedom' most people mean something more than 'plasticity'. For a human to be free is not to be theoretically manipulable by others. On the contrary, that seems to be the very definition of *bondage*. But I will not adjudicate that argument, since for our purposes here it suffices to point out that the logic of Suchocki's relational self eventuates in a situation in which individual responsibility is safeguarded by an appeal to a faculty anthropology. Such an appeal is a step backward in understanding the postmodern self.

Rosemary Radford Ruether

The thought of Rosemary Radford Ruether is slightly harder to classify than is Suchocki's work, but it certainly does belong in the relational type of rejection of individualism. It would be more accurate to say that

149. Suchocki, *God, Christ, Church*, 17.
150. Suchocki, *The Fall to Violence*, 134.
151. Ibid., 132.

Ruether's embrace of relationality is more a way of rejecting *dualism* than individualism. A compelling interpretation of Ruether's whole theological corpus can take the shape of a thorough uprooting of dualisms like male/female, nature/culture, good/evil and self/other. Yet I say that her work is hard to classify both because of its volume and because she deals substantially with the issue of structures. However, unlike most of the other writers considered in this chapter, Ruether sees more overlap between the relational self type and the structural sin type of social sin. For Ruether, 'sinful social structures' name most basically patterns of relation that are distorted and *make* people sinful. As Ruether puts it, 'What is appropriately called *sin* belongs to that sphere of human freedom where we have the possibility of enhancing life or stifling it. When this freedom is misused, patterns and organizational systems of relationships are generated where competitive hatred builds up.'[152] There is thus a complex interplay between distorted relationality, human freedom, and the social patterns and structures governing human relations. In this last section of feminist theologies of social sin I intend to sort out these complex interactions. I begin with a discussion of Ruether's rejection of dualism, proceed to an analysis of her threefold theory of sin as distorted relation, and end with a summary look at how she conceives of the relational self.

Dualisms

Christian theology has been gifted and cursed by the contributions of the ancient Greek philosophers. The ambiguous inheritance of powerful theology stemming from Plato and Aristotle takes a wrong turn when it joins too comfortably together the Greek dualisms of body and mind, spirit and matter, with putatively Christian notions of good and evil. This has the effect of absolutizing into one or the other a relative good or relative evil which ought to stay relative. Males were identified with the mind, females with the body. Males were culture, females nature. Men were spirit, women were matter. Little wonder, then, when in classic Christian theology, males were identified with the good, female with evil.[153] In the hands of St Augustine this led to an insistence that the original *imago dei* was truly present only in the male, and in the female it was derivative and obscured if present at all. As Ruether notes, 'Augustine sees female subordination, reflecting the subordination of the body to its ruling mind, as the original "order of creation."'[154] This leads Ruether to a rejection of what was,

---

152. Ruether, 'Feminist Metanoia and Soul-Making: The Journey of Conversion in Feminist Perspective', in *Introducing Redemption in Christian Feminism* (Sheffield: Sheffield Academic Press, 1998), 71.

153. Ruether, 'Dualism and the Nature of Evil in Feminist Theology', in *Studies in Christian Ethics* 5 (1992), 26–7.

154. Ibid., 29.

for Augustine, the logical conclusion to the dualism: Adam succumbed to Eve's temptation and the fall from a paradisiacal state of creation to an ambiguous state of fallen humanity resulted.[155] The remnant of good in this state was male, the cause of evil and the postlapsarian form it took were female. Thus, Ruether writes, 'I reject the Augustinian concept of "original sin" as a fallen state, caused by the sin of an original pair of human ancestors that caused the loss of original immortality, right relation with God, and freedom of the will to obey God.'[156] Thus rooting out dualisms is perhaps most important in the area of anthropology, since, as Ruether argues, 'The good potential of human nature ... is to be sought primarily in conversion to relationality. This means a *metanoia*, or "change in mind," in which the dialectics of human existence are converted from opposites into mutual interdependence.'[157]

Ruether's Alternative Vision of Sin

Thus Ruether is committed to conceiving both original and actual sin in different ways. The way she does this is to see sin as a threefold violation of right relation. In Augustine's thought and in that of most of his heirs, actual sin was essentially one-dimensional. Actual sin was the act which God did not want done. The effect of sin was thus separation or alienation from God. While Ruether allows (and in fact, later mandates) this religious dimension of sin, she does not start there.

> My understanding of what sin is does not begin with the concept of alienation from God, a concept that strikes me as either meaningless or highly misleading to people today. I think we need to start with our alienation from one another. We can then go on to understand how alienation from one another expresses itself in personal relations and social relations of negation of others, as well as self-negation, that are sick-making and violent.[158]

Ruether maps this set of negations into a threefold scheme. She writes, 'Sin as distorted relationship has three dimensions: there is a personal-interpersonal dimension, a social-historical dimension, and an ideological-cultural dimension.'[159] What we have here is a notion of the self in relation which is constructed in such a way that the terms of the relationship, which are genuinely present, are not arranged so that 'full humanity is promoted'.[160] Let us look briefly at the features Ruether locates in each of these dimensions.

155. Ruether, *Women and Redemption*, 72–4.
156. Ruether, 'Women and Sin: Response to Mary Lowe', *Dialog: A Journal of Theology* 39 (2000), 233.
157. Ruether, *Sexism and God Talk*, 163.
158. Ruether, 'Feminist Metanoia', 70.
159. Ibid., 71.
160. This is a common locution of Ruether's, which often functions criterially, as in her 'Critical Principle of Feminist Theology', in *Sexism and God-Talk*, 18–20.

First, there is subject-subject distortion. Ruether writes, 'On the interpersonal level, sin is the distortion of relationship, by which some persons absolutize their rights to life and potency at the expense of others with whom they are interdependent.'[161] This is a question of power. The proper use of power is *power with*, as opposed to *power over*. Humans exist in relationships. This is a fact. Power is by nature a relational concept – Force X exerts power Y over object Z – it cannot be different than this. But the kind of power which we exercise *can* vary. I can choose to care for my sick friend, who can then choose to thank me for my efforts by cooking me a meal, to which I can freely add a bottle of wine. These acts are genuinely exerted; one has to have power in order to perform them. Yet this is *power with*. In our interpersonal dealings, when they are not sinful, these centres of power interlock and cooperate to form systems of support and care, friendship and love. Sin, then, is the obverse of this. Sin is the distortion of power.

One of the ways that this has been construed in the dominant Christian theological tradition is to see the root sin as pride. As I have said above, we will not be dealing with the specific kinds of sin said to be typical of men or of women (since this tends to perpetuate dualistic essentialism). Yet Ruether does think that there is something to this tradition, despite the feminist objections to its formulation. What if we were to understand 'pride', Ruether asks, not in terms of egoistic self-aggrandizement, but in terms of the sinful cover-up of 'deep-seated dis-ease' with oneself?[162] In that case, both the sins of patriarchy and the sins of women are highlighted. Once one term in a relation has power, one is unwilling to give it up. The one with the power will stop at nothing to keep the one without power weak. The one who does not have power begins to be so closely identified with her powerlessness that she cannot, indeed – does not want to – become anything else. She is too ill-at-ease inhabiting any role other than the one she is comfortable with (since she has been sinfully socialized into it), that she will not resist the sin of domination, and thus complies or acquiesces in it. Both of these are forms of idolatrous pride. The powerful one falls in love with a phoney picture of himself as powerful, and the powerless one falls in love with the image of herself as powerless. This is far, far too simplistic to account for the complex distortions of relations among women and men, but Ruether does think that sin has at least one root in the insecurity which prompts the sinful cover-up of pride and victimization.

The second dimension of sin is social-historical. These sinfully distorted interpersonal relations are not created anew *ex nihilo* every time two persons come into contact. 'Rather, these ... patterns are themselves kept in place and re-enforced by the larger historical, social structures in which the [persons] are embedded as a dependent part. We are born into this system of patriarchal relations. We are socialized to accept our roles within

161. Ruether, 'Feminist Metanoia', 71.
162. Ibid., 72.

it.'[163] Sin names primarily the distortions that result from these structures or arrangements of relationships which condition our choosing, and so in a secondary kind of way, Ruether hints that the structures are sinful too. But not exactly. Ruether wants to keep sin fairly firmly seated in the human will. For example, she thinks, 'The capacity to sin is seen as based on the distinctively human characteristic of freedom ... Human beings, then, stand in the existential dialectic between the "is" and the "ought."'[164] Humans are free to act either in ways that promote living interdependency, or they can freely choose to cut themselves and others off from life-giving relationships. Each time one of these two alternatives happens, a vestige of the free choice is implanted in the patterns of relation people follow. The fact that we sense a difference between the 'is' and the 'ought' is itself good news, and testifies to our orientation to goodness. Ruether notes that 'Consciousness of evil, in fact, originates in the process of conversion itself. To locate and identify certain realities as "evil" means to already have taken the fundamental existential turn of disaffiliating oneself from them.'[165] This does not imply any kind of determinism, for Ruether, either on the side of fatalistic depravity or Pollyannaish Pelagianism; instead, she thinks this kind of active willing for or against proper relationality is built into the human condition: 'I view human capacities as ambivalent rather than depraved or in an irreparable condition of alienation. I prefer the traditional Jewish concept of the "two tendencies," the tendency to good and the tendency to evil, and believe that we retain the capacity to choose between them.'[166] This very structure is part of the goodness of our creation. And Ruether goes further to say, 'I also see the good tendency as that which connects us to our authentic existence, our true "nature," our "*imago dei*."'[167] So the 'sinfulness' of social and historical patterns of distorted relationship is connected to the freedom of the moral agent in choosing for herself which kind of relationality she will embrace. To put it in terms that Paul used, 'Powers and principalities exist as the precondition of evil choices. But these powers and principalities are precisely the heritage of systemic social evil, which conditions our personal choices before we choose and prevents us from fully understanding our own choices and actions.'[168]

The redemption of the sinner actually involves the embrace of right relationality, and the vindication of this misdirected freedom. Ruether elsewhere writes, 'Redeemed humanity, reconnected to the *imago dei*, means not only recovering aspects of our full psychic potential that have been repressed by gender stereotypes ... We need to recover our capacity for

163. Ibid., 73-4.
164. Ruether, *Sexism and God Talk*, 160.
165. Ruether, *Sexism and God-Talk*, 159.
166. Ruether, 'Feminist Metanoia', 69.
167. Ibid., 69–70.
168. Ruether, *Sexism and God-Talk*, 181-2.

relationality, for hearing, receiving, and being with others, but in a way that is no longer a tool of manipulation or self-abnegation.'[169]

It is tempting either to minimize or maximize the effects this social-historical dimension can have. Individualistic doctrines of sin either ignore it or relegate it to some version or another of 'original sin'. Or it can be maximized in the case of fatalism, where the self is such a product of its environment that when the environment is 'sinful' there is no responsibility when the self does sin. Ruether tries to stay squarely in the middle of these two extremes. She writes,

> To sort out our appropriate responsibility we have to recognize both the difference and the interconnection between individual and social evil. Sin always has a personal as well as a systemic side. But it is never just 'individual'; there is no evil that is not relational. Sin exists precisely in the distortion of relationality, including relation to oneself. Although there are sins that are committed primarily as personal self-violation or violation of another individual – abuse of one's body by intoxicants, rape, assault, or murder of another – even these very personal acts take place in a systemic, historical, and social context.[170]

There is a third dimension of sin, beyond its primary manifestation in sinful intersubjective relationships and the buttressing thereof by sinful social and historical patterns. This final aspect of sin is its ideological-cultural justification. 'Exploitative social systems are also maintained and reproduced through ideologies that make themselves the hegemonic culture. It is the purpose of this hegemonic culture to make such unjust relationships appear good natural, inevitable, and even divinely mandated.'[171] This is one of the most nefarious aspects of sin, in Ruether's view. It becomes so incredibly hard for the self to resist patterns of sin and distortion of relation because the self is on the one hand conditioned not to be able to do so, and is further conditioned not even to *want* to do so even if it were in her power to resist. And yet, inexplicably, resistance and positive transformation happens all the time. That it happens at all should come as a surprise, however, because the groups which are in power, and which thus are in a position to shape patterns of relation, often also control the cultural systems of ideology. They then set up ideologies valorizing the behaviours of the powerless which will allow the powerful to keep power. They insist on the maleness of God, on the virtue of feminine submissiveness, on the redemptive worth of suffering as such, and so on. Yet this system does not have the final word, thinks Ruether, for it is based on a lie. The lie is that we do not exist in relation to each other. The lie is that sin is individual only. To overcome it, we need to grow in our sense of connectedness and love.

We must now ask what kind of self this presupposes. We saw above that the notion of the self did not figure prominently in the doctrines of sin of women embracing the structural sin type of rejection of individualism

169. Ibid., 113.
170. Ibid., 181.
171. Ruether, 'Feminist Metanoia', 73–4.

(though this does not mean that their notions of selfhood are not relational). And in Suchocki the self was so relational as to nearly lack any kind of organizing centre. What about relationality in Ruether? How is it 'redemptive'? Relationality simply *as such* is not redemptive, though it is sometimes seen to be in feminist theology. The master–slave, abuser–abused relations are not magically less 'relational' than lover–beloved, or equal–equal. Those relationships vary in kind, not degree. Let us now look more specifically at what Ruether means by the relational self.

Whose Relationality? Which Self?

As far as I know, Ruether has not written an extended work on the human subject, but the theme is present enough in many of her writings that some useful conclusions can be drawn. It appears that Ruether wants to avoid two kinds of extremes in her conception of the self. The first is the subject that I have been cataloguing criticisms of for dozens of pages now. This is the individual self, whose character and whose sin are understandable apart from the relationships into which it enters. The other extreme is the form of relationality of which we saw hints in Suchocki's anthropology. This is the postmodern self which is such a product of its relations that there would appear to be no basis to resist the structures in which selfhood was formed. I will consider Ruether's objections to each in turn, and conclude with a note on her preferred model of 'individuation'.

Ruether seems to make two points about relationality and selfhood. The first is that the self simply is, indisputably, relational. This is a fact. The second point is that we need to alter our thinking and our theological formulations to align them with this reality. Consequently, this means that theological notions of selfhood which derive from desires to see the self as radically independent and self-contained must be rejected. Ruether writes about this need in several places. The theme comes into its most prominent relief when she is discussing the relationship of humans to the non-human environment. This has been denigrated by the individualistic self, which loses sight of the intense connection we have, as animals and creatures, with our natural environment. Ruether calls this constellation of commitments 'ecofeminism', since (as I noted above) the problem of dualism manifests itself in denigrating both nature and women, and so resistance to sexist realities must be thought into environmental concerns. Ruether writes that ecofeminists like her 'share a critique of western epistemology based on the isolated knower … Most of them are questioning a model of the self based on the isolated individual disconnected from relationships that ignores the actual support services that other humans and nature are providing to allow for this privileged appearance of the "autonomous self."'[172] Ruether also thinks that the autonomous view of the self necessarily objectifies the other

172. Rosemary Radford Ruether, *Integrating Globalization, Ecofeminism, and World Religions* (Lanham: Rowan and Littlefield), 123.

selves whom it encounters. That is, the modern self does not allow for the intersubjectivity that is necessary for a properly related and individuated self to emerge. 'It is characteristic of the male ideology of transcendent dualism that it cannot enter into reciprocity with the "other." Its view of what is over and against itself is not that of the conversation of two subjects, but of the conquest of an alien object.'[173] Or again, in still another ecofeminist work, 'Males need to overcome the illusion of autonomous individualism, with its extension of egocentric power over others, starting with the women with whom they relate.'[174]

On the other hand, Ruether strenuously objects to the radical de-centring of the subject in much postmodernism.[175] Ruether rejects the radically socialized, perhaps *over-related* self of typically postmodern sensibilities. If human selfhood were entirely constituted by and exhausted in their socialized relationships, then Ruether worries that there would be no centre of action that could rise up against the systems of oppression that socialize selves sinfully.

> I agree that we need to go beyond an androcentric reduction of the human qualities traditionally associated with the male and notions of femininity associated with leisure-class females. But the postmodern insistence on infinite particularity, its view that all definitions of self and group identity are 'mere' social construction can easily lead, not to a more inclusive justice for poor women of color and non-Western culture, but, rather, new ways of justifying women's subjugation in societies which are not postmodern but still premodern.[176]

In the contexts said to be postmodern, further, Ruether says, 'I am skeptical about the postmodernist attack on an existence of a "pre-linguistic self." This seems to me absurdly anthropocentric, ignoring our own roots as animals in a pre-linguistic world. Nor do I see myself as operating with an Enlightenment view of an individual, autonomous self.'[177]

Ruether on Individuation

How is it that relationality should then be conceived? Too little relationship breeds sin by the domination of the autonomous self. Too much enfeebles resistance to sinful systems. I follow the helpful suggestions of Mary Elise

---

173. Rosemary Radford Ruether, *New Woman, New Earth: Sexist Ideologies and Human Liberation* (New York: Seabury, 1983), 195.

174. Ruether, *Gaia and God*, 266.

175. Rosemary Radford Ruether, 'Gender Equity and Christianity: Premodern Roots, Modern and Postmodern Perspectives', in *Faith and Praxis in a Postmodern Age*, ed. Ursula King (London: Cassell, 1998), 70.

176. Ibid.

177. Rosemary Radford Ruether, 'Dialogue in *dialog*: Women and Sin', in *Dialog: A Journal of Theology* 39 (2000): 235.

Lowe that Ruether articulates a self which is 'individuated', as opposed to individual.[178] To be individuated as a self means that one is cognizant of both one's separation from and connection to what is other-than-self. As Ruether puts is, 'We need to think of men and women as both relational *and* individuated ... Feminist anthropology must reject both the patriarchal family ... and liberal individualism, where all are assumed to be autonomous but isolated from relationships.'[179] Ruether identifies three sources for thinking about the kind of relationality that is useful for conceiving of the individuated self: feminist theory generally, nature and God. First, like Suchocki, Ruether thinks that there may just be something about the perspective women tend to take that lends them well to perceiving the reality of relationships. 'Feminist Theology bases itself on just relationality. On this basis it seeks relations between men and women, between some women and other women, between men and women of different classes and races, and between humans and nonhumans.'[180] This perspective is a gift feminist theologians can offer to the world. Men and women can be saved from the myth of their supposed independence. Second, Ruether draws on biological metaphors to discuss appropriate types and amounts of relationality in selfhood. 'Life is sustained by a biotic relationality in which the whole attains well-being through mutually affirming interdependency.'[181] Just as the health of an ecosystem depends on the proper functioning and health of all of its parts, so must the self integrate whole and part. Ruether elsewhere writes, 'Good and evil, and hence ethics, are rooted in relationality itself, life-sustaining and renewing relationality versus a distorted relationality that destroys both sides of the relationship.'[182] And finally, Ruether finds appropriate relationality in her picture of God. In Ruether's view, God is 'the living matrix of matter/energy itself, from which this process [of the universe] continually arises and returns and which also holds the whole together in mutually interacting relationality.'[183] While I would welcome more explicitly Trinitarian formulations of this kind of constitutive relationality, the point Ruether is making is on target. The doctrine of the *imago dei* requires that if God is essentially relational, so are we.[184]

---

178. Mary Elise Lowe, 'The Human Subject and Sin: Autonomy, Relationality, or Constitution?' (PhD diss., Graduate Theological Union, 2004), 119–31.

179. Rosemary Radford Ruether, 'Christian Understandings of the Human Person', in Ann Carr and Mary Stewart Van Leeuwen, eds, *Religion, Feminism and the Family* (Louisville: Westminster John Knox Press, 1996), 108.

180. Rosemary Radford Ruether, 'Feminist Hermeneutics', in *Radical Pluralism and Truth: David Tracy and the Hermeneutics of Religion*, Werner Jeanrond and Jennifer Rilke, eds (New York: Crossroad, 1991), 103.

181. Ruether, 'Feminist Metanoia', 71.

182. Ruether, *Gaia and God*, 256.

183. Ruether, 'Dualism', 35.

184. For an insightful programmatic essay on the connection between the *imago dei*, relationality, and sin, cf. LeRon Shults, *Reforming Theological Anthropology: After the Philosophical Turn to Relationality* (Grand Rapids: Eerdmans, 2003), 217–42.

The understanding of human selves as individuated is best summed up in the following quotation from Ruether's ecofeminist writings.

> An ecofeminist understanding of the human person ... starts with the person in a network of relationships. The person does not exist first and then assumes relationships, but the person is constituted in and by relationships. One does not seek to extricate oneself from relationships in order to become more 'autonomous' ... Rather, one seeks to become ever more deeply aware of the interconnections on which one's own life depends, ultimately the network of relations of the whole cosmos.[185]

Thus it is the case both that the self realizes its intense connections with the other-than-self, but that there is still an honest-to-goodness self present to do this knowing. This is an individuated, as opposed to an individual, self. Ruether describes this development of individuation from two perspectives. One aspect involves the definition of 'boundaries of the self over the non-self'.[186] This slow coming to awareness of our embodiedness, our historicity, our relation to the world around us – this makes the self 'individuated'. One might also describe consciousness as 'the gradual differentiation between subject and object, rooted in the distinction between the internal awareness of oneself thinking and feeling and that which the sense, particularly that of sight, locates as external objects'.[187] Being individuated thus means a growing sense of self-consciousness that highlights appropriately the continuities and discontinuities with other selves and with one's natural environs.

Conclusion and Assessment

In this chapter I have given a broad introduction to the basic types of options available for discussing sin in terms that are not strictly individualistic in several different feminist and womanist theologies. The two main types of sin helpfully organize what can be an overwhelming amount of diversity, breadth and depth of proposals into evaluable groups. As I showed above, the first wave of feminist theology was primarily preoccupied with exposing the androcentrism of traditional doctrines of sin. Saiving, Plaskow, Nelson-Dunfee, Hampson and others laboured to show how facilely male theologians had taken the sins that were typical of men, like pride or self-assertion, and universalized them into notions of sin that were held to obtain for all people. After this initial mode of critique, many feminists realized that a deeper problem was actually beneath this surface one: the male dominance of theology had too much valorized the independence and solitariness of human existence, which led to an excessive individualization

185. Ruether, *Integrating Globalization*, 112–13.
186. Ruether, 'Dualism', 30–31.
187. Ibid., 31.

of sin. I showed how such feminist theologians as Elisabeth Schüssler Fiorenza, Mary Potter Engel, Serene Jones and Deanna Thompson and womanist theologians Jacquelyn Grant, Delores Williams and Emilie Townes reacted to this emphasis on the individual by asserting or reasserting that sin must name phenomena which are fundamentally *structural*, and therefore transpersonal, or at least not individualistic. I then showed that the other available option was pursued by such feminist theologians as Marjorie Suchocki and Rosemary Ruether. Ruether's relational view of sin was found to be particularly helpful, because it blended effectively elements from each of the two kinds of ways around individualism.

Despite the manifold and searching accomplishments of the feminist critiques of sin, we have been confronted with several shortcomings in the alternative models examined in this chapter. Let us begin with the examples of the structural sin type of rejection of individualism. Engel asserts that wickedness comprises evil and sin, and that sin is to be emphasized when speaking to abusers and evil to the abused. As I pointed out in the last chapter, this approach tends to rigidify people into one category or the other. What begins as a helpful therapeutic and pastoral strategy quickly becomes an inappropriately static theological concept. This also overstates the distinction between evil and sin. Evil is not merely experienced and sin committed. As I showed in Chapter 2, Ritschl pointed out sharply in his critique that Schleiermacher (who basically used sin and evil in this way) was too individualistic. Thus Engel does not go far enough in showing the corporate nature of *both* sin and evil.

Schüssler Fiorenza's thought also has unfortunate limits. While she is ready to name any structure which perpetuates *kyriarchy* as unjust or wrong, the bounds of New Testament exegesis prevent her from making the much stronger statement that those structures are *sinful*. That is, their endurance is simply against God, and their downfall will be the work of God.[188] What is also unclear in Schüssler Fiorenza's writing is the agential status of the structure. It is at least counter-intuitive, and may be simply false, that a structure or system could act. A more careful way to describe what is meant as a sinful social structure, then, would be to describe it as a series of constraints on or stimuli for certain kinds of human action. If this is what Schüssler Fiorenza means when she decries the *kyriarchal* turn taken by Christianity after the Jesus movement, her rhetoric of 'active structures' frustrates her aims. This is not a mortal flaw of her notion of *kyriarchy*; it simply prompts serious clarification and specification as to what is meant by such a structure.

Grant, Williams and Townes display significant divergences for putatively being in the same (womanist) 'school of thought'. As I pointed out, Grant seems to be in the uncomfortable position of trying to draw on two very

---

188. The compatibility of divine and human action will, I predict, become a preoccupation of feminist theology in the future. This emphasis could go far to reconnect the activist social tendency in feminism with a rich conception of God's grace.

different traditions. She wants to continue to use the ideas of 'troubling', 'suffering', 'servanthood' or 'tragedy' to get at what traditional Christian theology denotes in categories like evil and sin. This restricts her to vague assertions about racism, classism, sexism, and so on as social sins, yet leaves her without any clear vocabulary to describe what this means. Are they *sins* because they are against God? Are they *social* because more than a few people are racist? Williams commits some of these same errors. Her insistence on the need for the black community to resist the structures she calls sinful is so strong that it almost makes God irrelevant. There is no account for what it is in people that makes such resistance possible at all, and not sinful when actual. This leads to a kind of Pelagianizing tendency that eclipses God's role both as the one sinned against and as the one powerful enough to redeem so grave a sin as the structural distortion Williams condemns.

Grant, Williams and Townes, like many of the women theologians considered in this chapter, tend to embrace a kind of common-sense criterion for what counts as 'sinful'. It is as though we all know what racism, sexism, classism, and so forth basically *are*, and could stop them if we wanted to, but we just do not see the need to stop them. I highly doubt that this is the case. Williams and Townes spend many pages describing the horrors of gang-raped black women, lynched black men and institutionalized racial violence across America. To the extent that their work is profile raising and is part of the process of conscientization, I applaud their efforts and wish them well. But these ideologies are often so subtly manifested that their description in such broad strokes is not terribly helpful. I attribute this lack of subtlety in the womanists' proposals to the relative inattention paid to the self which is (or anyway can be) racist, classist, sexist, and so forth. What is it about human nature that makes us prone to do such awful, and such faintly wicked, acts? What would the transformation of such a wicked self look like? Is *metanoia* really possible for a structure? May a system be forgiven? Since it has been one of the theses of this book that sin is best known in its overcoming, questions such as these will have to occupy the fore of womanist theology if even more contributions towards a non-individualistic notion of sin can come from these quarters.

I shall make three brief criticisms of the other approach assessed in this chapter, the relational self. The first objection I have, to which Suchocki seems particularly susceptible, is the absence of culpability. When the self is conceived so thoroughly in relational terms, it becomes harder and harder to see how the relational self is a responsible moral agent. Victims of childhood abuse internalize their abuse as it forms their sense of identity or their sense of self. Those sinful relations contribute to making the self who it really it is (even as that self is not as it 'should' be), and it is logical that future actions of this self will stem from its own self-understanding. Thus it is, in a way, understandable when a childhood sexual abuse victim becomes a sexual abuser of children. Yet the Christian doctrine of sin simply must (if anywhere, here!) say that this is simply wrong. Child sexual abuse is against

God, is against God's creature, and is unequivocally sin. Thus Suchocki and other postmodernists know that the radical de-centring of subjectivity, of the correlative emphasis on relationality, makes them susceptible to charges of exculpation. Again, this is not necessarily a mortal flaw in their reasoning, it simply prompts the open question of how to admit properly of relationality while not sacrificing responsibility.

The form which this takes in Suchocki, and to a lesser extent, in Ruether, I find to be slightly objectionable. This is my second criticism of their projects. The point of moving to relationality in theological anthropology is, in part, to move away from conceptions of the human person which distance them from nature, from others, from themselves, and from God, in relation to which all people are in fact constituted. This involves an appropriate rejection of the former methods of theological anthropology which sought to locate and identify the single characteristic (or group of characteristics) said to make one truly *human*, truly *oneself*. These were usually characteristics like reason, consciousness, the soul, the intellect, free will and so on. It appears as though this tendency to rely on a certain 'faculty' to maintain a sense of human nature is still present in views of the relational self. At *the* critical point in Suchocki's argument concerning moral responsibility for sin, she seems simply to pull freedom out of a hat in order to secure individual culpability. Ruether uses the concept of 'two tendencies' to good and to evil, which we are said to exercise freely, but does not really give an account of what these tendencies are, what their 'free' use (as opposed simply to their abuse) would consist in. This is the problem in Protestant theology which is called the bondage of the will. Ruether has gone a long way in explaining the social-historical dimensions of sin which can, as a Protestant might put it, enslave our will. Yet Ruether insists that we remain free to resist these structures. The question I would pose to her is just what capacity it is that accounts for such resistance. If it is freedom, I confess that I do not know precisely in what freedom consists in her thought, and I do not know how it could be formulated in a non-essentialist way that would not take back much of the relationality Ruether labours so admirably to procure.

This leads to my third and final objection. It is similar to the criticism above made of Williams, Grant and Townes. The criterion against which relationships are measured and found to be 'sinful' in views of the relational self remains, in my view, exceedingly vague. Ruether is fond of giving stark examples which highlight the genuine differences between life-giving and death-dealing relations. 'The difference between starving a child or torturing a prisoner and nurturing their lives is real, and reflects decisions made by actual people.'[189] Yet in my experience, the line between godly relationality and its sinful distortion is painfully, maddeningly more blurry. I hope that future works on the relational self and sin can account more clearly for what would count as positive relationship and what not. More

189. Ruether, *Gaia and God*, 256.

extensive engagement with these themes will follow in the conclusion, but for now let us bracket our concerns about and our appreciation for the commitment to social sin manifest in feminist and womanist theologies and look at a third context for thinking about individualism and sin. This is the exciting context of Christian theology in Asia, particularly as it takes shape in the Korean *Minjung* theology.

Chapter 6

INDIVIDUAL AND SOCIAL SIN IN SELECTED ASIAN THEOLOGIES

'Asia' as a Category?

Even the briefest, most cursory examination of topics headed under the category of 'Asian theology' prompts serious reservations about the effectiveness, or even the applicability, of that geographic designator. Covering a third of the world's land mass and comprising about three-fifths of its people, 'Asia' is both a place and a concept so large as to risk vacuity. This chapter proceeds with only the heaviest reservations that the term 'Asian' still has explanatory power. I will continue to use this designation, but let me first offer some qualms about the propriety of its sustained usage. Asia stretches from the Ural Mountains in the northwest, through Muslim former Soviet Republics to the Indian subcontinent, and from Sri Lanka through the Southeast Asian peninsula up through China, Japan and Korea. Traversing this course one would meet thousands of different ethnic or cultural groups, hear hundreds of languages and encounter dozens of religions and myriad forms of each religion. Little wonder, then, that some scholars doubt that anything is helpfully named as 'the Asian perspective' on any topic.[1] After all, what could a conservative Filipino Catholic theologian demonstrably have in common with a syncretistic Confucian-Christian theologian in China? Would a Siberian Russian Orthodox churchgoer group herself in any significantly 'Asian' way with her fellow minority-group Christians in Indonesia?

Still, the designator 'Asian' may yet be useful and appropriate. Many theologians and lay people continue to self-identify in one form or another as Asian, and certainly enough Westerners use it descriptively to refer not just to a geographical area and its residents, but also to a constellation of values. Asian theologians have, on the whole, dealt with issues like acculturation, globalization, religious pluralism and principles of contextualization with perhaps more sensitivity and precision than their European and North

---

1.   This is perhaps one of the leading edges in Asian Christian theology today. A burgeoning literature exists and will continue to develop. Cf., for example, Namsoon Kang, 'Who/What is Asian? A Postcolonial Theological Reading of Orientalism and Neo-Orientalism' in Catherine Keller, et al., eds, *Postcolonial Theologies: Divinity and Empire* (St Louis: Chalice Press, 2004). Kang is extremely critical of most current descriptive uses of the term 'Asian'.

American counterparts. This is virtually a necessity given their context. 'Asian' as a descriptor has more use outside Asia than it does within, where the cultural and theological differences are more proximate, and therefore more noticeable. Many theologians from underdeveloped countries like those in Asia struggle to be taken seriously by the rest of the world, and to have their positions regarded as 'orthodox'. Since this is the case, theologians from these regions often have banded together, the better to present a united front for the purpose of furthering their important agenda. This is the reason for the existence of such groups as EATWOT (Ecumenical Association of Third World Theologians) and the Federation of Asian Bishops' Conference (of Roman Catholic bishops). Since these names are self-applied and serve a positive purpose, it is appropriate for Western theologians to use the concept of Asia, so long as one is properly chastised about the levelling of difference and potential for hegemony in attempting an Asian theological discourse.[2]

Scope

While I think the conclusions I draw from my analyses in this chapter will have some modest worth for making sense of 'Asian' Christian theologies, my scope here will be much narrower. I will be focusing on what seems to me to be the branch of Asian theology that has thought the most carefully about social and individual sin. This is the *Minjung* theology that took root in Korea in the 1960s and 1970s, flourished for a time, and has since basically run its course and petered out. Naming reasons for this theology's demise is in itself an interesting project, and is also relevant for our concerns in this book, since we want to know what kinds of formulations of social sin will work and which will not. Even more pressing is the need to identify the usable and insightful theological contributions that the *Minjung* theologians made which can be recovered.

Of course, many theologians writing from other places in Asia have fascinating points to make about sin. For example, Aloysius Pieris, a Sri Lankan born Jesuit theologian, has done much to develop what he considers to be a distinctly 'Asian' view of human sin and its overcoming.[3] He was one of the first Asians to point out that the poverty of Asia (and particularly of Sri Lanka and India) was not only, or even primarily, an issue of economics, but was instead a product of interlocking systems of socio-political and

2.   This is an approach structurally similar to Gayatri Spivak's 'strategic essentialism,' in *A Critique of Post-Colonial Reason: Toward a History of the Vanishing Present* (Cambridge: Cambridge University Press, 1999), which was borrowed by Serene Jones to describe her pragmatic view of feminist theory and theology, on which, see Chapter 5 above. For many of the insights contained in the above reflection on 'Asia,' I am grateful for many conversations with Kei Kato, Abraham Laurence Kadaliyil and Joseph Dayam Prabhakar.

3.   Aloysius Pieris, *An Asian Theology of Liberation* (Maryknoll: Orbis, 1988).

religious phenomena. Tissa Balasuriya, OMI, another Catholic theologian
from Sri Lanka, links a corporate understanding of sin with a corporate
view of redemption, symbolized in a re-interpretation of the church and
its sacraments.[4] T. C. Chao (Zhao Zichen) in China would also have to be
included on a list of important re-interpreters of Christian theology in Asia,
aside from the Koreans who will be examined here.[5] I have not, however, on
the whole found the kind of extended mediation on the particular *concept*
of sin that I have found in the *Minjung* theologians' writings. This does not
mean that sin does not have a function in these other theological works,
nor that they do not invest 'sin' with characteristically Asian content. It
only means that this chapter will be a sampling of selected major themes in
Asian doctrines of sin, and among those primarily ones with a rich notion
of 'social sin', and will not be a survey of all such doctrines.

Finally, I have had to make the painful decision not to include a full
discussion of Christian theology on the Indian sub-continent. This is not
because it is not interesting or intellectually rigorous. It is certainly both of
those. For example, Raimundo Panikkar[6] and Madathilparampil Thomas[7]

---

4.   Tissa Balasuriya, *Human Liberation and the Eucharist* (Maryknoll: Orbis, 1977),
Planetary Theology (Maryknoll: Orbis, 1984), and the insightful essays on sin and evil,
'World Apartheid: Our Greatest Structural Evil,' in Mary Hembrow Snyder, ed., *Spiritual
Questions for the Twenty-First Century: Essays in Honor of Joan D. Chitester* (Maryknoll:
Orbis, 2001) and 'Women and Men: Insights from Struggles for Human Liberation,' in
Mid-Stream 21 (1982): 311–23. Balasuriya was excommunicated from the Catholic
church for some of these views, but he was later reinstated. Since his reinstatement he has
been significantly more muted in his pursuit of these theological themes, which is quite
unfortunate.

5.   Tzu-Chen Chao was an early figure (1888–1979) in Christian theology in China
(by which I mean obviously not that he was one of the first Christians in China, but that
was one of the first to think through explicitly and in detail what a Chinese Christian
theology would be, as opposed to how to adapt Western theologies to the Chinese context.
Educated in China and at Vanderbilt University, Chao was one of the first directly to relate
both his new and traditional Christian thought (Protestant) to the emerging social needs
of China first before, and then during, the Communist Revolution. He was also a president
of the World Council of Churches in the late 1940s. Cf. especially the fascinating *Christian
Philosophy* (Shanghai: CCLP, 1926) and *My Prison Experience* (Shanghai: CCLP, 1948)
and on Chao, Winfried Glüer, *Christliche Theologie in China: T.C. Chao, 1918–1959*
(Gütersloh: Mohn, 1979).

6.   Panikkar's most important and up-to-date work relevant to an understanding of
sin and the human person is *Christophany: The Fullness of Man* (Maryknoll: Orbis, 2004),
and specifically with reference to a pluralistic understanding of moral culpability, cf. his
Invisible Harmony: Essays on Contemplation and Responsibility (Minneapolis: Fortress,
1995), and especially the provocative essay 'Sunyata and Pleroma: Buddhist and Christian
Response to the Human Predicament', in *The Intrareligious Dialogue* (New York: Paulist,
1999).

7.   Many of Thomas' works are elliptically anthropological in nature, operating
under an assumed Marxist analysis of human possibility tempered with a typically Indian
sensibility regarding the cycles of human misery. Representative works include *Human
Person, Society and State*, ed. M. M. Thomas and P. D. Devandandan (Bangalore:
Committee on Literature for Social Concerns, 1957), and *Salvation and Humanisation*

in India have written widely on all sorts of topics at least somewhat related to sin, and there exists a burgeoning secondary literature on their work.[8] But their work is well known, and thus would not benefit much from treatment here, and opening the door to Indian texts would require a look at the now substantial literature on Dalit Christianity. The Dalits are the 'untouchables' of Indian culture, and have obviously experienced exactly the kind of massive oppression and suffering which would be relevant to an interpretation of 'social sin'. What is more, it is in the Dalit circles that Christianity is most rapidly growing in India, and Dalit Christians are the majority of Christians in India. Thus the number of theological views espoused on any topic, particularly sin, is simply massive. That reality, coupled with the fact that most of these texts are extant only in their original languages, has made treatment in this brief chapter impossible.

The Origins of Minjung *Theology*

There is not a consensus as to the appropriateness of transferring the name 'liberation theology' out of its original context in Latin America and applying it to other theologies.[9] While I do not have anything at stake in taking a side in this debate, it is enough to say for now that African-American, Asian, Feminist and Womanist, and other theologies concerned primarily with the poor and socially oppressed share enough family resemblances to be considered together. *Minjung* theology is the name of the most developed and intellectually sophisticated movement in Christian theology coming from Northeast Asia, and inasmuch as it concerns itself with the social and economic liberation of the *Minjung*, it is a kind of a theology of liberation. The word *Minjung* is a combination of two shorter Korean words: *min* means something like 'the people' and *jung* means something like 'the masses'. It does not mean the Korean nation as a whole (this is *Minjok*), nor does it mean 'the Proletariat' (this is *InMin*).[10] It refers

(Madras: CLS, 1971). His views on sin are coincidentally quite consonant with early Latin American liberation theologians', though Thomas himself was very forthcoming about his elite status in his own culture.

8.   The most up-to-date work on Panikkar is Anthoniraj Thumma, *Breaking Barriers: Liberation of Dialogue and Dialogue of Liberation – The Quest of R. Panikkar and Beyond* (Dehli: ISPCK, 2000), and on Thomas, Thannikapurathoot Jacob Thomas, *Ethics of a World Community: Contributions of Dr. M.M. Thomas Based on Indian Reality* (Calcutta: Punthi Pustak, 1993).

9.   For one discussion of this, cf. Christopher Rowland, 'Introduction: The Theology of Liberation', in idem, ed., *The Cambridge Companion to Liberation Theology* (Cambridge: Cambridge University Press, 1999), 1–16.

10.   Chang-Nack Kim notes how important it was for the oppressed of Korea to be able to name themselves as *Minjung*, since 'Calling the majority of Koreans by the name given to them by the ruler is binding them in the relationship of ruling and being ruled.' 'Korean Minjung Theology: An Overview', in *Chicago Theological Seminary Register* 85 (1995): 2.

instead to the great mass of people who have been historically oppressed in Korea (and the lands which predate the formation of 'Korea'). They have not been, as the later proponents of *Minjung* theology put it, the 'subjects of history'.[11] Instead, they have been merely the objects of manipulation by the powerful in their society. The *Minjung* are the nameless, faceless masses held under the thumb of one oppressive regime after another. In the late 1960s and early 1970s Korean Christian theologians began to recognize in the proclamation of Jesus a particular concern for the *Minjung*, and they determined to lay out some principles regarding how theology might address the 'objectification' and oppression of the Korean *Minjung*. The view of these first *Minjung* theologians was that the suffering of the people at the hands of and due to the policies of the South Korean dictator Park Chung Hee was simply becoming unbearable.[12] The *Minjung* movement in response to this oppression was broader than just theology. The early period of post-colonialism in Korea witnessed a rise in literature and art that was basically nationalistic, but this began to be replaced by poetry, literature and art centred on the themes of marginality, suffering and resistance to power.

We should be careful not to correlate too closely the *Minjung* movement with its structural analogues in Marxist movements. As one of the earlier exponents of *Minjung* theology notes, '[One] difference between the *Minjung* and the proletariat is [its] different view of history. Minjung history has a strong transcendental or transcending dimension – a beyond-history – that is often expressed in religious form. There is a close relation between religion and the Minjung perception of history.'[13] Unlike leaders of many of the coeval revolutions then underway, the theologians of Minjung thought religion could be helpfully employed in the service of genuine cultural change. To that end, in 1971 a group of Catholic and Protestant religious leaders formed a coalition called 'The Christian Social Action Council'. They drafted a document outlining their understanding of the Minjung and the theology implied by it, and made a statement of purpose based on four principles.

1. All the churches and clergy and intellectuals must stand up for the oppressed Minjung and fight for social justice.

---

11.   Such as, for example Andrew Sung Park, 'Theology of Han (The Abyss of Pain)', in *Quarterly Review* 9 (1989): 49ff, and especially Commission on Theological Concerns of the Christian Conference of Asia, *Minjung Theology: People as the Subjects of History* (Maryknoll: Orbis, 1983).

12.   For an interesting and relatively balanced look at this controversial ruler, cf. Sung Chul Yang, *Korea and Two Regimes: Kim Il Sung and Park Chung Hee* (Cambridge: Schenkman, 1981). He is both hated by many Koreans for his human rights violations, and respected by some for his role in growing the South Korean economy.

13.   Kim Yong-bock, *Messiah and Minjung: Christ's Solidarity with the People for New Life* (Hong Kong: Christian Conference of Asia, 1992), 184.

2. All corporate powers must stop exploiting the *Minjung* and must operate under the principle of equal distribution.
3. The mass media must not submit to financial or political power, but should stand on the side of the *Minjung* and to their duty of reporting fairly and accurately.
4. The three million Christians must be on the side of oppressed and powerless *Minjung* and resolutely struggle for social justice.[14]

We should note two things about this declaration. The oppression in Korea was becoming so severe that Catholics and Protestants were able to come together with no problems in order to try to stop the bloodshed, and this was to be done in very concrete and practical ways.[15] The idea that the churches should unite their powers (such that they be) to further a unanimously held social agenda was so obvious as not to require articulation.[16] Second, while the statement was written by Christians and directed in some measure toward Christians[17] there is nothing particularly Christian about its content. This would be true of much of the official promulgations of church bodies and many of the early theologians of the *Minjung* movement.[18] One might infer from this fact there was not really any serious theology going on among these people. After all, social structures are usually named publicly by those within the early years of the *Minjung* movement as 'unjust', not as specifically 'sinful', little mention is made of the Kingdom of God, and the particularity of Jesus Christ does not factor significantly into their public teachings.[19] But that inference would be completely wrong. As a

14.   Quoted in Chang-Nack Kim, 'Minjung Theology', 5. Kim has discussed these labour issues more fully in his essay 'Arbeitskämpfe in der Dritten Welt, am Beispiel der Arbeiterbewegung in Südkorea' in Luise and Willy Schottrof, eds, *Mitarbeiter der Schöpfung: das Bibel und Arbeitswelt* (München: Kaiser Verlag, 1983), 301–23.
15.   And there was massive bloodshed. The most famous example of the violence of the time is the case of Chun Tae Il. He worked fifteen hours a day for twenty-eight days a month in a sewing shop in virtual darkness. Despite these hours, he could not earn enough to survive. One day when he could take no more he covered himself in gasoline and set himself on fire, dying during a labour protest. He held a sign in his hands insisting on the genuine humanity of the *Minjung*.
16.   This stands in stark, and perhaps sad, contrast to the experience of many Western church groups where either the unanimity supporting particular cultural change is not present, or there is dissent regarding the propriety of the church(es) acting as an agent of such change.
17.   Although it is relevant to note that the immediate predecessor to Park Chung Hee was a man named Syngman Rhee, who was actually a Christian and who tended to appoint Christians to the kinds of positions relevant to policies addressed by the decrees. Park removed almost all of those people immediately after taking power.
18.   One notable exception would be the 'Theological Declaration of Korean Christians' of May 1973.
19.   Suh Nam-Dong had reservations about the propriety of the Kingdom of God concept, however. 'While the kingdom of God is used in the ideology of the ruler, the millennium is the symbol of the aspiration of the *Minjung*.' 'Historical References for a Theology of *Minjung*', *Minjung Theology*, 177. His position is not necessarily the norm.

matter of fact, lying in the background of much of this social activism and the denunciation of structures of oppression is a very nuanced and careful interpretation of the New Testament. While there are several figures I could have selected to analyse more closely, I have chosen to focus on perhaps *Minjung* theology's greatest exponent, and certainly its greatest biblical exegete, Ahn Byung-Mu.[20]

Ahn Byung-Mu and the Exegesis of ὁ ὄχλος

Ahn Byung-Mu was a New Testament scholar of the first rate. He grew up in Pyongnam in what is now North Korea before moving to Japan to study philosophy in college.[21] During World War II he was sent to Manchuria and later returned to Korea to teach English. Ahn had had a conversion experience some time before this, but was unable fully to explore his faith in the oppressive post-war conditions.[22] He finally made what would be a life-changing move by deciding to go to Germany to study the New Testament. He studied with some of the greatest scholars of the world, coming particularly under the influence of Rudolf Bultmann and Ernst Käsemann. He wrote a doctoral dissertation under the supervision of Günther Bornkamm on the possibility of an existential interpretation of the concept of love and the historical Jesus (which was provocative, given Bultmann's insistence on the existential appropriation of the kerygmatic Christ alone). This was a difficult time for Ahn, because while he was so appreciative of the importance of the European hermeneutical tradition and their biblical scholarship, Ahn found that he could not make this fit with his experiences in Korea. So he began to try to read the New Testament afresh with the concrete situation of the *Minjung* in mind, and was particularly concerned with how the notion of sin could be rethought in service to the *Minjung*.

20.   Suh Nam-Dong would have been the other most likely candidate for exemplar status, but he does not use the concept of sin much in his writings. Cf. his *In Search of Minjung Theology* (Seoul: Hang-Il Sa, 1984).

21.   A full intellectual biography is available: Andreas Hoffmann Richter, *Ahn Byung-Mu als Minjung Theologe* (Gütersloh: Mohn, 1990). A shorter sketch can be found in idem, 'Biographische Hinweise und Erläuterung zu den Texten, in Ahn Byung-Mu, *Draussen vor dem Tor: Kirche und Minjung in Korea*, ed. Winfried Glüer (Göttingen: Vandenhoeck and Ruprect, 1986), 151–6.

22.   The story is compellingly told by Richter and warrants quoting. 'Der christlichen Kirche war er bereits frühzeitig begegnet. Er sah als Kind, bevor er eingeschult wurde, ein Kreuz in einem Dorf und bekam von einem anderen Kind die Erklärung, "Da ist jemand für uns gestorben." Als er während seines fünften Schuljahres auf einem Gebäude wieder das Kreuz sah, wurde ihm das Vergessene neu bewusst: "Da ist wieder jemand für andere gestorben." Dabei dachte er, jemand aus seiner Umwelt sei gekreuzigt worden. Diese shockierte ihn so, dass er sich entschloss, zur Kirche zu gehen.' 'Biographische Hinweise', 152.

Ahn's breakthrough discovery came in his study of the Gospel of Mark, and centres on his interpretation of the term ὁ ὄχλος (ho ochlos). The word is usually translated into English as 'the people' or 'the crowd' or 'the ones gathered'. This word appears over forty times in the Gospel of Mark. Traditional scholarship more or less ignored this curious fact, though it is of clear importance. The word does not exist in the New Testament in any of the writings earlier than Mark (for example, in the letters of Paul). When scholars did discuss ὄχλος[23] it was seen primarily as simply the bystanders who happened to be present when Jesus was saying or doing something, and it was that saying and doing that was held to be the really important part of the passage. Form critics and, to a lesser extent, redaction critics tended to draw parallels to the 'chorus' that was often in the background in an ancient play. They said their lines dutifully stayed out of the way, and let the important players have the centre of the stage. Ahn began to wonder about this interpretation. Might there not be something more going on here? There were many other words that could refer to 'people' in the New Testament. For example, the masses of people who are not Israelites are often designated 'εθνοι' (ethnoi). And when the other gospel writers want to talk about the people of God, or the people of Jesus, the most common word would have been 'λαος' (laos). If the connotation was these people were 'the unruly masses' there is a perfectly good New Testament word for this, too: 'ὁι πολλοί' (hoi polloi).[24] Yet Mark very self-consciously, in Ahn's opinion, chose ochlos. Why could this be? And for the present purpose the question must be asked, what does all of this (admittedly interesting) New Testament literature have to do with social and individual sin?

Ahn thought something much more important was going on in the interactions between Jesus and the ochlos than simply those of the lead player and the chorus in a drama. In fact, Ahn would go so far as to say that the content of Jesus' preaching and actions could not be understood apart from the context of those words and actions in the presence of the ochlos.

The Features of ὁ ὄχλος

Ahn wrote extensively on the ochlos in Mark and in the New Testament as a whole, but a summary of his basic position is possible. First, the ochlos was not omnipresent in Jesus' ministry, but it is present at nearly every major public event in Jesus' life, especially during his ministry in the cities and countryside of Galilee (cf. Mk 2:4, 2:13, 3:9, 3:20, 3:32, 4:1, 5:21, 5:24, 5:31, 8:1, 10:1). It is not clear whether the same people followed Jesus from place to place. This seems unlikely – he probably went to the places in each new town he travelled to and sought out the ochlos. Socially, in the second

23. Hereafter for convenience transliterated into English.

24. For an extended discussion of these terms and their implications, see Ahn Byung-Mu, 'Nation, Volk, Minjung und Kirche', in *Draussen vor dem Tor*, 79–84.

place, the ochlos were considered to be on the fringes of the dominant social group. They were the outcasts. In Mark's terms, they were tax collectors and 'sinners'.[25] Jesus is criticized for spending time with the ochlos, since they are not worthy of the company of an otherwise 'righteous' person (Mark 2:13–17). The contrast with *polloi* is here quite evident. When the crowd surrounding Jesus is being chastised for unrighteousness by one of the gospel writers, the term used for the crowd is almost always *hoi polloi*. Mark's decision to use a more neutral word like ochlos for these people thus represents a conscious decision to show that the characters in the story who are denigrating the crowd are in the wrong to do so. Mark upholds the basic righteousness of the ochlos, implying that if there are sinners in the midst of Jesus, the sinners are not to be identified too easily with the ochlos. I have devoted a whole section to the relationship between the ochlos, sin and the *Minjung* below.

The third feature in Ahn's writings about the ochlos is its differentiation from the disciples. One might be tempted to say that Jesus had a closer relationship with his named followers than with the unnamed masses. Ahn himself notes that there a few times where Jesus teaches only the disciples, with the ochlos not present (e.g. Mk. 4:36, 6:46, 7:17, 7:33).[26] However, this fact should be tempered by the correlative one that Jesus constantly criticizes his disciples in Mark's gospel, but there is not even one instance of him criticizing the ochlos. Jesus seems ambiguously *for* the disciples, and unequivocally *for* the ochlos. Further, Ahn notes that Matthew and Luke depict Jesus either steadfastly praising or vehemently berating the disciples. Whether Jesus' reaction to the disciples is positive or negative often correlates to the disciples' treatment of the ochlos.[27] In Mark 3, where Jesus is giving an extended sermon in the countryside of Galilee, he refers specifically to the ochlos gathered about him, and refers to them as his brothers and sisters. This would have been a fairly shocking thing to say, for it implied a negation of the authenticity of Jesus' ties with his own (blood) family. Luke and Matthew are unable to cope with this radicality. Matthew, in a parallel passage just before the sermon on the mount, replaces the indirect object of Jesus' remark with μαθέται (disciples), and Luke excises it all together. Thus theological readings which try to find an exegetical basis for an ecclesiology would be better off doing so by reference to the ochlos, not by Petrine or Pauline apostolicity, and persons considering the justness of social structures should note the unequivocal support Jesus gives the ochlos, over and against the rather more muted praise of the disciples.

Fourth, the ochlos were primarily the outsiders of Galilee, but this should not be understood only in contrast to the insiders of Galilee, but

---

25.   That there must be a distinction between these two will become apparent below, in the section on *dan* and *han-puri*.

26.   Ahn Byung-Mu, 'Jesus and the Minjung', in *Minjung Theology*, 141.

27.   Although, of course, Matthew and Luke use the word less often than Mark does. They use it nine and eleven times, respectively.

also in contrast to the hierarchy in Jerusalem. The ochlos understood themselves to be in opposition to Jerusalem, and tried to align themselves with Jesus, whom they saw as sharing their viewpoint (cf. Mk. 2:4–6, 3:2-21, 4:1, 11;18, 11:27, 11:31). Thus the expanse of the critique of sinful 'structures' in the gospel of Mark is quite broad. This does not mean that the relationship between the ochlos and Jerusalem was purely antagonistic, however. Mark says in 15:8–15 that the rulers were able to bribe the ochlos in order to turn them against Jesus. Yet Mark's position seems to be that this is simply a lamentable aspect of the extreme poverty of the ochlos, and does not represent a thoughtful repudiation of Jesus' message and person. On the contrary, they were the people whom Jesus taught most often, and to whom Jesus promised the coming Kingdom of God. This was met with great resistance both by the religious and secular authorities of the time (the Pharisees, Sadducees and Roman officials) and even by rival religious groups which were also anti-Jerusalem (like the Essenes and the followers of John the Baptist).[28]

ὁ ὄχλος *and Sin*

Given what I have said about *Minjung* theology (before our adventure into New Testament exegesis), it should not come as a surprising revelation to learn that Ahn translated ochlos into Korean as *Minjung*. In the lives of these downcast and oppressed people who yet were uniquely loved by Jesus, Ahn saw his fellow beleaguered Koreans. When he moved from exegesis to theology, he found that he had to have recourse to an idea of *sin* in order to makes sense of this new picture of Jesus and the ochlos. He quickly found that the traditional interpretations of sin he had learned in Korea and especially in Germany could not account for what he took to be a major biblical approach to what it is that is wrong with human nature and society. That is, his exegesis of Mark and the ochlos led directly to a new way of thinking about social, as opposed to individual, sin.

   Ahn's main point is that though the ochlos/*Minjung* are called sinners, they really are not sinners. Instead, sin is seen as the system or structures which create the ochlos/*Minjung* and perpetuate their oppression. Put simply sin names, for Ahn, the structure or social system which maintains an oppressive power dynamic between the subjects of history and their manipulated objects. While the characters in Mark name the ochlos as sinners, Mark himself, Ahn maintains, names the very existence of an ochlos as sinful.[29] The social makeup of the ochlos is composed of people who are forced out of the in-group because of structures that are sinful. These structures are mostly legal systems. For example, the people of the ochlos are often not able to abide by the law because of their occupations.

   28.   Ahn, 'Jesus and Minjung', 142.
   29.   Ahn Byung-Mu, 'Leidendes und bekennendes Christsein', in *Draussen vor dem Tor*, 26–9.

Boatmen, prostitutes and shepherds could not easily keep the Sabbath, for example, due to the nature of their jobs. Ahn maintains that boatmen, prostitutes and shepherds may not have been considered sinful because of their moral character (though this is possible), but rather simply due to the fact that their work did not easily accord with the law, against which sin was measured. This feature of sin became more prominent with the rise of the Pharisees. To generalize extremely broadly, the Pharisees brought the law, and a stress on the adherence of the law, out of its central location surrounding the temple and required all people to uphold the law.[30] What is more, they advocated a form of 'oral Torah' that extended the reach of the law even further, as it gave the Pharisees the right and the ability to extrapolate from the Torah extensions of the old law to cover new situations. The Sadducees, on the other hand, tended to think that the law, personal purity and righteousness before God were issues for the priests and in temple life.[31] When the actions of all people were then strictly measured against the standard of the law by the Pharisees, the number of people considered 'sinners' was bound to increase. Sometimes the people who were being held responsible for their 'sinful' actions did not even have any idea what the law really required of them. In Ahn's view, this is what Jesus had in mind when he said that he had not come to call the righteous, but to call the sinners (Mark 2:17). Jesus' act of 'healing' or 'saving' the sinners would thus be interpreted socially. He would not save the individual (for example, a shepherd) from his sin by reforming his heart after bringing him to repentance. Rather, he would save him from his sin by restructuring society in such a way that a dominant group would not be able to exclude the shepherd from the community on account of his social standing.

Sin is not made into a social category for Ahn only along the lines of occupation. The ochlos also contained people who were *sick*. Many Jews of Jesus' time considered sickness to be punishment for unrighteousness. It was usually, though not always, the individual penalty for an individual offence. When someone was sick, they by definition often violated the 'purity' codes of ancient Israel. They were not allowed to go to the Temple and be purified, and often were not able to continue in their work. Sometimes they were completely cast out of the community, thus making the situation even worse because it separated them from people who could care for them. Jesus took a particular initiative toward lepers, haemophiliacs and the mentally ill. Mark is full of examples of Jesus healing these people. While this could be viewed as an individual remedy of an individual sin (purging the effects of one's own sin), Ahn argues instead that this is really a social remedy of a social ill. When the leper is healed, he can rejoin society. He can work again, be in community and family again. This is all part of the unfolding

---

30. Lawrence Boadt, *Reading the Old Testament* (New York: Paulist Press, 1984), 522–4.

31. On this, cf. Raymond Brown, *Introduction to the New Testament* (New York: Doubleday, 1997), 77–80.

of the Kingdom of God, which is, for Ahn, predictably social and structural in nature. 'The Kingdom of God must be regarded as bringing liberation not just from sins but rather from the whole dominating system and from the ideas upon which it is founded.'[32]

Ahn reads not only Mark but all of the gospels with this social idea of sin in mind. Space will not permit inclusion of the many fecund reinterpretations of biblical texts on 'sin' that Ahn is able to make. He takes a basically 'materialist' rather than a 'spiritual' stance on such issues as the interpretation of the Sermon on the Mount and on Jesus' parables about the Kingdom of God. In a telling example, Ahn rereads the parables in Mk 2:23–3:6 about Jesus allowing the picking of grain on the Sabbath. This is an example of structural sin, not individual sin, in Ahn's view. The disciples and the ochlos pick grain as they are walking through the fields. They do this because they are hungry. The Pharisees see this and ask Jesus why he allows them to sin, by breaking the Sabbath injunction against gathering food. Jesus implies that it is not the arbitrary rule that is in the wrong, but the social *fact* that the people who are following him are so poor that they are forced to break an otherwise acceptable law. Thus the parable is not primarily about Jesus antagonizing the Pharisees nor making self-aggrandizing claims about his own superiority to the law, but about the social sins of poverty, hunger and exclusion.

Throughout his writings, Ahn is very careful not to rigidify the ochlos into a stagnate 'group'. The ochlos emerges as an event between Jesus and his followers. In fact, one of Ahn's more famous dictums is 'In the beginning was the event.'[33] The dynamic interchange between Jesus and the ochlos both names sin as such and emphatically *is* grace itself. In this sense, Ahn thinks, the ochlos become subjects of their own history. Later in his life Ahn would go further than this to say that the relation between the ochlos and Jesus is so close that the attributes of one can be predicated of the other. In this restricted sense, then, Ahn can say that Jesus is the *Minjung*, and the *Minjung* are Jesus.[34] The implication, which Ahn later made explicit, was that the *Minjung* can actually redeem the world by overcoming the structures of sin.[35]

While this is a fascinating movement in contemporary theology, I do have some serious reservations about Ahn's approach to sin. First, there is the risk that the role of the individual in sin will be eclipsed. This is perhaps a necessary consequence of an exegetical theology drawing from

32.   Ahn, 'Jesus and the Minjung', 146.

33.   Ahn Byung-Mu, *Jesus of Galilee* (Seoul: Christian Conference of Asia, 2004), vii.

34.   For relevant texts on this matter, cf. Sang Jin Ahn, *Continuity and Transformation: Religious Synthesis in East Asia* (New York: Peter Lang, 2001), 88–94.

35.   This has been one of the most contentious aspects of the reception of *Minjung* theology in the West. For a representative appreciation and critique, cf. Jürgen Moltmann, *Experiences in Theology: Ways and Forms of Christian Theology*, trans. Margaret Kohl (Minneapolis: Fortress Press, 2000), 252–67.

a fairly narrow slice of the biblical pie. Just as the doctrine of sin was plagued for years by an exegetical emphasis on the individualistic passages of the Apostle Paul,[36] so too does a theological concept of sin taken almost entirely from one aspect of one of the gospels (no matter how important an aspect) risk myopia. Second, while Ahn is extremely careful not to make the idea of *Minjung* into an us vs them dichotomy, with everyone in society divided up and placed into either the *Minjung* or the oppressive participants in the structure of domination, it is clear that one less careful with Ahn's *event* language regarding the interface between Jesus and the ochlos/*Minjung* could easily slip into this antagonistic idiom. If that were the case, then Ahn's work would be its own undoing. It would purchase the solidarity of the *Minjung* at the cost of perpetuating permanently antagonistic relationships between governor and governed. The concept of sin would move from being a liberating recognition of the universality and commonness of the human condition and would become a reason for ever-more sinful division. To test out the *Minjung* theology against these risks, we will now turn to a second-generation *Minjung* theologian and look at where a more explicit doctrine of sin ends up on the trajectory launched by Ahn Byung-Mu.

Andrew Sung Park on Sin and Han

Andrew Sung Park is the one Asian-American theologian who has taken Ahn Byung-Mu's theological programme the furthest in the United States, especially in the area of the doctrine of sin. Park, who is Methodist, has written or edited several books and penned many other chapters and articles, but he essentially is a one-issue thinker centred on a main problematic: the relationship between suffering, particularly the suffering of the *Minjung*, and sin.[37] The key to understanding Park's theology is a concept he borrows

---

36.   This is mildly ironic, since Paul's notion and use of the categories of principalities and powers have proven to be rich resources in contemporary doctrines of social sin. Maybe Paul can be used to rescue Paul from himself!

37.   The most representative works, not all of which will be discussed here, are Andrew Sung Park, *The Wounded Heart of God: The Asian Concept of Han and the Christian Doctrine of Sin* (Nashville: Abingdon, 1992), idem et al., eds, *The Other Side of Sin: Woundedness from the Perspective of the Sinned Against* (Albany: SUNY Press, 2001), 'A Theology of Enhancement: Multiculturality in Self and Community', in *Journal of Pastoral Theology* 13 (2003): 14–33, 'The Formation of Multicultural Religious Identity within Persons in Korean-American Experience', in *Journal of Pastoral Theology* 13 (2003): 34–50, 'A Theology of Transmutation', in Fernando Segovia and Eleazar Fernandez, eds, *A Dream Unfinished* (Maryknoll: Orbis, 2001), 152–66, 'Sin and Han: The Pain of a Victim', in *Living Pulpit* 9 (1999): 22–3, 'Holiness and Healing: An Asian-American Voice Shaping the Methodist Traditions', in Joerg Rieger and John Vincent, eds, *Methodist and Radical: Rejuvenating a Tradition* (Nashville: Abingdon, 2003), 'Theology of Han (The Abyss of Pain)', in *Quarterly Review* 9 (1989): 48–62.

from Buddhist philosophy, which is *han*. *Han* is a difficult to describe notion. When it is described by those who wish to employ it for the service of theology, it is usually couched in the form of a story or a poem, for it is best understood allusively and intuitively.[38] Still, some things can be said fairly directly about *han*. Park describes *han* as 'frustrated hope', 'the collapsed feeling of pain', 'letting go', 'resentful bitterness' and finally as 'the wounded heart'.[39] Christian theological engagement with the Asian concept of *han* can shore up what Park believes to be a fundamental problem with traditional doctrines of sin. Not only is the problem that these notions of sin have been overly individualized, which is of obvious relevance to the current project, but there is a further shortcoming, too. This problem is that systematic theologians, when discussing sin, focus so much on the perpetration of acts of sin that they are blinded to the depths of the painful experience of those acts. In other words, doctrines of sin traditionally focus on the sinner, and not on the 'sinned-against'. The old ways of conceiving of sin create an essentially subject–object scheme between sinner and sinned-against. *Han* replaces this with a more appropriately intersubjective scheme. The sinned-against is reckoned to have been a full person in the encounter with the sinner. He or she fully 'participates' in the act which sin names. Since traditional models of sin ignore this, we must replace them with new models of sin in conjunction with *han*.

Clearly one of the risks of *Minjung* theology I named above could be at play here. Has Park already neatly divided up the world into sinners and the sinned against – into those with sin and those with *han*? We should not be too hasty in coming to this conclusion, because, as Park notes, 'Sin and han are complex, entangled realities. While sin and guilt belong to oppressors, and han and shame belong to the oppressed, the two realities often overlap. Frequently – indeed, probably most of the time – they exist side by side in individuals; ... sometimes we commit sin and sometimes we experience han.'[40] The fact that Park needs to mention this, however, belies the fact that he knows his theology is subject to the criticisms he attempts to forestall. As we shall soon see, the fuzzy nature of this 'overlap' between those who sin and those who experience *han* causes Park great problems.

Park maintains that there are four basic kinds of *han*. *Han* has corporate and individual expressions, and within these groups there are active and passive manifestations. Individual passive *han* could be something like the festering frustration of a victim of abuse.[41] This could be made active when the pattern of abuse becomes so intolerable that the victim lashes out in

---

38. This is a strategy followed quite widely by Asian-American theologians, particularly C. S. Song, in works such as *The Believing Heart: An Invitation to Story Theology* (Minneapolis: Fortress, 1999) and *Third Eye Theology: Theology in Formation in Asian Settings* (Maryknoll: Orbis, 1991).
39. Park, *The Wounded Heart of God*, 15–20.
40. Park, *The Wounded Heart of God*, 13.
41. Ibid., 33.

vengeance.[42] Passive corporate *han* expresses itself primarily as despair in the face of continued oppression. This is the kind of generalized mentality or *zeitgeist* of hopelessness inculcated in the *Minjung* through centuries of exploitation.[43] Active or conscious corporate *han* takes the shape of bloody or violent social revolution and war.[44]

Park identifies three major roots of the *han* of our time. First there is the global capitalist economy wherein the most powerful and wealthy few grow more powerful and wealthier at the expense of the suffering of the individuals and groups on the underside of society. In the second place there is patriarchy, which Park links closely with all kinds of typically Western dualisms (male/female, culture/nature, self/other). This part of Park's analysis is among his most perceptive, as he weaves together threads of traditional 'Asian' *han* into a single fabric – infanticide, foot binding, crimes of 'honour' and the institutionalized abuse of women by their mothers-in-law (*Si-jip Gahn-Da*). The third major root of *han* is racial and cultural discrimination. All of these roots of *han* are the result and future cause of continued power discrepancies between the oppressors and the oppressed. These roots of *han* both presuppose themselves (racist systems beget racists) and reinforce each other (a male victim of racism may be more prone to turn to sexism to gather power). In traditional Christian theology, these sorts of themes are often grouped together under the heading of 'original sin'. But Park rejects this doctrine for he thinks that 'the concept of original sin undermines the guilt of oppressors by universalizing the guilt of humanity. The idea of original sin inevitably projects the idea of original guilt.'[45] Park finds this both illogical and counterproductive; illogical because since sin is purely volitional, in his thinking, it makes no sense to say that the sin of one is borne by the guilt of another,[46] and counterproductive because it obscures, rather than establishes, the nature of genuine guilt.[47]

The notion of *han* helps here. While sin cannot be transmitted from generation to generation, *han* can be. If one were to replace the doctrine of original sin with original *han*, one could maintain an appreciation for the gravity of human misery (which the doctrine of original sin rightly seeks to do) while not insensitively blurring the distinction between perpetrators and sufferers of sinful actions. Yet now we see the fundamental problem of Park's theory. The line between sinner and sinned against must not be inappropriately blurred, yet the vast majority of the time, *han* and sin 'overlap' in the self. Couple this paradox with a strong defence of the

---

42.   Ibid., 32.
43.   Ibid., 37–8.
44.   Ibid., 36.
45.   Ibid., 79.
46.   'Sin is something one commits and for which one is responsible ... Sin involves a willful act'. Ibid., 79.
47.   'This idea (original sin) has misdirected the course of Christian theology by placing a smokescreen before the reality of the suffering of the wronged; it has created the *han* of the suffering in the church'. Park, *The Wounded Heart of God*, 79.

voluntaristic notion of sin, and the idea of a non-individualistic doctrine of sin comes completely undone.

Sin Known in Its Overcoming: Dan *and* Han-puri

Park does not only rethink the doctrine of original sin in terms of *han*. He also rejects the traditional formulation of justification by grace through faith, particularly in Luther's approach thereto. He cites three reasons for this dismissal. It takes the perspective of the wrongdoer only, since it is only one who has sinned who needs to be justified. This implies, second, that the sinned against have no recourse to salvation, since suffering is not redeemed – transgression is. Taken together, these two data imply that, third, justification is only a transaction between the sinner and God, conceived without reference to the 'significance of our relation with our neighbor'.[48] To anyone who has ever actually read Luther, the shocking distortion of his views by Park will be obvious.[49] But we will put aside this objection for now and concentrate on the logic of his position. Instead of relying on the justifying grace of God to transform the sinner, Park thinks that the sinner must effect his or her own justification by empathetically imagining him or herself into the mind of the victim of sin. Park suggests developing a deeper notion of Jesus 'rebuking commandment' (Matt. 18:15–17; Luke 17:3) which would highlight the 'forgivingness' of victims rather than the 'forgiveness' of wrongdoers.[50]

The point Park is trying to make is that absent the initiative towards reconciliation taken by either the wrongdoer, the victim, or both, sin and *han* will fester and multiply. Sin can be forgiven, and *han* can be 'resolved', the name for which is *han pu-ri*, but this is only realized after a genuinely self-effected change in both wrongdoer and victim. Park stresses,

> It is not feasible to change our status before God from sinners to saints without changing our natures. With such unchanged nature, we will never experience God's peace and salvation, for salvation is not a *status* but a *state of our nature*. If we are supposedly justified by our faith, yet live in sinfulness, that justification helps no one in actuality and loses its significance. When we change our perspective from our self-centeredness to a victim's view and live in love with others, we come to *justify* our existence and abide in salvation.[51]

This is another way of formulating Thomas' dictum *agere sequitur esse*: doing follows from being. If we are to change ourselves from sinful to

---

48. Ibid., 95.

49. For a powerful restatement on the intensely ethical ramification of Luther's allegedly morally enfeebling doctrine of justification, cf. Carter Lindberg, 'Luther's Struggle with Social-Ethical Issues', in Donald K. McKim, ed., *The Cambridge Companion to Martin Luther* (Cambridge: Cambridge University Press, 2003), 165–78.

50. Park, *The Wounded Heart of God*, 92.

51. Park, *The Wounded Heart of God*, 98, emphasis his.

righteous (and Park is clear that we are the ones who must do this; relying on 'grace' for such things 'debilitates' sinners and victims), we must first perform acts which serve to 'resolve' the *han* of those we victimize. This (*han-pu-ri*; the resolution of *han*) can only happen in two ways. Either the sinner comes to the victim in a show of repentance and earnestly tries to make amends for the suffering, or the victim is able to change the circumstances of his existence such that his suffering loses its bite. Thus *han* would be resolved without the repentance of the sinner (and consequently, without the sinner being forgiven).

Park also tries to distinguish between two kinds of repentance. First there is what is normally thought of by repentance, which is the awakening in the mind of the individual that comes with knowledge of wrongdoing. This is followed in some way by an attitude of contrition or sorrow. But then there is also social repentance, which is neither cognitive nor conscious. Thus real forgiveness, or genuine redemption requires both kinds of repentance – at the individual and social levels. Social repentance is identified by Park as the cessation of oppressive systems of economic and cultural exploitation.[52] Yet this is problematic for the same reasons besetting Park's reinterpretation of justification by grace. Whence comes the power to transform social structures, such that forgiveness for their past sinfulness could be granted? Either it is not possible for sinful persons to change the structures, in which case forgiveness would never come, or sinful people would change the structures by themselves, in which case God, and by extension God's forgiveness, would be superfluous. Here again is the fundamental problem with Park's theology: the need to distinguish sinner from sinned against eventually simply cuts God and God's grace out of the picture.

Perhaps Park omits God from the drama of human sin and redemption because God could not really do much anyway. Park thinks that salvation is such an interpersonal dynamic that God, who also suffers *han* from the sin of the world, is in need of it. He writes, 'The cross of Jesus is a symbol of God's crying for salvation (*Eli Eli, lama sabachtini?*), because God cannot save Godself. *God needs salvation!*'[53] Park evidently does not think that the doctrine of the Trinity makes God 'relational' enough to be saved by Godself. Since God is not relational enough to save Godself, individual humans are at even more of a disadvantage. The more comprehensive word in *Minjung* theology for salvation is *dan* (*han-pu-ri* resolves the *han* of victims; *dan* refers to the salvation of both victims and sinners), and *dan* is, in Park's view, a 'participatory dialectic'. Of *dan* Park writes,

This dialectical salvation is the relational, dynamic and affective interaction between sinners and their victims, and the cooperative efforts of the two to dissolve *han* and sin. The oppressors (sinners) cannot be saved unless the oppressed (victims) are saved or made whole, and vice versa. In other words, no one is actually saved

52. Ibid., 89–90.
53. Ibid., emphasis his.

until all are saved. Salvation is wholeness, and no one can actualize wholeness by him or herself.[54]

Thus we are left, if Park is right about the trajectory of *Minjung* theology and sin, in a profoundly difficult situation. We need to save each other from each other's sin, and we need our neighbours to initiate reconciliation with us to resolve our *han*. God is unable or unwilling to help make this possible, since forgiveness is only made available to those who have already done the good work of effecting genuine reconciliation of their own accord. There is no explanation given for what it is that might make us willing or able to effect this real change, other than perhaps reading and taking to heart Park's own work. Thus an unsympathetic reader would have to conclude that Park has hit for the heretical cycle: that we need to save ourselves and others is Pelagian, that we do so by our knowledge that we ought to do so is Gnostic, that God cannot help is Manichean and that Jesus is in need of salvation by Godself is Arian.

Conclusion

In this chapter I have described the theologies of the most prominent and most conceptually subtle thinker of the first generation of *Minjung* theology, Ahn Byung-Mu, and the thought of a third-generation disciple. The fact that just these two theologians were discussed has limitations, but wide and careful reading ensures that their views are significantly representative of trends in Korean and Asian-American theology. The first generation of *Minjung* thinkers were incredibly careful in maintaining a dynamic tension between the *Minjung* and the ruling classes. *Minjung* was not simply a political term neatly dividing the world into oppressors and oppressed. It had its roots in the event of Jesus meeting the downtrodden, identifying with them, and promising them the kingdom of God. These themes are nearly ubiquitous in the first-generation thinkers.[55]

I have tried to show how Andrew Sung Park's work exemplifies a precipitous fall from this caution and subtlety. The distinction between the *han* of the victims and the sin of the oppressors is drawn so sharply that any fluidity between the two groups is lost in antagonistic relationships, despite Park's claim that sin and *han* overlap in people. Sin is brought back into voluntaristic focus, making it hard to see how it could be social. Recall that Ahn had stated that the Gospel of Mark implied that the existence of

---

54.   Ibid., 101.

55.   Cf. David Kwang-sun Suh, *Theology, Ideology and Culture* (Hong Kong: World Student Christian Fedearation, 1983), and 'Korean Theological Development in the 1970's' in *Minjung Theology: People as the Subjects of History*, Kim Yong-Bock, 'The Social Biography of the Minjung and Theology', in *Minjung and Theology in Korea* (Hong Kong: World Student Christian Fedearation, 1979) and Kim Chung-choon, 'The Old Testament Basis for Minjung Theology', in *Minjung and Theology in Korea*.

the ochlos was sin, not the discrete acts of its members, or even the discrete acts of those who antagonized the ochlos. Sin named a social reality that was against God. Park ends up disallowing this by insisting on the volitional character of sin and replacing God as the object of sin solely with one's neighbour. Park is by no means alone in this regard.[56] If it is true that *Minjung* theology has now essentially run its course (and I think that this is true), I hope I have made clear that the development of *Minjung* thoughts on sin contributed to its demise, though I do not thereby intend to argue anything like a historical thesis, as the actual historical reasons for the ending of any theological epoch are never reducible to a single doctrine or event.[57]

What relevance may we draw for other Asian Christian doctrines of social and individual sin? As even this brief chapter shows, the proper way to speak about social and individual sin in Asia is very much up for grabs. There are strong undercurrents even within *Minjung* theology about whether and how to move forward. To cite just one example, some Asian feminists have shown how insufficient was the original critical analysis undertaken by Ahn Byung-Mu and others, for it ignored the plight of women.[58] They particularly omitted to extend the implications of the egalitarian proclamation of Jesus to include women, thus exposing a deficient Christology. Noted commentator Edmond Tang thinks that *Minjung* theology has simply exceeded the limits it set for itself as a particular contextual theology, and the way forward for Christians in Korea must be along completely different lines.[59]

Yet the demise of the *Minjung* theology need not imply that it cannot still have some lessons both for doctrines of sin in Asia and in America. For

---

56.　On this particular point, Park has parallels like Young-Hak Hyun, 'Minjung Theology and the Religion of Han', *East Asia Journal of Religion* 3 (1985): 354–9, and Heup-Young Kim, 'A Tao of Asian Theology in the 21st Century', *CTC Bulletin* XV (1998): 60–73.

57.　The indigenous Christian theology in China inaugurated first by Y. T. Wu in the 1950s and his protégé Bishop K. H. Ting followed much the same path. Ting tried to reinterpret the doctrine of sin along the lines of sinners and sinned against (thought *han* did not play a role in his reformulation) and the essential 'Christlikeness' of God. 'What was new to many Chinese Christians (in Ting's theology) is the awareness that people are not only sinners but are also sinned against. The task of evangelism is not only to convince persons of their sin but to stand alongside those who are sinned against in our society. To dwell on sin is not evangelism proper; it does not necessarily move a person to repentance and to the acceptance of Christ as saviour'. In *No Longer Strangers: Selected Writings of Bishop K.H. Ting*, ed. Raymond L. Whitehead (Maryknoll: Orbis, 1989), 126. Cf. also his massive *Love Never Ends: Papers by K.H. Ting*, ed. Janet Wickeri (Nanjing: Yillin Press, 2000).

58.　The best introduction to this perspective can be found in Chung Hyun Kyung, *Struggling to Be the Sun Again: Introducing Asian Women's Theology* (Maryknoll: Orbis, 1990).

59.　Tang, 'East Asia', in John Parratt, ed., *An Introduction to Third World Theologies* (Cambridge: Cambridge University Press, 2004), 100–101.

example, the commitment to deal positively with other religious traditions and their language of human misery and depravity is a laudable one, and is not destined to fail as Park's has.[60] Yet the inter-religious nature, or at least context, of these characteristically Asian approaches to the doctrine of sin has also been the cause for dispute. Many Westerners are often suspicious of Asian Christian theology, wary that acceptance of it implies acceptance of what they feel is an improperly syncretistic approach to faith. This may be especially problematic in the case of writers like Park, who, despite their best intentions for opening up Christianity for inter-religious dialogue, sometimes lose any kind of recognizably Christian particularity, especially on such a contentious doctrine as sin.[61]

Contextual Asian theologies in general, and *Minjung* theology in particular, have evinced a careful refusal to import an inappropriately individualistic Western conception of sin which cannot address the vaster issues of globalization, economic tyranny, the environmental crisis, and the breakdown of traditional cultures which currently take the centre of the social stage in Asia. Of course, in the wake of the recent devastation of the 2004 tsunami, there is reason to believe that theologians may appropriately devote more energy to an analysis of natural instead of moral evil, if a traditionally Western distinction may be superimposed on an Asian experience.[62]

Despite these divergences within various branches of Asian theologies, and despite the reservations enunciated above regarding the propriety of 'Asia' as a category under which theologians could be helpfully grouped, I think that the Asian perspectives can be valuable contributors to the ongoing theological construction of non-individualistic doctrines of sin, particularly in the case of *Minjung* theology, and its exemplification of the structural sin type of rejection of individualism in sin.

60.   One interesting recent discussion of this matter is found in Hans Ucko, *The People and the People of God: Minjung and Dalit Theology in Interaction with Jewish-Christian Dialogue* (Münster: Lit Verlag, 2002).

61.   Park devotes a chapter to 'Han: The Point of Interreligious Dialogue', *Wounded Heart of God*, 129–35.

62.   On this point reference must be made to the eloquent essay by David Bentley Hart, *The Doors of the Sea: Where Was God in the Tsunami?* (Grand Rapids: Eerdmans, 2005).

Chapter 7

CONCLUSION

Re-viewing the Map

The reader has borne a special burden in the preceding pages. The charting of so much unknown theological territory, the features of which changed so much from region to region, and chapter to chapter, has been taxing. I have asked the reader to keep in mind the characteristic strengths and weaknesses of two incredibly sophisticated nineteenth-century proposals on sin, including one by theologian extremely unfamiliar even to most theologically trained ears. Before summing up the learning I take from the whole foregoing book, it will be helpful to review a final time the preliminary conclusions to which we have thus far come.

Ritschl's critique of Schleiermacher provided our point of departure. Schleiermacher rendered an invaluable service to systematic theology by daring to provide his own map of previously uncharted territory, particularly in the area of sin and grace. Schleiermacher was one of the very first Christian theologians to embrace a thoroughly developmental theological anthropology. We saw how this affected his doctrine of sin; sin is the failure to integrate one's higher self-consciousness and God-consciousness with one's sensible self-consciousness. The developmental anteriority of the sensible self-consciousness made humans prone to such disintegration. This does not mean that humans are not created good, for the perfection of creation means, for Schleiermacher, that perfection is possible, not actual. Schleiermacher's focus on the psychological development of the individual gives him problems in the doctrine of sin, too, for he is forced to defend a position where what evil one undergoes is basically relative to the sin one commits. Besides being an indecent thing to say, we can see how susceptible to attack this kind of logic is to liberationist critique, which sees the suffering caused by the sins of a few borne in the suffering of the many.

Ritschl saw the shortcomings in all of this with uncommon perception. Schleiermacher had started down the road to a communal understanding of sin by re-emphasizing the centrality of the kingdom of God as a theological symbol. However, Ritschl held that Schleiermacher did not go far enough in this direction, stopping short of saying that the intersubjective resistance to the Kingdom of God on earth created something like a Kingdom of sin or Kingdom of evil. He thus relied too much, in Ritschl's view, on the psychological account of the origin of sin in the individual, and could not see its social dimensions. Drawing on Kant and Rothe, Ritschl strived to show that the symbol of the Kingdom of God should be both immanent and eschatological, religious and ethical, gift of God and task of the human community. This thoroughly social view of the good is accompanied by a thoroughly social view of the good's privation. Thus we have an insistence that a doctrine of sin take into serious consideration the *social structures* of sin.

This was not the only way to resist individualism in sin in the nineteenth century. In Chapter 3 I highlighted the salient features of a debate between two American Reformed theologians, Charles Finney and John Nevin. Finney's view of sin was as consistent as it was individualistic; a person sinned when he or she directly and consciously acted in a way inconsistent with the eternal law of God. Any act stemming from a motive other than 'disinterested benevolence' was a sinful act. Even gross corporate distortions like slavery and enforced economic exploitation of the poor were individualist ills with accordingly individualist cures.

In Nevin's view, this description of sin was too simplistic and too individualistic. Finney had simply posited the metaphysical concepts of God's absolute and eternal moral law and moral government and did not account for how knowledge of the law was possible, such that sin could occur. Nevin thus developed a fuller notion of the self-in-relation, the purpose of which was to show that it is only in concrete relations with other subjects, particularly in the contexts of the family, church and state, that one could come to know the law, and could thus be said wilfully to contradict it. Yet even when one sinned, thereby contradicting God's law, Nevin argued that this had very real, practical, concrete effects in the relational spheres in which one's selfhood had formed. Thus those effects (which would be a form of 'social sin') were rightly shown to be sinful. Further, Nevin took issue with the notion of the self presupposed in the revivals of Finney and others. Nevin thought that the only part of the person which was actually being addressed in the revivals of the Second Great Awakening, of which Finney and his anxious bench were emblematic, was the *will*. Nevin thought that it was more than the will which was involved in sin, and therefore the whole person, not just the will, should be called to conversion and repentance for sin.

One factor that frustrates adoption of Nevin's theory of the self for a contemporary doctrine of sin is his idealism. Were one to ask Nevin what it was specifically about the relational self that brought a human from infant to moral agent to sinner and finally to redeemed child of God, Nevin would respond that the same thing brings humans along all these stages that brings an oak from acorn to tree. All of reality is the gradual externalization of the ideal in the actual. As an acorn needs soil, water and sunlight to externalize its organic nature into a tree, so the human needs relationships in family, state and church to become a self. Despite the reliance on idealism implicit in this formulation and the attendant difficulties in appropriating the idealistic, relational self in an age where idealism is no longer the *lingua franca* of philosophical theology, I pointed to the great strengths of Nevin's neglected theology.

Taken together, Nevin's and Ritschl's rejections of individualism provide us with a road map for reading liberationist doctrines of sin in the late twentieth century. The dizzying variety of perspectives taken in describing sin in non-individualistic terms is made manageable by seeing the basic approaches to sin, as well as the relative strengths and weaknesses of each approach. In Chapter 4 I showed that most of the Latin American liberation theologies could be fitted under the 'structural sin' type of rejection of individualism. Gutiérrez was extremely successful in showing the sinfulness of human social structures while neither granting those structures agency nor exculpating the sinner at the individual level. He described sin as the 'breach of friendship with God' that could not but have serious social effects. Those effects were seen as derivative consequences of the primary religious dimension of sin, but they were sinful nonetheless specifically because they violated God's intentions for full human flourishing. I showed that Gutiérrez' view of social sin was essentially embraced by the Vatican.

However, theologians writing after Gutiérrez have not been as careful in thinking through the implications of the structural sin type of non-individualistic sin. Leonardo Boff and Juan Luis Segundo offer fascinating and novel frameworks in which to conceive of social sin, in the form of a 'fundamental project' and evolutionary categories, respectively. Yet these approaches almost thoroughly blur the distinction between 'human nature' and 'sin'. Segundo simply admits that he thinks sin is a constitutive low-level structure of all human being and doing. If we are to evolve collectively into structures which are maximally loving and minimally sinful, we have to 'sin in the right way' in order to achieve this by turning our inherent egotism towards the good. In the case of Boff, I showed that his close linkage of the fundamental project of a culture and the projects of its inhabitants means that when a culture is fundamentally sinful (which Boff does not really define), its inhabitants necessarily must be as well, since they absorb the orientation of the culture which surrounds them. Boff uses the traditional language of habitual grace to describe the re-orientation of the individual, yet I showed this approach to be lacking a way to describe what must be the logically prior move of re-orienting the fundamental project of a social system. Both of these thinkers, Boff and Segundo, thus have hypostatized social sin into individual sin. I also showed in Chapter 4 that many other thinkers in the Latin American liberationist tradition encounter problems in their doctrines of social sin either by vagueness in proposing an alternative understanding of how to conceive of sin socially (Alfaro), the agency of structures (Chopp and Etchegoyen), and the clean demarcation between oppressor and oppressed (Gonzalez). I showed that all of these theologians have made terribly important advances in thinking about sin in non-individualistic ways, but that their proposals must be superseded in future doctrines of social sin.

In Chapter 5 the strengths of the map of social sin derived from nineteenth-century theology again proved its usefulness in making sense of contemporary proposals. Feminist contributions to doctrines of social sin actually exemplify both types. The structural sin type organized writings on sin from Mary Potter Engel, Elisabeth Schüssler Fiorenza, womanist theologies (Jacquelyn Grant, Delores Williams and Emilie Townes), and neo-Reformation proposals (Serene Jones and Deanna Thompson). In discussing these works I noted how carefully they were able to attend to the implicit sexism of traditional individualistic notions of sin, which was valuable in its own right, but that they were able to go beyond this critique to make the positive point that it was precisely sinful social structures which perpetuate sexism, racism, classism and other sins. Yet each of these versions of social sin had problems of their own. Schüssler Fiorenza was unable to account for the way in which *kyriarchy* is against God, and therefore more positively why it is wrong. For most Christians, when it is definitively shown that some act, orientation, structure, relationship or anything else is demonstrably contrary to Jesus' teachings, the link must also be made that this is a uniquely serious offence because Jesus and God are linked in some determinate way. Thus the 'against-God-ness' of sin is a genuinely open matter which must be considered. This partial eclipse of God from the picture of social sin plagues the three womanist theologies considered in Chapter 5 in similar ways.

Two feminist theologians were our exemplars of the relational self type of rejection of individualism in sin. Marjorie Suchocki's adduction of Whiteheadian relationality as a model for selfhood was detailed in depth. I showed how thoroughly successful this attempt was at rooting out individualism, since by definition a myopic focus on just one aspect (the individual self) is practically disallowed in her process scheme. Yet I raised significant concerns about the status of the process-relational self as moral agent. At what point in the teleological development of the self has 'enough' development occurred such that a culpable moral agent is in place? And if this does not happen, is the only way to secure the moral responsibility of the individual the strategy of positing some latent non-relational faculty like human free will? If so, the advances in relationality are undone in the doctrine of sin.

I then showed Rosemary Ruether's contributions to be more successful in moving forward the discussion of the relational self type of rejection of individualistic sin. Instead of relying on an abstract notion of free will to account for the genuinely culpable actions of sin, she uses the idea of two orientations, drawn from Jewish thought. Ruether does not normally accord structures with agency, seeing them rather as the effects of sins like domination and patriarchy, which are themselves distortions of 'life-giving' relations. Thus the two types of rejections of individualism are brought critically into conversation for the first time – the distortions in relationship which lie at the root of sin in the self lie also at the root of sin in society. As I will show below, this is a terribly important contribution to future doctrines of social sin. Yet I remained critical of the imprecision in Ruether's model of the relational self. By what criterion are relationships said to be life-giving or death-dealing? That is, how would one know that one's relationships were sinful? This is by no means a mortal wound in Ruether's view of the self, but it is one which calls for more clarification. She refers explicitly to the centrality of the *imago dei* for theological anthropology. This would imply that the Trinitarian structure of relationality constitutive of divine personhood may also be reflected in human personhood. But this possibility is left undeveloped. This will have to be mapped into a future doctrine of social sin.

Finally, our last stop through previously uncharted territory brought us to Asia, and there specifically to the Korean form of *Minjung* theology. While I plotted a kind of cul-de-sac at the end of that road, I did labour to show that there still are some significant lessons to be drawn from the *Minjung* formulation of sin. The dangers of rigidifying oppressor–oppressed distinctions was the clearest danger uncovered that we must avoid in the future, as was omitting to offer an account of the self which contributes to the perpetuation of sinful social structures. More positively, *Minjung* theology confirmed for us that biblical research into the religious meaning of sin will reward those efforts with ever new understanding of sin in non-individualistic ways. Further, the seriousness with which *Minjung* theologians engaged in inter-religious thinking about human misery and fallenness represents a trend which should be developed and continued.

Prolegomenon to a Future Doctrine of Social Sin

None of what follows is material that has not already been developed in my appreciations and criticisms of doctrines of social sin located in the previous chapters, yet it may be helpful to enumerate some of the lessons that we may take from our mapping of social sin in the last two centuries of Christian thought. In this very last brief section, then, I will offer some recommendations for theologians who wish to conceive of sin in non-individualistic ways without repeating the errors and without neglecting the treasures in past theological formulations of social sin.

Recommendations drawn from the use of the structural sin type:

1. The agential status of structures must be clarified. It is one thing for a theologian occasionally to slip rhetorically into an idiom wherein sinful actions are predicated of social arrangements as such. This is understandable, though not to be encouraged. I am thinking here of something like the practice of naming 'unchecked global capitalism' as the source of suffering and evil, or the reification of 'racism', in a way disconnected from the discrete, concrete actions of robber barons and bigots. Yet it is another thing entirely to assert that these structures actively and actually sin. Thus a corollary of this first lesson must be a push for

greater clarity in what it means to 'sin' and to 'be sinful'. Structures may be both of these, but it is at least not clear how. Future engagement with the topic of social sin must deal urgently with this issue.

2. The object of sin in sinful social structures must be clarified. Are structures sinful because they are in some way *against* God? If so, in what way is this to be understood? Are they sinful because they harm people? If so, in what way is this to be understood? It is not clear to me in what way value is added to the idea that the sins of people harm other people when it is asserted that structures harm people. Can an individual's participation in a sinful social structure cause one to sin against oneself? Or against creation, broadly understood? As I noted throughout the book, this vagueness does not seem to me to a fatal flaw in the use of the structural sin type to reject individualism in doctrines of sin. It is only an area that deserves much more careful scrutiny and emendation.

3. The sinfulness of the situation in which the self is located (once the meaning of this is clarified per recommendation 1) must not be tied so directly to the sinfulness of the self that we become unable to differentiate between created human goodness and actual (i.e., sinful) human life. This is another way of saying that we should not hypostatize sin. One of the positive threads of traditional theology on the subject of sin that I am simply unwilling to give up is the conviction that human nature is one thing, and sin is quite another. Hypostatizing sin from the social realm to the core of individual human nature threatens this critical distinction.

Recommendations drawn from the relational self type:

1. The ways in which relationality is seen in the formation of the self must continue to be developed in non-trivial ways. This is becoming increasingly axiomatic in systematic theology. Yet the precise way in which this relationality is to be understood is completely up for grabs. There are almost as many versions of relationality in selfhood on offer as there are people who write about it. Nonetheless, being honest about the deeply interconnected nature of the whole world, with regard both to persons and non-persons, promises to be a stratum of thought which will be richly mined. As with any mine, however, there seems to be at least as much slag and dross as there is usable ore in recent thinking about relationality. The precise forms relationality takes in forming selfhood simply must be further specified. To say that the self exists 'in relationship' seems to me incontrovertible. Yet everything hinges on what *kind* of relationality with *which* terms of relation. The problems we encounter here seem legion. There is, first, the drawback of vacuity. In many cases, to say that two (or more) things 'exist in relationship' is to say utterly nothing. I could rightly say, to take a completely bizarre example, that my pet fish, Pete, exists 'in relationship' to the square root of 3. Now, what kind of relationship do we have here? Obviously there is not much of one, but inasmuch as they are, say, both objects of my

thought, or both nouns in the previous sentence, or both things I am acquainted with in my daily life, it is accurate to say they exist in some kind of relationship. If that is all that is meant by the indispensability of relational thinking for understanding the universe, however, it is certainly not enough to be helpful for understanding any phenomenon, let alone one as intricate as personal identity and human sin.

There is also the problem that understanding the human person in a thoroughly relational way risks instrumentalizing those with whom we are in relationship. If I need you to be you in order for me to be most fully me, we have a precarious situation in which I will inevitably try to manipulate you to further my project of self-identity. When we diminish or even lose the 'centredness' characteristic of less relational anthropologies, we open the door to exploitation and distortion of relationship. Again, this is no fatal flaw of the relational self type, but rather is an avenue for increased clarity and specificity in our thinking about social sin.

2. One appropriate avenue to follow in pursuing this necessary specification of relationality that I have advocated above is the closer connection of Trinitarian relationality with human selfhood. This is by no means the only way forward in this matter. Yet the renaissance of Trinitarian theology in the twentieth century should have as its next goal the reinterpretation of human relationality along the lines of the *imago dei*. Recent Trinitarian theology has taken up such themes as unity-in-diversity, constitutive otherness, the relationship of divine being with divine action, and temporality in the divine life. All of these issues bear directly on the problem of the relational self and sin. Future work, mine included, will do well to incorporate these Trinitarian insights into our doctrines of social sin.

3. Relationality must be construed in such a way that it does not become a threat to moral culpability at the individual level. My discussion of Suchocki's Whiteheadian relationality above provided an extended critique of this problem, which I will not repeat here, except to say that this seems to me to be the most pressing issue in the whole constellation of problems associated with the doctrine of social sin. Self-identity and morally evaluable action are indissolubly linked. This is uncontestable. Self-identity and relationality are intimately linked. This is equally uncontestable. Yet these facts make mischief at their intersection. When my self-identity is forged in the context of, or constituted in part by, relations with others that are not my responsibility (such as in the case of victims of abuse), and my subsequent actions are determinately linked to that identity (as in the case when abuse victims perpetuate this abuse against others), how on earth can we find a way to say that relational self is still responsible for sin? Answering that question even provisionally would take another book. What I am recommending here, then, is simply a way in which continued thinking about social sin should *not* go. When the relational self is so decentred that no culpable moral

agent can be seen as the source of a sinful act, the wrong way to move forward is suddenly to posit some vestige of a 'faculty anthropology' like freedom or consciousness, to maintain responsibility at the individual level. Resorting to such faculties represents a retreat from the necessary advances we have made toward relationality.

Concluding Note

Future doctrines of sin need not choose between either pursuing the structural sin type or the relational self type. In fact, they must not. What is needed is the proper integration of *both* of these approaches, coupled with usable material from the rich traditions on how the individual sins. Lacking in all this rich (and necessary!) emphasis on the structures of sin is something like an account of what it is like actually *to sin*. Presumably, Latin American theologians think that neo-liberal capitalist robber-barons are sinning when they order wages cut in Factory X below the poverty line in order to increase profit margins by a fraction of a per cent. Yet there exists relatively little in the way of analysis for why this might be so. To shore up this potential lacuna in the adequacy of structural sin we could bring in the insights of the relational self. Perhaps the pendulum shift towards social sin, while a necessary movement, swung a bit too far. Future deliberation on social sin will have to account for the contributions of nearly all of these liberationist perspectives, and great thinkers like Ritschl and Nevin, too, if we are to inch closer to a relatively adequate formulation of the Christian doctrine of sin in both its individual and social dimensions. It is my hope and my belief that this book will be a helpful map for charting that still-to-be-explored terrain.

BIBLIOGRAPHY

Adams, Marilyn McCord. *Horrendous Evils and the Goodness of God*. Ithaca: Cornell University Press, 2000.

Ahlstrom, Sidney W. 'The Scottish Philosophy and American Theology', in *Church History* 24 (1955): 257–72.

— 'Theology in America', in James W. Smith, et al., eds, *The Shaping of American Religion*. Princeton: Princeton University Press, 1961, 232–321.

— *Theology in America: The Major Protestant Voices from Puritanism to Neo-Orthodoxy*. Indianapolis: Bobbs-Merrill, 1967.

— *A Religious History of the American People*. New Haven: Yale University Press, 1972.

Ahn, Byung-Mu. *Draussen vor dem Tor: Kirche und Minjung in Korea – Theologische Beiträge und Reflexionen*, ed. Winfried Glüer. Göttingen: Vandenhoeck and Ruprecht, 1983.

— 'The Korean Church's Understanding of Jesus: An Historical Overview', in *International Review of Mission* 74 (1985): 81–91.

— 'Minjung Bewegung und Minjung Theologie', in *Zeitschrift für Mission* 15 (1989): 18–26.

— 'Jesus and People Minjung', in R. S. Sugirtharajah, ed., *Asian Faces of Jesus*. Maryknoll: Orbis Press, 1993.

— *Jesus of Galilee*. Chai Wan, Hong Kong: Christian Conference of Asia, 2004.

Ahn, Sang Jin. *Continuity and Transformation: Religious Synthesis in East Asia*. New York: Peter Lang, 2001.

Alfaro, Juan. *Christian Liberation and Sin*. San Antonio: Mexican American Cultural Center, 1975.

— 'God Protects and Liberates the Poor', in *Option for the Poor: Challenge to the Rich Countries*, ed. Virgilio Elizondo and Leonardo Boff. Edinburgh: T&T Clark, 1986.

Alison, James. *Raising Abel: The Recovery of the Eschatological Imagination*. New York, Crossroad, 1996.

— *The Joy of Being Wrong: Original Sin through Easter Eyes*. New York: Crossroad, 1998.

Althaus, Paul. *The Ethics of Martin Luther*, trans. Robert C. Schulz. Philadelphia: Fortress, 1972.

Anscombe, G. E. M. *Intention*. Oxford: Basil Blackwell, 1979.

Appel, Theodore. *The Life and Work of John Williamson Nevin*. New York: Arno Press, 1969.

Aquino, Maria Pilar. *Our Cry for Life*, trans. Dinah Livingstone. Maryknoll: Orbis, 1993.

Arendt, Hannah. *The Human Condition*. Chicago: University of Chicago, 1958.

— *Eichmann in Jerusalem: A Report on the Banality of Evil*. New York: Viking, 1963.

— *On Violence*. New York: Harcourt, Brace and World, 1970.

Aune, Michael B. 'Removing The Barthian Spectacles', in *Dialog* 43 (2004): 223–32 and 44 (2005): 56–68.

Balasuriya, Tissa. *Human Liberation and the Eucharist*. Maryknoll: Orbis, 1977.

— 'Women and Men: Insights from Struggles for Human Liberation', in *Mid-Stream* 21 (1982): 311–23.

— *Planetary Theology*. Maryknoll: Orbis, 1984.

— 'World Apartheid: Our Greatest Structural Evil', in Mary Hembrow Snyder, ed., *Spiritual Questions for the Twenty-First Century: Essays in Honor of Joan D. Chitester.* Maryknoll: Orbis, 2001.

von Balthasar, Hans Urs. *The Theology of Karl Barth.* Ed. John Drury. New York: Anchor, 1972.

Baltzer, Klaus. *Deutero-Jesaja: Kommentar zum Alten Testament.* Gütersloh: Gütersloher Verlagshaus, 1999.

Barnes, Gilbert. *The Antislavery Impulse, 1830–44.* Gloucester: Peter Smith, 1957.

Barth, Karl. *Church Dogmatics,* 14 vols, ed. T. F. Torrance and Geoffrey Bromiley. Edinburgh: T&T Clark, 1936–77.

— *Protestantische Theologie im 19. Jahrhundert: ihre Vorgeschichte und ihre Geschichte.* Zürich: Evangelischer Verlag, 1947.

— *Protestant Thought from Rousseau to Ritschl,* trans. Brian Cozens. New York: Harper and Row, 1959.

— *The Theology of Schleiermacher,* trans. Geoffrey Bromiley. Grand Rapids: Eerdmans, 1982.

Baum, Gregory. 'Structures of Sin', in idem and Robert Ellsberg, eds, *The Logic of Solidarity: Commentaries on Pope John Paul II's Encyclical* On Social Concern. Maryknoll: Orbis, 1989.

Bauman, Zygmunt. *Postmodern Ethics.* Oxford: Blackwell, 1993.

Beardsley, Frank. *A History of American Revivals.* New York: American Tract Society, 1912.

— *A Mighty Winner of Souls: Charles Grandison Finney.* New York: American Tract Society, 1937.

Belt, R. A. *Charles Finney: A Great Evangelist.* Des Moines: Boone, 1944.

Blickle, Peter. *The Revolution of 1525: The German Peasants' War from a New Perspective* trans. Thomas A. Brady, Jr and Erik Midelfort. Baltimore: Johns Hopkins University Press, 1981.

Boadt, Lawrence. *Reading the Old Testament.* New York: Paulist Press, 1984.

Bodo, John. *The Protestant Clergy and Public Issues, 1812–1848.* New York: Random House, 1965.

Boff, Leonardo. *Jesus Christ, Liberator: A Critical Christology for Our Time,* trans. Patrick Hughes. Maryknoll: Orbis, 1978.

— *Way of the Cross – Way of Justice,* trans. John Drury. Maryknoll: Orbis, 1980.

— *The Lord's Prayer: The Prayer of Integral Liberation,* trans. Theodore Morrow. Melbourne: Dove Communications, 1983.

— *Church, Charism and Power: Liberation Theology and the Institutional Church,* trans. John Drury. Maryknoll: Crossroad, 1985.

— *Liberating Grace,* trans. John Drury. Maryknoll: Orbis, 1988.

— *Faith on the Edge,* trans. Robert B. Barr. San Francisco: Harper, 1989.

Bonino, Jose Miguez. *Doing Theology in a Revolutionary Situation.* Philadelphia: Fortress Press, 1975.

— 'A Covenant of Life', *Ecumenical Review* 33 (1981): 341–5.

— 'Love and Social Transformation in Liberation Theology', in *The Future of Liberation Theology: Essays in Honor of Gustavo Gutiérrez,* ed. Marc H. Ellis and Otto Maduro. Maryknoll, NY: Orbis Books, 1989, 121–9.

Boorstein, Daniel. *The Americans: The National Experience.* New York, Random House, 1965.

Bozeman, Theodore Dwight. *Protestants in an Age of Science: The Baconian Ideal and Antebellum American Religious Thought.* Chapel Hill: University of North Carolina Press, 1977.

Brandt, James M. 'Ritschl's Critique of Schleiermacher's Theological Ethics', in *The Journal of Religious Ethics* 17 (1989): 51–72.

Brenner, Scott Francis. 'Nevin and the Mercersburg Theology', in *Theology Today* 12 (1955): 43–56.

Brown, Raymond. *Introduction to the New Testament.* New York: Doubleday, 1997.

Brown, Robert McAfee. 'Who Is This Jesus Who Frees and Unites?' in *Ecumenical Review* 26 (1978): 6–21.

Brunner, Emil. *Der Mensch im Widerspruch: Die christliche Lehre vom wahren und vom wirklichen Menschen.* Zürich: Zwingli Verlag, 1941.

Burghardt, Walter, SJ. 'All Sin Is Social', in *Living Pulpit* 8 (1999): 42–6.

Burns, J. Patout, ed. *Theological Anthropology.* Philadelphia: Fortress Press, 1981.

Capps, Donald. *The Depleted Self: Sin in a Narcissistic Age.* Minneapolis: Fortress Press, 1993.

Carlough, William L. 'German Idealism and the Theology of John W. Nevin', in *Reformed Review* 15 (1962): 37–45.

Chai, Soo-Il. 'Einige Ansätze zum kritische Dialog mid der Minjung-Theologie', in *Zeitschrift für Mission* 17 (1991): 197–206.

Chao, Zu-Chen. *Christian Philosophy.* Shanghai: CCLP, 1926.

— *My Prison Experience.* Shanghai: CCLP, 1948.

Chapman, Mark. 'The Kingdom of God and Ethics: From Ritschl to Liberation Theology', in Robin Barbour, ed., *The Kingdom of God and Society.* Edinburgh: T&T Clark, 1993.

Chesebrough, David B. *Charles G. Finney: Revivalistic Rhetoric.* Westport, CT: Greenwood Press, 2002.

Cheeseman, Lewis. *Differences between Old School and New School Presbyterians.* Rochester: Darrow, 1848.

Chopp, Rebecca. *The Praxis of Suffering: An Interpretation of Liberation and Political Theologies.* Maryknoll, NY: Orbis, 1986.

— 'Latin American Liberation Theology', in *The Modern Theologians*, ed. David F. Ford. Oxford: Blackwell, 1997.

Christian, William A. *An Interpretation of Whitehead's Metaphysics.* New Haven: Yale University Press, 1959.

Chung Hyun Kyung. *Struggling to Be the Sun Again: Introducing Asian Women's Theology.* Maryknoll: Orbis, 1990.

Cole, Charles C. *The Social Ideas of the Northern Evangelists, 1826–1860.* New York: Columbia University Press, 1957.

Comblin, Jose. 'The Situation of Violence', in Padraig Flanagan, ed., *New Missionary Era* Maryknoll, NY: Orbis, 1982, 159–62.

— *Retrieving the Human: A Christian Anthropology*, trans. Robert R. Barr. Maryknoll, NY: Orbis, 1990.

— 'Grace', trans. Dinah Livinstone, in Jon Sobrino and Ignacio Ellacuria, eds, *Systematic Theology: Perspectives from Liberation Theology* Maryknoll, NY: Orbis, 1993.

Cone, James. 'Black Theology and the Black Church: Where Do We Go from Here?' in *Cross Currents* 13 (1977): 147–56.

— *A Black Theology of Liberation.* Maryknoll: Orbis, 1990.

Connolly, Hugh. *Sin.* London: Continuum, 2001.

Costas, Orlando E. 'Sin and Salvation in Latin America', *Theological Fraternity Bulletin* 3 (1981): 1–16.

Courth, Frank. *Das Wesen des Christentums in der liberalen Theologie: dargestellt am Werk Friedrich Schleiermachers, F.C. Baurs und A. Ritschls.* Frankfurt: Lang, 1977.

Cross, Whitney R. *The Burned-Over District: Social and Intellectual History of Enthusiastic Religion in Western New York, 1800–1850.* New York: Harper and Row, 1965.

Daly, Mary. *The Church and the Second Sex.* Boston: Beacon, 1967.

Davidson, Donald. *Essays on Actions and Events.* Oxford: Clarendon, 1980.

Davis, William. 'Davis' Plea', in *Lutheran Observer* 12 (1843): 32.

Dayton, Donald W. 'Engaging the World: The Evangelism of Charles Finney', in *Sojourners* 15 (March, 1984): 17–19.

Deddo, Gary W. *Karl Barth's Theology of Relations*. New York: Peter Lang, 1999.

Deegan, Daniel L. 'The Ritschlian School: The Essence of Christianity and Karl Barth', in *Scottish Journal of Theology* 16 (1963): 390–414.

DeVries, Dawn, ed. and trans., *Servant of the Word: Selected Sermons of Friedrich Schleiermacher.* Philadelphia: Fortress, 1987.

DiPuccio, William. 'Nevin's Idealistic Philosophy', in Sam Hamstra, Jr and Arie J. Griffioen, eds, *Reformed Confessionalism in Nineteenth Century America: Essays on the Thought of John Williamson Nevin.* Lanham, MD: Scarecrow Press, 1995, 43–68.

Dorner, Isaak A. *Entwicklungsgeschichte der Lehre von der Person Christi von den ältesten Zeiten bis auf die neueste dargestellt,* 2 vols. Berlin, Schlawitz, 1851–3.

Drummond, Lewis A. *Charles Grandison Finney and the Birth of Modern Evangelism.* London: Hodder and Stoughton, 1983.

Duke, James. 'The Christian and the Ethical in Schleiermacher's Christian Ethics', in *Encounter* 46 (1985): 51–69.

Dunfee, Susan Nelson. 'The Sin of Hiding', in *Soundings* 65 (1982): 316–27.

Dyson, Michael Eric. *I May Not Get There With You: The True Martin Luther King, Jr.* New York: Touchstone, 2001.

Ehrhard, James. 'Asahel Nettleton: Forgotten Evangelist', in *Reformation and Revival* 6 (1997): 62–79.

Elliot, Charles. 'Structures, Sin and Personal Holiness', in Haddon Willmer, ed., *Christian Faith and Political Hopes*. London, Epworth, 1979.

Ely, Ezra Stiles. *A Contrast between Calvinism and Hopkinsianism.* New York: S. Whiting, 1811.

Engel, Mary Potter. 'Evil, Sin, and the Violation of the Vulnerable', in *Lift Every Voice: Constructing Christian Theologies from the Underside,* idem and Susan Brooks Thistlethwaite, eds San Francisco: Harper, 1990, 152–164.

Etchegoyen, Aldo. 'Theology of Sin and Structures of Oppression', in Dow Kirkpatrick, ed., *Faith Born in the Struggle for Life: A Reading of Protestant Faith in Latin America Today.* Grand Rapids: Eerdmans, 1988.

Farley, Edward. *Good and Evil: Interpreting a Human Condition.* Minneapolis: Fortress, 1990.

Fernandez, Eleazar. *Toward a Theology of Struggle.* Maryknoll: Orbis, 1994.

— *Reimagining the Human: Theological Anthropology in Response to Systemic Evils.* St. Louis: Chalice Press, 2003.

— and Fernando Segovia, eds, *A Dream Unfinished: Theological Reflections on America from the Margins.* Maryknoll: Orbis, 2001.

Finney, Charles Grandison. *Skeletons of a Course of Theological Lectures.* Oberlin: James Steele, 1840.

— *Views on Sanctification.* Oberlin: James Steele, 1840.

— 'Recent Discussions on the Subject of Entire Sanctification in This Life', in *Oberlin Quarterly Review* 2 (1847): 449–72.

— *Lectures on Systematic Theology,* ed. J. H. Fairchild. Grand Rapids: Eerdmans, 1957.

— *So Great Salvation: Evangelistic Messages.* Grand Rapids: Kredel Publishing, 1965.

— *Sermons on Gospel Themes.* Oberlin: E. J. Goodrich, 1876.

— *Lectures to Professing Christians.* New York: Fleming H. Revell, 1878.

— *Lectures on Revival.* St Paul: Bethany, 1988.

— *The Original Memoirs of Charles G. Finney,* ed. Garth M. Rossell and Richard G. Dupuis. Grand Rapids: Zondervan, 2002.

Fischer, Hermann. *Subjektivität und Sünde: Kierkegaards Begriff der Sünde mit ständiger Rücksicht auf Schleiermachers Lehre von der Sünde.* Itzehoe: Spur Verlag, 1963.

Ford, David. *Self and Salvation: Being Transformed*. Cambridge: Cambridge University Press, 1999.

Frei, Hans W. *Types of Christian Theology*, William C. Placher and George Hunsinger. New Haven: Yale University Press, 1992.

Fulkerson, Mary McClintock. 'Sexism as Original Sin: Developing a Theacentric Discourse', in *Journal of the American Academy of Religion* 59 (1991): 653–75.

— *Changing the Subject: Women's Discourses and Feminist Theology*. Minneapolis: Fortress, 1994.

— 'Contesting the Gendered Subject: A Feminist Account of the *Imago Dei*', in Rebecca S. Chopp and Sheila Grave Devaney, eds, *Horizons in Feminist Theology: Identity, Tradition and Norms*. Minneapolis: Fortress, 1997, 99–115.

Garvie, Alfred E. *The Ritschlian Theology: Critical and Constructive*. Edinburgh: T&T Clark, 1902.

Gebara, Ivonne, 'Option for the Poor as an Option for Poor Women', in Elisabeth Schüssler Fiorenza, ed., *The Power of Naming: A* Concilium *Reader in Feminist Liberation Theology*. Maryknoll: Orbis, 1996.

— 'The Trinity and Human Experience: An Ecofeminist Approach', in Rosemary Radford Ruether, ed., *Women Healing Earth: Third World Women on Ecology, Feminism and Religion*. Maryknoll: Orbis, 1996.

— *Longing for Running Water: Ecofeminism and Liberation*, trans. David Molineaux. Minneapolis: Fortress, 1999.

— *Out of the Depths: Women's Experience of Evil and Salvation*, trans. Ann Patrick Ware. Minneapolis: Fortress, 2002.

Gerrish, Brian A. *Tradition and the Modern World: Reformed Theology in the Nineteenth Century*. Chicago: University of Chicago Press, 1978.

— *Grace and Gratitude: The Eucharistic Theology of John Calvin*. Minneapolis: Fortress, 1993.

Gestrich, Christof. *Wiederkehr des Glanzes in der Welt die christliche Lehre von der Sünde und ihrer Vergebung in gegenwärtiger Verantwortung*. Tübingen: Mohr, 1989.

— *Peccatum – Studien zur Sündenlehre*. Tübingen: Mohr Siebeck, 2003.

Girard, Rene. *The Scapegoat*, trans. Yvonne Frecerro. Baltimore: Johns Hopkins University Press, 1986.

— *Things Hidden since the Foundation of the World*, trans. Stephen Bann. Palo Alto: Stanford University Press, 1987.

— *I See Satan Fall Like Lightning*, trans. James G. Williams. Maryknoll: Orbis, 2001.

Glüer, Winfried. *Christliche Theologie in China: T.C. Chao, 1918–1959*. Gütersloh: Mohn, 1979.

Goldsmith, Timothy. *The Biological Roots of Human Nature: Forging Links between Evolution and Behavior*. New York: Oxford University Press, 1991.

— *Biology, Evolution, and Human Nature*. New York: John Wiley, 2001.

González, Justo L. 'Searching for a Liberating Anthropology', in *Theology Today* 34 (1978): 386–94.

— *Mañana: Christian Theology from a Hispanic Perspective*. Nashville: Abingdon, 1990.

— 'The Alienation of Alienation', in Andrew Sung Park and Susan L. Nelson, eds, *The Other Side of Sin: Woundedness from the Perspective of the Sinned-Against*. Albany: SUNY Press, 2001.

— and Catherine G. Gonzalez, *Liberation Preaching*. Nashville: Abingdon, 1980.

Graby, James K. 'The Problem of Ritschl's Relationship to Schleiermacher', in *The Scottish Journal of Theology* 19 (1966): 257–68.

Graff, Ann O'Hara. *In the Embrace of God: Feminist Approaches to Theological Anthropology*. Maryknoll: Orbis, 1995.

Grant, Jacquelyn. 'Black Theology and the Black Woman', in Gayraud S. Wilmore and James H. Cone, eds, *Black Theology: A Documentary History, 1966–1979*. Maryknoll: Orbis, 1979.

— 'Womanist Theology: Black Women's Experience as a Source for Doing Theology, with Special Reference to Christology', in *Journal of the Interdenominational Theology Center* 13 (1985): 189–204.

— *White Women's Christ and Black Women's Jesus*. Atlanta: Scholar's Press, 1989.

— 'The Sin of Servanthood: And the Deliverance of Discipleship', in Emilie Townes, ed., *A Troubling in My Soul: Womanist Perspectives on Evil and Suffering*. Maryknoll: Orbis, 1993, 199–218.

Green, Bonnie. 'Women, Men, and Corporate Sin', in Roberta Hestenes, et al., eds, *Women and the Ministry of Christ*. Pasadena: Fuller Theological Seminary, 1979.

Grenz, Stanley. *The Social God and the Relational Self*. Louisville: Westminster John Knox, 2000.

Grover, Norman 'The Church and Social Action in Finney, Bushnell, and Gladden', PhD diss., Vanderbilt University, 1957.

Gudorf, Christine. 'Admonishing the Sinner: Owning Structural Sin' in Francis A. Eigo, ed., *Rethinking the Spiritual Works of Mercy*. Villanova: Villanova University Press, 1983.

Gutiérrez, Gustavo. *The Power of the Poor in History*, trans. Robert B. Barr. Maryknoll, NY: Orbis, 1983.

— *We Drink from Our Own Wells: The Spiritual Journey of a People*, trans. Matthew J. O'Connell. Maryknoll, NY: Orbis, 1984.

— *On Job: God-Talk and the Suffering of the Innocent*, trans. Matthew J. O'Connell. Maryknoll: Orbis, 1987.

— *A Theology of Liberation: History, Politics, Salvation*, trans. Sister Caridad Inda and John Eagleson. London: SCM, 1988.

— 'Toward a Theology of Liberation', trans. Jeffrey Klaiber, SJ, in Alfred Hennelly, SJ, ed., *Liberation History: A Documentary History*. Maryknoll: Orbis Books, 1990, 62–76.

— *The Truth Shall Make You Free: Confrontations*, trans. Matthew J. O'Connell. Maryknoll, NY: Orbis, 1990.

Hambrick-Stowe, Charles E. *Charles G. Finney and the Spirit of American Evangelicalism*. Grand Rapids: Eerdmans, 1996.

Hampson, Daphne. 'Reinhold Niebuhr on Sin: A Critique', in *Reinhold Niebuhr and the Issues of Our Time*, ed. Richard Harries. London: Mowbray, 1986.

— 'Luther on the Self: A Feminist Critique', in *Feminist Theology: A Reader*. Louisville: Westminster John Knox, 1990, 215–25.

Hardman, Keith J. *Charles Grandison Finney, 1792–1875: Revivalist and Reformer*. Syracuse, Syracuse University Press, 1987.

Häring, Bernard. *Sünde im Zeitalter der Säkularisation*. Graz: Verlag Styria, 1974.

Hart, David Bentley. *The Doors of the Sea: Where Was God in the Tsunami?* Grand Rapids: Eerdmans, 2005.

Hatch, Nathan. *The Democratization of American Religion*. New Haven: Yale University Press, 1989.

Heesch, Matthias. 'Transzendentale Individualität? Schleiermacher und sein Schüler Rothe im Streit um das Wesen des Endlich-Gegebenen', in *Neue Zeitschrift fur Systematische Theologie* 35 (1993): 259–95.

Hefner, Philip. *Faith and the Vitalities of History: A Theological Study Based on the Work of Albrecht Ritschl*. New York: Harper and Row, 1966.

— 'The Concreteness of the Kingdom: A Problem for the Christian Life', in *Journal of Religion* 51 (1971): 188–205.

— 'Albrecht Ritschl: An Introduction', in idem, ed., *Three Essays*. Philadelphia: Fortress, 1972, 1–51.

— *The Human Factor: Evolution, Culture and Religion*. Minneapolis: Fortress Press, 1993.

Hemmenway, Moses. *Vindication of the Power, Obligation, etc., of the Unregenerate to Attend the Means of Grace, against the Exceptions of Samuel Hopkins in His Reply to Mills*. Boston: Kneeland, 1772.

Hennelly, Alfred T., SJ. 'The Red-Hot Issue: Liberation Theology', in *America* 157 (May 24, 1986): 424–31.

— ed. *Liberation History: A Documentary History*. Maryknoll: Orbis Books, 1990.

Henriot, Peter. 'Social Sin: The Recovery of a Christian Tradition', in James D. Whitehead, ed., *Method in Ministry*. New York: Seabury, 1980.

Heron, Alasdair I. C. *A Century of Protestant Theology*. Philadelphia: Westminster Press, 1980.

Hewitt, Glenn A. *Regeneration and Morality: A Study of Charles Finney, Charles Hodge, John W. Nevin and Horace Bushnell*. Brooklyn: Carlson Publishing, 1991.

— 'Nevin on Regeneration', in Sam Hamstra, Jr and Arie J. Griffioen, eds, *Reformed Confessionalism in Nineteenth Century America: Essays on the Thought of John Williamson Nevin*. Lanham, MD: Scarecrow Press, 1995, 153–68.

Heyward, Carter. *The Redemption of God: A Theology of Mutual Relation*. Washington, DC: University Press of America, 1982.

— *Saving Jesus from Those Who Are Right*. Minneapolis: Fortress, 1999.

Hick, John. *Evil and the God of Love*. London: Macmillan, 1960.

Hille, Rolf. 'The Radical Modernizing of the Christian Doctrine of Reconciliation and Redemption', in *Evangelical Review of Theology* 23 (1999): 222–37.

Himes, Kenneth. 'Social Sin and the Role of the Individual', in *Annual of the Society* 6 (1986): 183–218.

Hinkelammert, Franz. 'Befreiung, soziale Sünde und subjektive Verantwortlichkeit: Anmerkungen zu einem politischen Dokument' in Herbert Vorgrimler, et al., eds, *Das Lehramt der Kirche und der Schrei der Armen: Analysen zur Instruktion der Kongregation für die Glaubenslehre über einige Aspekte der 'Theologie der Befreiung'*. Freiburg: Editions Exodus, 1985.

Hodge, Charles. *Systematic Theology*, 3 vols, London: Clarke, 1960.

Hofmann, Franz. *Albrecht Ritschls Lutherrezeption*. Gütersloh: Gütersloher Verlagshaus, 1998.

Hoffmann-Richter, Andreas. *Ahn Byung-Mu als Minjung Theologe*. Gütersloh: Gütersloher Verlagshaus Gerd Mohn, 1990.

Hofstadter, Richard. *Anti-Intellectualism in American Life*. New York: Knopf, 1966.

Hök, Gösta. *Die elliptische Theologie Albrecht Ritschls*. Uppsala: Appelbergs, 1942.

Hoitenga, Dewey. 'The Noetic Effects of Sin: A Review Article', in *Calvin Theological Journal* 38 (2003): 68–102.

Holifield, E. Brooks. *Theology in America: Christian Thought from the Age of the Puritans to the Civil War*. New Haven: Yale University Press, 2003.

Hopkins, Dwight. *Heart and Head: Black Theology – Past, Present, and Future*. New York: Palgrave, 2002.

Husserl, Edmund. *Ideas: General Introduction to Pure Phenomenology*, trans. W. R. Boyce Gibson. London: Allen, 1931.

Hyun, Young-Hak. 'Minjung Theology and the Religion of Han', *East Asia Journal of Religion* 3 (1985): 354–9.

Isai-Diaz, Ada Maria. *En la Lucha: Elaborating a* Mujerista *Theology*. Minneapolis: Fortress, 1993.

Ishida, Manabu. 'Doing Theology in Japan: The Alternative Way of Reading the Scriptures as the Book of Sacred Drama in Dialogue with Minjung Theology', in *Missiology: An International Review* 22 (1994): 55–63.

Jepson, J. W., ed. *A Digest of Finney's Systematic Theology*. Ashland: Jepson, 1970.

Jodock, Darrell, ed. *Ritschl in Retrospect: History, Community and Science.* Minneapolis: Fortress Press, 1995.

Johnson, Elizabeth. *She Who Is.* New York: Crossroad, 1992.

Johnson, William Stacy, *The Mystery of God: Karl Barth and the Postmodern Foundations of Theology.* Louisville: Westminster John Knox, 1997.

Jones, Serene. *Calvin and the Rhetoric of Piety.* Louisville: Westminster John Knox Press, 1995.

— *Feminist Theory and Christian Theology: Cartographies of Grace.* Minneapolis: Fortress, 2000.

— 'Bounded Openness: Postmodernism, Feminism and the Church Today', in *Interpretation* 55 (2001), 49–59.

— 'Companionable Wisdoms: What Insights Might Feminist Theorists Gather from Feminist Theologians?' in *Blackwell Companion to Postmodern Theology.* Oxford: Blackwell, 2001, 294–308.

— 'Graced Practices', in *Practicing Theology.* Dorothy Bass, et al., eds, Grand Rapids: Eerdmans, 2002, 51–71.

Julian of Norwich. *Revelations of Divine Love*, trans. Elizabeth Spearing. London, Penguin, 1998.

Junker, Maureen. *Das Urbild des Gottesbewusstseins: zur Entwicklung der Religionstheorie und Christologie Schleiermachers von der ersten zur zweiten Auflage der Glaubenslehre.* Berlin: Walter de Gruyter, 1990.

Kang, Namsoon. 'Who/What is Asian? A Postcolonial Theological Reading of Orientalism and Neo-Orientalism' in Catherine Keller, et al., eds, *Postcolonial Theologies: Divinity and Empire.* St Louis: Chalice Press, 2004.

Kant, Immanuel. *Religion within the Bounds of Reason Alone*, trans. Hoyt Hudson and Theodore Green. New York: Harper, 1960.

— *Groundwork of the Metaphysics of Morals*, trans. H. J. Patton. New York, Harper, 1964.

— *Critique of Pure Reason*, trans. P. Guyer and Allen Wood. Cambridge: Cambridge University Press, 1998.

Kasper, Walter. 'Die Lehre der Kirche vom Bösen', in *Macht des Bösen und der Glaube der Kirche*, ed. Rudolf Schnackenburg. Düsseldorf: Patmos, 1979, 68–84.

Keller, Catherine. *From a Broken Web: Separation, Sexism, and Self.* Boston: Beacon, 1986.

— *Postcolonial Theologies: Divinity and Empire.* St Louis: Chalice Press, 2004.

Kelsey, David. 'Whatever Happened to the Doctrine of Sin?' in *Theology Today* 50 (1993): 169–78.

— *Imagining Redemption.* Louisville: Westminster John Knox Press, 2005.

Kendall, Anthony Barrett. 'Riding the Anxious Bench: Enthusiasm, Conversion and Performance in Early American Revivals', PhD diss., Stanford University, 2008.

Kerans, Patrick. *Sinful Social Structures.* New York: Paulist, 1974.

Kierkegaard, Søren. *The Concept of Anxiety*, trans. Reidar Thomte. Princeton: Princeton University Press, 1980.

— *The Sickness unto Death*, trans. Alastair Hannay. London: Penguin, 1989.

— *Works of Love*, trans. Howard V. Hong and Edna H. Hong. Princeton: Princeton University Press, 1995.

Kim, Chang-Nack. 'Arbeitskämpfe in der Dritten Welt, am Beispiel der Arbeiterbewegung in Südkorea', in Luise und Willy Schottrof, eds, *Mitarbeiter der Schöpfung: Bibel und Arbeitswelt.* München: Christian Kaiser Verlag, 1983.

— 'Korean Minjung Theology: An Overview', in *Register* 85 (1995): 1–13.

— 'Justification by Faith – A Minjung Perspective', in *Register* 85 (1995): 14–23.

Kim, Kirsteen. 'India', in John Parratt, ed., *An Introduction to Third World Theologies.* Cambridge: Cambridge University Press, 2004.

Kim, Heup-Young. 'A Tao of Asian Theology in the 21st Century', *CTC Bulletin* 15 (1998): 60–73.

Kim, Myung Hyuk. 'The Concept of God in Minjung Theology and Its Socio-Economic and Historical Characteristics', in *Evangelical Review of Theology* (1990): 126–49.

Kim, Won-Bae. 'Bonhoeffer and Barth in the Light of Liberation and Minjung Theologies: An Attempt to Bring Together Living Traditions', in Paul S. Chung and Frank D. Macchia, eds, *Theology Between East and West: A Radical Heritage*. Eugene, OR: Wipf and Stock, 2003.

Kim, Yong-Bock. 'The Social Biography of the Minjung and Theology', in *Minjung and Theology in Korea*. Hong Kong: World Student Christian Fedearation, 1979.

— 'Minjung and Power: A Biblical and Theological Perspective on *Doularchy* Servanthood', in Nantawan Boonprasat Lewis, ed., *Revolution of Spirit: Ecumenical Theology in Global Context*. Grand Rapids, MI: Eerdmans, 1998.

Kim Chung-choon. 'The Old Testament Basis for Minjung Theology', in *Minjung and Theology in Korea*. Singapore: CTC, 1981.

Krötke, Wolf. *Sünde und Nichtige bei Karl Barth*. Berlin: Neukirchener Verlag, 1983.

Kuhlmann, Helga. *Die theologische Ethik Albrecht Ritschls*. München: Kaiser Verlag, 1992.

Küster, Volker. *Jesus und das Volk im Markusevangelium: Ein Beitrag zum interkulturellen Gespräch in der Exegese*. Neukirchen-Vluyn: Neukirchener Verlag, 1996.

Lee, Jae Hoon. *The Exploration of the Inner Wounds – Han*. Atlanta: Scholars Press, 1994.

Lee, Jung Young. *The I: A Christian Doctrine of Man*. New York: Philosophical Library, 1971.

— ed. *An Emerging Theology in World Perspective: Commentary on Korean Minjung Theology*. Mystic, CT: Twenty Third Publications, 1988.

Lee-Linke, Sung-Hee. 'Jesus und Minjung ὄχλος: Kontextualisierung des Evangeliums in der Minjung-Theologie', in Ingo Baldermann, et al., eds *Glaube und Öffentlichkeit*. Neukirchen-Vluyn: Neukirchener Verlag, 1996.

Lindberg, Carter. 'Luther's Struggle with Social-Ethical Issues', in Donald K. McKim, ed., *The Cambridge Companion to Martin Luther*. Cambridge: Cambridge University Press, 2003, 165–78.

Littlefair, Duncan. *Sin Comes of Age*. Philadelphia: Westminster, 1975.

Lochmann, Jan Milic. 'Das so genannte Böse: zur Aktualität des biblischen Sündenbegriffs', in *Reformatio* 32 (1983): 465–71.

Lotz, David W. *Ritschl and Luther: A Fresh Perspective on Albrecht Ritschl's Theology in Light of His Luther Study*. Nashville: Abingdon, 1974.

— 'Albrecht Ritschl and the Heritage of the Reformation', in *Revisioning the Past: Prospects in Historical Theology*, ed. Mary Potter Engel and Walter E. Wyman, Jr. Minneapolis: Fortress Press, 1992.

Lowe, Mary Elise. 'Woman Oriented Hamartiologies: A Survey of the Shift from Powerlessness to Right Relationship', in *Dialog* 39 (2000): 119–39.

— 'The Human Subject and Sin: Autonomy, Relation, or Constitution?' PhD diss., Graduate Theological Union, 2004.

McAfee Brown, Robert. 'The Roman Curia and Liberation Theology: The Second (and Final?) Round', in *Christian Century* 103 (1986): 552–6.

Macartney, Clarence E. 'Finney and the Atonement', in *The Presbyterian* July 30, 1942: 6–43.

McDowell, James. 'Learning Where to Place One's Hope: The Eschatological Significance of Election in Barth', *Scottish Journal of Theology* 53 no. 3 (2000), 320–56.

McFague, Sallie. *The Body of God: An Ecological Theology*. Minneapolis: Fortress, 1993.

McFadyen, Alistair. *The Call to Personhood: A Christian Theory of the Individual in Social Relationships*. Cambridge: Cambridge University Press, 1990.

— *Bound to Sin: Abuse, Holocaust and the Christian Doctrine of Sin*. Cambridge, UK: Cambridge University Press, 2000.

McFarland, Ian A. *Difference and Identity: A Theological Anthropology*. Cleveland: Pilgrim Press, 2001.

McGill, Arthur C. 'Structures of Inhumanity', in Alan M. Olson, ed., *Disguises of the Demonic: Contemporary Perspectives on the Power of Evil*. New York: Association Press, 1975.

Mackie, Steven. 'God's People in Asia: A Key Concept in Asian Theology', in *Scottish Journal of Theology* 42 (1990): 215–40.

MacKinnon, Mary Heather and Moni McIntyre, eds, *Readings in Ecology and Feminist Theology*. Kansas City: Sheed and Ward, 1995.

Madden, Edward H. 'Holiness Thought and the Moral Image of Man', in *The Asbury Theological Journal* 43 (1988): 45–61.

Mallow, Vernon R. *The Demonic: An Examination into the Theology of Edwin Lewis, Karl Barth and Paul Tillich*. New York: University Press of America, 1983.

Marsden, George. *The Evangelical Mind and the New School Presbyterian Expereince: A Case Study of Thought and Theology in Nineteenth Century America*. New Haven: Yale University Press, 1970.

Marty, Martin E. *Religious Empire: The Protestant Experience in America*. New York: Dial Press, 1970.

Mathewes, Charles. *Evil and the Augustinian Tradition*. Cambridge, UK: Cambridge University Press, 2000.

Matsuoka, Fumitaka, and Eleazar Fernandez, eds, *Realizing the America of our Hearts: Theological Voices of Asian Americans*. St Louis: Chalice, 2003.

Mechthild of Magdeburg. *The Flowing Light of Godhead*, trans. Christiane Mesch Galvani. New York: Garland, 1991.

Mercadante, Linda. *Victims and Sinners: Spiritual Roots of Addiction and Recovery*. Louisville: Westminster John Knox, 1996.

Menninger, Karl, *Whatever Became of Sin?* New York: Hawthorn, 1973.

Miller, Perry. *The Life of the Mind in America: From the Revolution to the Civil War*. New York: Harcourt, Brace and World, 1965.

Millet, Olivier. *Calvin et la dynamique de la parole: Etude de la rhetorique reformee*. Genève: *Editions Slatkine*, 1992.

Moltmann, Jürgen. *Experiences in Theology: Ways and Forms of Christian Theology*, trans. Margaret Kohl. Minneapolis: Fortress Press, 2000.

Mott, Stephen Charles. 'Biblical Faith and the Reality of Social Evil', in *Christian Scholar's Review* 9 (1980): 225–40.

Mueller, David L. *An Introduction to the Theology of Albrecht Ritschl*. Philadelphia: Westminster, 1969.

— 'Albrecht Ritschl 1822–89: Prophet of a New Christianity?' in *Review and Expositor* 67 (1970): 353–67.

Nevin, John Williamson. 'Our Union with Christ', in *Weekly Messenger of the German Reformed Church* 13 (1848), 23–43.

— 'True and False Protestantism', in *Mercersburg Review* 1 (1849): 83–104.

— *Human Freedom and a Plea for Philosophy*. Mercersburg: Rice, 1850.

— 'Moral Philosophy', Notes prepared by Benjamin Bausman, 5 September 1850. Lancaster, PA: Historical Society of the Evangelical and Reformed Church, n.d.

— 'The New Creation in Christ', in *Mercersburg Review* 2 (1850): 1–11.

— 'Man's True Destiny', in *Mercersburg Review* 5 (1853): 492–520.

— 'The Moral Order of Sex', in *Mercersburg Review* 2 (1850): 549–73.

— 'Natural and Supernatural', in *Mercersburg Review* 11 (1859): 176–210.

— 'The Wonderful Nature of Man', in *Mercersburg Review* 11 (1859): 317–37.

— 'Answer to Professor Dorner', in *Mercersburg Review* 15 (1868): 532–646.

— 'Nature and Grace', in *Mercersburg Review* 19 (1872): 485–509.
— 'Christianity and Humanity', in *Mercersburg Review* 20 (1873): 469–86.
— 'Biblical Anthropology', in *Mercersburg Review* 24 (1877): 329–65.
— *The Anxious Bench, Antichrist, and Sermon on Catholic Unity*, ed. Augustine Thompson, OP. Eugene: Wipf and Stock, 2000.
— *The Mystical Presence: A Vindication of the Reformed or Calvinistic Doctrine of the Holy Eucharist*, ed. Augustine Thompson, OP. Eugene: Wipf and Stock, 2000.
Nichols, James Hastings. *Romanticism in American Theology: Nevin and Schaff at Mercersburg*. Chicago: University of Chicago Press, 1961.
— ed. *The Mercersburg Theology*. New York: Oxford University Press, 1966.
Nicolaisen, Poul Juul. *Samfund og individ i Albrecht Ritschls teologi*. Copenhagen: Gads, 1972.
Niebuhr, H. Richard. *Christ and Culture*. San Francisco: Harper, 2001.
Niebuhr, Reinhold. *Moral Man and Immoral Society*. New York: Charles Scribner's Sons, 1932.
— *The Nature and Destiny of Man*, 2 vols. New York, Charles Scribner's Sons, 1941.
— *Man's Nature and His Communities*. New York: Charles Scribner's Sons, 1965.
Niebuhr, Richard R. *Schleiermacher on Christ and Religion*. New York: Charles Scribner's Sons, 1964.
Ogden, Schubert. *Faith and Freedom: Toward a Theology of Liberation*. Nashville: Abingdon, 1979.
— 'The Concept of a Theology of Liberation: Must a Christian Theology Today Be So Conceived?' in Brian Mahan and L. Dale Richesin, eds, *The Challenge of Liberation Theology: A First World Response*. Maryknoll, NY: Orbis, 1981, 127–40.
O'Keefe, Mark. *What Are They Saying About Social Sin?* New York: Paulist Press, 1990.
— 'Social Sin and Fundamental Option', in Clayton N. Jefford, ed., *Christian Freedom* New York: Peter Lang, 1993.
Orchard, W. E. *Modern Theories of Sin*. London: James Clarke, 1909.
Panikkar, Raimundo. *Invisible Harmony: Essays on Contemplation and Responsibility*. Minneapolis: Fortress, 1995.
— 'Sunyata and Pleroma: Buddhist and Christian Response to the Human Predicament', in *The Intrareligious Dialogue*. New York: Paulist, 1999.
— *Christophany: The Fullness of Man*. Maryknoll: Orbis, 2004.
Pannenberg, Wolfhart. *Theology and the Kingdom of God*, ed. Richard John Neuhaus. Philadelphia: Westminster Press, 1969.
— *What is Man?*, trans. Duane A. Priebe. Philadelphia: Fortress, 1970.
— *The Idea of God and Human Freedom*, trans. R. A. Wilson. Philadelphia: Westminster, 1973.
— 'Person und Subjekt', in *Neue Zeitschrift für Systematische Theologie und Religionsphilosophie* 18:2 (1976), 133–48.
— *Human Nature, Election and History*. Philadelphia: Westminster, 1977.
— *Grundfragen Systematischer Theologie*, vol. 2. Göttingen: Vandenhoeck and Ruprecht, 1980.
— *Anthropology in Theological Perspective*, trans. Matthew J. O'Connell. Philadelphia: Westminster, 1985.
— *Sind wir von Natur aus religiös?*, Düsseldorf: Patmos, 1986.
— 'Sünde, Freiheit, Idenität: Eine Antwort an Thomas Pröpper', *Theolgogische Quartalschrift* 174:4 (1990), 289–98.
— *Systematic Theology* 3 vols., trans. Geoffrey W. Bromiley. Grand Rapids: Eerdmans, 1991–8.
Park, Andrew Sung. 'Minjung and Process Hermeneutics', in *Process Studies* 17 (1988): 118–26.
— 'Theology of Han: The Abyss of Pain', in *Quarterly Review* 9 (1989): 48–62.

— *The Wounded Heart of God: The Asian Concept of Han and the Christian Doctrine of Sin*. Nashville: Abingdon, 1992.

— 'Sin and Han: The Pain of a Victim', in *Living Pulpit* 9 (1999): 22–3,

— 'A Theology of the Way (*Tao*)', in *Interpretation: A Journal of Bible and Theology* 55 (2001): 389–99.

— 'A Theology of Transmutation', in Fernando Segovia and Eleazar Fernandez, eds, *A Dream Unfinished*. Maryknoll: Orbis, 2001, 152–66,

— 'A Theology of Enhancement: Multiculturality in Self and Community', in *Journal of Pastoral Theology* 13 (2003): 14–33.

— 'The Formation of Multicultural Religious Identity within Persons in Korean-American Experience', in *Journal of Pastoral Theology* 13 (2003): 34–50.

— 'Holiness and Healing: An Asian American Voice Shaping the Methodist Tradition', in Joerg Rieger and John Vincent, eds, *Methodist and Radical: Rejuvenating a Tradition*. Nashville: Kingswood Books, 2003.

— 'Sin', in Miguel A. De La Torre, ed., *Handbook of U.S. Theologies of Liberation*. St. Louis: Chalice Press, 2004.

— and Susan L. Nelson, eds, *The Other Side of Sin: Woundedness from the Perspective of the Sinned Against*. Albany: SUNY Press, 2001.

Peters, Ted. *Sin: Radical Evil in Soul and Society*. Grand Rapids: Eerdmans, 1994.

Phelps, Jamie T. 'Joy Came in the Morning Risking Joy for the Resurrection: Confronting the Evil of Social Sin and Socially Sinful Structures', in Emilie Townes, ed., *A Troubling in My Soul: Womanist Perspectives on Evil and Suffering*. Maryknoll: Orbis, 1993.

Pieper, Josef. *Über den Begriff der Sünde*. München: Kösel, 1977.

Pieris, Aloysius. 'Das Christentum des Westens und die Religionen des Ostens: Ein theologische Vortrag über historische Begegnungen', in Franz Lembeck, ed., *Theologie in der Dritten Welt*. Hamburg: Evangelisches Missionswerk, 1979, 4–39.

— *An Asian Theology of Liberation*. Maryknoll: Orbis, 1988.

Placher, William C. *A History of Christian Theology* Louisville: Westminster John Knox Press, 1983.

— *The Domestication of Transcendence: Where Modern Thinking about God Went Wrong*. Louisville: Westminster John Knox, 1996.

Plantinga, Cornelius, Jr. *Not the Way It's Supposed to Be: A Breviary of Sin*. Grand Rapids: Eerdmans, 1995.

Plaskow, Judith. *Sex, Sin and Grace: Women's Experience and the Theologies of Reinhold Niebuhr and Paul Tillich*. Lanham: University Press of America, 1980.

Portman, John. *In Defense of Sin*. New York: Palgrave, 2001.

Preus, Robert D. *The Theology of Post-Reformation Lutheranism*, 2 vols. St Louis: Concordia, 1970.

Pröpper, Thomas. 'Schleiermachers Bestimmung des Christentums und der Erlösung', in *Theologische Quartalschrift* 168 (1988): 193–214.

Purvis, Sally B. *The Power of the Cross: Foundations for a Christian Feminist Ethic of Community*. Nashville: Abingdon, 1993.

Rahner, Karl, SJ. *Foundations of Christian Faith*, trans William van Dych. New York: Crossroad, 1978.

Ramm, Bernard. *An Offense to Reason: A Theology of Sin*. San Francisco: Harper and Row, 1986.

Rauch, Friedrich Augustus. *Psychology, Or a View of the Human Soul*. New York: Dodd, 1841.

Rauschenbusch, Walter. *A Theology for the Social Gospel*. Nashville: Abingdon, 1978.

Ray, Stephen G. *Do No Harm: Social Sin and Christian Responsibility*. Minneapolis: Fortress, 2003.

Reed, Duncan and Mark Worthing, eds *Sin and Salvation*. Hindmarsh, Australia: ATF Press, 2003.

Richmond, James. *Ritschl: A Reappraisal – A Study in Systematic Theology.* London: Collins, 1978.

Richter, Andreas Hoffmann. 'Biographische Hinweise und Erläuterung zu den Texten', in Ahn Byung-Mu, *Draussen vor dem Tor: Kirche und Minjung in Korea* , ed. Winfried Glüer. Göttingen: Vandenhoeck and Ruprect, 1986, 151–6.

— *Ahn Byung-Mu als Minjung Theologe.* Gütersloh: Mohn, 1990.

Ricoeur, Paul. *Oneself as Another*, trans. Kathleen Blamey. Chicago: University of Chicago Press, 1992.

Ringleben, Joachim. *Reich Gottes und menschliche Freibet.* Göttingen: Vandenhoeck und Ruprecht, 1990.

Ritschl, Albrecht. *Entstehung der altkatolischen Kirche: Eine kirchen- und dogmengeschichtliche Monographie.* Bonn: Adolph Marcus, 1850.

— *A Critical History of the Christian Doctrine of Justification and Reconciliation*, trans. John S. Black. Edinburgh: Edmonston and Douglas, 1872.

— *Rechtfertigung und Versöhnung*, vol. II. Bonn: Adolph Marcus, 1872.

— *Schleiermachers Reden über die Religion und ihre Nachwirkungen auf die evangelsishe Kirche Deutschlands.* Bonn: Adolph Marcus, 1874.

— *The Christian Doctrine of Justification and Reconciliation*, trans. H. R. Mackintosh and A. B. Macaulay. Edinburgh: T&T Clark, 1900.

— 'Instruction in the Christian Religion', 'Prolegomena to *The History of Pietism*', and 'Theology and Metaphysics', in Philip Hefner, ed., *Three Essays*. Philadelphia: Fortress Press, 1971.

Rodin, Scott. *Evil and Theodicy in the Theology of Karl Barth.* New York: Peter Lang, 1997.

Ritschl, Otto. *Albrecht Ritschls Leben*, 2 vols. Freiburg im Breisgau: Mohr, 1892.

Romero, Oscar. 'The Political Dimension of the Faith from the Perspective of the Option for the Poor', in *Voice of the Voiceless' The Four Pastoral Letters and Other Statements*, trans. Michael Walsh. Maryknoll: Orbis, 1985.

Rössler, Dietrich. 'Richard Rothe', in Martin Greschat, ed., *Theologen des Protestantismus im 19. und 20. Jahrhundert.* Stuttgart: Kohlhammer, 1978, 74–83.

Rothe, Richard. *Die Anfänge Der christlichen Kirche und ihrer Verfassung.* Wittenberg: Zimmerman, 1837.

— *Theologische Ethik* 3 vols. Wittenberg: Zimmerman, 1845.

Rowland, Christopher, ed. *The Cambridge Companion to Liberation Theology.* Cambridge: Cambridge University Press, 1999.

Ruether, Rosemary Radford. *Liberation Theology.* New York: Paulist, 1972.

— ed., *Religion and Sexism: Images of Woman in the Jewish and Christian Traditions.* New York: Simon and Schuster, 1974.

— *New Woman, New Earth: Sexist Ideologies and Human Liberation.* New York: Seabury, 1983.

— 'Dualism and the Nature of Evil in Feminist Theology', in *Studies in Christian Ethics* 5 (1992): 26–39.

— *Gaia and God: An Ecofeminist Theology of Earth Healing.* New York: HarperCollins, 1992.

— *Sexism and God-Talk.* Boston: Beacon, 1993.

— 'Feminist Metanoia and Soul-Making: The Journey of Conversion in Feminist Perspective', in *Introducing Redemption in Christian Feminism.* Sheffield: Sheffield Academic Press, 1998.

— *Women and Redemption: A Theological History.* (Minneapolis: Fortress Press, 1998.

— 'Women and Sin: Response to Mary Lowe', in *Dialog: A Journal of Theology* 39 (2000): 229–35.

— *Integrating Globalization, Ecofeminism, and World Religions* Lanham: Rowan and Littlefield, 2005.

Ruhe, Bernd. *Dialektik der Erbsünde: das Problem von Freiheit und Natur in der neueren Diskussion um die katholische Erbsündenlehre.* Freiburg: Universitätsverlag, 1997.

Russell, Letty. *Human Liberation in a Feminist Perspective: A Theology.* Louisville: Westminster, 1974.

Saiving, Valerie. 'The Human Situation: A Feminine View', in *Journal of Religion* 40 (1960): 100–12.

Schäfer, Rolf. *Ritschl: Grundlinien eines fast verschollenen dogmatischen Systems.* Tübingen: J. C. B. Mohr, 1968.

Scherzberg, Lucia. *Sünde und Gnade in der Feministischen Theologie.* Mainz: Matthias Grünewald, 1992.

Schleiermacher, F. D. E. *Die christliche Sitte nach den Grundsätzen der evangelischen Kirche im Zusammenhänge dargestellt,* in L. Jonas, ed., *Friedrich Schleiermachers sämtliche Werke,* I.12. Berlin: G. Reimer, 1843.

— *On Religion: Speeches to Its Cultured Despisers,* trans. John Onan. New York: Harper, 1958.

— *The Christian Faith,* trans. H.R. Mackintosh and J.S. Stewart. Edinburgh: T&T Clark, 1960.

Schmitz-Moorman, Karl. *Die Erbsünde: Überholte Vorstellung – bleibende Glaube.* Olten, Freiburg im Breisgau: Walter, 1969.

Schoof, T. M., OP, *A Survey of Catholic Theology: 1800–1970,* trans. N. D. Smith. New York: Paulist, 1970.

Schoonenberg, Piet. *Man and Sin: A Theological View.* trans. Joseph Donceel Notre Dame: Notre Dame University Press, 1965.

Schulweis, Harold M. 'Karl Barth's Job: Morality and Theodicy', in *Jewish Quarterly Review* 65 (1975): 156–67.

Schüssler Fiorenza, Elisabeth. 'Emanzipation aus der Bibel: Gegen patriarchalisches Christentum', in *Evangelisches Kommentar* 16 (1983): 185–6.

— *In Memory of Her: A Feminist Theological Reconstruction of Christian Origins.* New York: Crossroad, 1983.

— *Bread, Not Stone – The Challenge of Feminist Biblical Interpretation.* Boston: Beacon, 1984.

— 'Das Schweigen brechen sichtbar werden', in *Concilium* 21 (1985): 380–9.

— *But She Said: Feminist Practices of Biblical Interpretation.* Boston: Beacon Press, 1992.

— 'The Ties that Bind: Domestic Violence against Women', in Mary John Manzanan, et al., eds, *Women Resisting Violence: Spirituality for Life.* Maryknoll: Orbis, 1996, 42–6.

Schütte, Hans Walter. 'Die Ausscheidung der Lehre vom Zorn Gottes in der Theologie Schleiermachers und Ritschls', in *Neue Zeitschrift für Systematische Theologie und Religionsphilosophie* 10 (1968): 387–97.

Searle, John. *Intentionality: An Essay in the Philosophy of Mind.* Cambridge: Cambridge University Press, 1983.

Segundo, Juan Luis. *Evolution and Guilt,* trans. John Drury. Maryknoll: Orbis, 1974.

— *The Liberation of Theology,* trans. John Drury. Maryknoll: Orbis Books, 1976.

— *Grace and the Human Situation,* trans. John Drury. Maryknoll: Orbis Books, 1980.

Senft, Christoph. *Wahrhaftigkeit und Wahrheit: die Theologie des 19. Jahrhunderts zwischen Orthodoxie und Aufklärung.* Tübingen: Mohr Siebeck, 1956.

Shea, John. *What a Modern Catholic Believes about Sin.* Chicago: Thomas More Press, 1971.

Shults, F. LeRon. *Reforming Theological Anthropology: After the Philosophical Turn to Relationality.* Grand Rapids: Eerdmans, 2003.

Shuster, Marguerite, *The Fall and Sin: What We Have Become as Sinners.* Grand Rapids: Eerdmans, 2004.

Sievernich, Michael. *Schuld und Sünde in der Theologie der Gegenwart*. Frankfurt: Knecht, 1982.

Smith, H. Shelton. *Changing Conceptions of Original Sin: A Study in American Theology since 1750*. New York: Charles Scribners Sons, 1955.

Smith, Timothy L. *Revivalism and Social Reform in Mid-Nineteenth Century America*. New York: Abingdon, 1957.

— 'A Higher Law: Finney's Social Vision', in *Sojourners* 13 (March 1984): 19–21.

Smylie, James H. *A Brief History of the Presbyterians*. Louisville: Geneva, 1996.

Sobrino, Jon. 'Christianity and Reconciliation: A Way to Utopia', trans. Paul Burns, in Maria Pilar Aquino, et al., eds, *Reconciliation in a World of Conflicts*. London: SCM, 2003.

— and Ignacio Ellacuria, eds *Systematic Theology: Perspectives from Liberation Theology*. Maryknoll: Orbis, 1993.

Son, Chang-Hee. Haan *of Minjung Theology and Han of Han Philosophy: In the Paradigm of Process Philosophy and Metaphysics of Relatedness*. Lanham, MD: University Press of America, 2002.

Song, C. S. *Third Eye Theology: Theology in Formation in Asian Settings*. Maryknoll: Orbis, 1991.

— *The Believing Heart: An Invitation to Story Theology*. Minneapolis: Fortress, 1999.

Spivak, Gayatri. *A Critique of Post-Colonial Reason: Toward a History of the Vanishing Present*. Cambridge: Cambridge University Press, 1999.

Stefano, Frances. 'The Evolutionary Categories of Juan Luis Segundo's Theology of Grace', in *Horizons* 19 (1992): 14–39.

Stendahl, Krister. 'The Apostle Paul and the Introspective Conscience of the West', *Harvard Theological Review* 56 (1963): 199–215.

Stewart-Gambino Hannah W. and Edward L. Cleary, eds, *Power, Politics and Pentecostals in Latin America*. Boulder, CO: Westview Press, 1997.

Stone, Ronald H. Review of *Do No Harm*, in *Theology Today* 61:4 (2004): 268.

Strohl, Jane. 'Luther's Spiritual Journey', in Donald McKim, ed., *The Cambridge Companion to Martin Luther*. Cambridge: Cambridge University Press, 2003.

Strong, Augustus Hopkins. 'Reminiscences of Charles G. Finney', in *Christ in Creation and Ethical Monism*. Philadelphia: Williams, 1899, 364–87.

Suchocki, Marjorie. *God – Christ – Church*. New York, Crossroad, 1982.

— 'Weaving the World', in *Process Studies* 14 (1985): 76–86.

— *The End of Evil: Process Eschatology in Historical Context*. Albany: SUNY Press, 1988.

— *The Fall to Violence: Original Sin in Relational Theology*. New York: Continuum, 1996.

— 'Sin in Feminist and Process Thought', in Terrence Fretheim, et al., eds, *God, Evil and Human Suffering*. Saint Paul: Luther Seminary, 2001.

Suh, David Kwang-sun. 'Korean Theological Development in the 1970's' in *Minjung Theology: People as the Subjects of History*. Maryknoll: Orbis, 1983.

— *Theology, Ideology and Culture*. Hong Kong: World Student Christian Fedearation, 1983.

Suh, Nam-Dong. *In Search of Minjung Theology*. Seoul: Hang-Il Sa, 1984.

Sullivan, Roger J. *Kant's Moral Theory*. New York: Cambridge University Press, 1989.

Sweet, Leonard. 'The View of Man Inherent in New Measures Revivalism', in *Church History* 45 (1976): 206–21.

Tamez, Elsa. *Bible of the Oppressed*, trans. Matthew J. O'Connell. Maryknoll, Orbis, 1982.

— *The Amnesty of Grace: Justification by Faith from a Latin American Perspective*, trans. Sharon Ringe. Nashville: Abingdon, 1993.

Tang, Edmond. 'East Asia', in John Parratt, ed., *An Introduction to Third World Theologies*. Cambridge: Cambridge University Press, 2004.

Taylor, James. *Sin: A New Understanding of Virtue and Vice*. Kelowna, BC: Northstone, 1997.

Taylor, Michael J., ed. *The Mystery of Sin and Forgiveness*. Staten Island: Alba House, 1971.

Taylor, Richard S. 'The Doctrine of Sin in the Theology of Charles Grandison Finney', PhD diss., Boston University, 1953.

Teilhard de Chardin, Pierre. *The Phenomenon of Man*, trans. Bernard Wall. New York: Harper, 1959

Theisen, Jerome. *Community and Disunity: Symbols of Grace and Sin*. Collegeville, MN: Saint John's University Press, 1985.

Thomas, Madathilparampil M. *Salvation and Humanisation*. Madras: CLS, 1971.

— and P. D. Devandandan, eds, *Human Person, Society and State*. Bangalore: Committee on Literature for Social Concerns, 1957.

Thomas, Thannikapurathoot Jacob. *Ethics of a World Community: Contributions of Dr. M. M. Thomas Based on Indian Reality*. Calcutta: Punthi Pustak, 1993.

Thompson, Deanna A. *Crossing the Divide: Luther, Feminism, and the Cross*. Minneapolis: Fortress, 2004.

Thumma, Anthoniraj. *Breaking Barriers: Liberation of Dialogue and Dialogue of Liberation – The Quest of R. Panikkar and Beyond*. Dehli: ISPCK, 2000.

Tillich, Paul. *Perspectives on 19th and 20th Century Protestant Theology*. New York: Harper and Row, 1967.

Timm, Hermann. *Theorie und Praxis in der Theologie Albrecht Ritschls und Wilhelm Herrmanns: ein Beitrag zur Entwicklungsgeschichte des Kulturprotestantismus*. Gütersloh: Gütersloher Verlagshaus, 1967.

Townes, Emilie. 'Living in the New Jerusalem: The Rhetoric and Movement of Liberation in the House of Evil', in idem, ed. *Troubling in My Soul: Womanist Perspectives on Evil and Suffering*. Maryknoll: Orbis, 1993.

— *Womanist Justice, Womanist Ethics*. Atlanta: Scholars Press, 1993.

— 'The Doctor Ain't Taking No Sticks' in idem, ed., *Embracing the Spirit: Womanist Perspectives on Hope, Salvation and Transformation*. Maryknoll: Orbis, 1997.

Tirimanna, Vimal, CSsR. 'The Concept of "Sin" in Catholic Moral Theology', in *Asia Journal of Theology* 15 (2001): 52–66.

Troeltsch, Ernst. *The Social Teachings of the Christian Churches*, 2 vols, trans. Olive Wyon. Louisville: Westminster John Knox, 1992.

Trotman, Charles. *The Structures of Good and Evil*. Columbus, GA: Brentwood Christian Publications, 1984.

Ucko, Hans. *The People and the People of God: Minjung and Dalit Theology in Interaction with Jewish-Christian Dialogue*. Münster: Lit Verlag, 2002.

Vance, Robert. 'Sin and Consciousness of Sin in Schleiermacher', in *Perspectives in Religious Studies* 13:3 (1986): 241–62.

— *Sin and Self-Consciousness in the Thought of Friedrich Schleiermacher*. New York: Mellen Press, 1994.

Vidal, Marciano. 'Structural Sin: A New Category in Moral Theology?', in Raphael Gallagher, ed., *History and Conscience: Studies in Honour of Seán O'Riordan, CSsR*. Dublin: Gill and McMillan, 1989.

Volf, Miroslav. *Exclusion and Embrace: A Theological Exploration of Identity, Otherness, and Reconciliation*. Nashville: Abingdon, 1996.

Vulgamore, Melvin. 'Social Reform in the Theology of Charles Finney', PhD diss., Boston University, 1961.

Wallmann, Johannes. *Der Pietismus*. Göttingen: Vandenhoeck & Ruprecht, 1990.

Walther, Christian. 'Der Reich-Gottes-Begriff in der Theologie Richard Rothes und Albrecht Ritschls' in *Kerygma und Dogma* 2 (1956): 115–38.

Webster, John. '"The Firmest Grasp of the Real:" Barth on Original Sin'. *Toronto Journal of Theology* 4 (1988): 19–29.

Weddle, David L. 'The Liberator as Exorcist: James Cone and the Classic Doctrine of Atonement', in *Religion in Life* 9 (1980): 477–87.

— *The Law as Gospel: Revival and Reform in the Theology of Charles G. Finney.* Metuchen, NJ: Scarecrow Press, 1985.

Westhelle, Vitor. 'O Tamanho do Paraiso: Presupostos do Conceito de Pecado na Theologia Latino-Americana', in *Estudos Teologicos* 38 (1998): 239–51.

Weiss, Johannes. *Die Predigt Jesu vom Reich Gottes.* Göttingen: Vandenhoeck and Ruprecht, 1892.

Welch, Claude. *Protestant Thought in the Nineteenth Century*, 2 vols. New Haven: Yale University Press, 1972–85.

Wells, David F., ed. *Reformed Theology in America: A History of Its Modern Development.* Grand Rapids: Eerdmans, 1995.

Wentz, Richard E. 'Nevin and American Nationalism', in Sam Hamstra, Jr and Arie J. Griffioen, eds, *Reformed Confessionalism in Nineteenth Century America: Essays on the Thought of John Williamson Nevin.* Lanham, MD: Scarecrow Press, 1995, 23–42.

— *John Williamson Nevin: American Theologian.* Oxford: Oxford University Press, 1997, esp. 98–111.

West, Angela. *Deadly Innocence: Feminist Theology and the Mythology of Sin.* London: Cassell, 1995.

Whitehead, Alfred North. *Process and Reality.* Ed. David Ray Griffin and Donald W. Sherburne. New York: Free Press, 1978.

Whitehead, Raymond L., ed. *No Longer Strangers: Selected Writings of Bishop K.H. Ting,* Maryknoll: Orbis, 1989.

Wickeri, Janet, ed. *Love Never Ends: Papers by K.H. Ting.* Nanjing: Yillin Press, 2000.

Wilberforce, Robert I. *The Doctrine of the Incarnation of Our Lord Jesus Christ in Its Relation to Mankind and to the Church.* London: Murray, 1849.

Williams, Delores. 'The Color of Feminism: Or Speaking the Black Woman's Tongue', in *Journal of Religious Thought* 43 (1986): 42–58.

— 'Womanist Theology: Black Women's Voices', in *Yearning to Breathe Free: Liberation Theology in the U.S.*, ed. Linda Rennie Forcey, et al. Maryknoll: Orbis, 1990.

— *Sisters in the Wilderness: The Challenge of Womanist God-Talk.* Maryknoll: Orbis, 1993.

— 'A Womanist Perspective on Sin', in Emilie Townes, ed., *A Troubling in My Soul: Womanist Perspectives on Evil and Suffering.* Maryknoll: Orbis, 1993.

— 'Straight Talk, Plain Talk: Womanist Words about Salvation in a Social Context', in Emilie Townes, ed., *Embracing the Spirit: Womanist Perspectives on Hope, Salvation and Transformation.* Maryknoll: Orbis, 1997.

Williams, Patricia. *Doing without Adam and Eve: Sociobiology and Original Sin.* Minneapolis: Fortress, 2001.

Williamson, Clark. 'Did Ritschl's Critics Read Ritschl?' in *Evangelical Quarterly* 44 (1972): 159–68.

Willimon, William H. *Sighing for the Faith: Sin, Evil, and the Christian Faith.* Nashville: Abingdon, 1985.

Willis, Robert. 'Bonhoeffer and Barth on Jewish Suffering: Reflections on the Relationship between Theology and Moral Sensibility'. *Journal of Ecumenical Studies* 24 no. 4 (1987): 598–615.

Wingren, Gustaf. 'Tre Motforestillinger', *Norsk Teologisk Tidskrift* 79 (1978): 203–14.

Wolterstorff, Nicholas. 'Barth on Evil', in *Faith and Philosophy* 13 (1996): 584–608.

Wood, Allen. *Kant's Moral Religion.* Ithaca, NY: Cornell University Press, 1970.

Wyman, Jr, Walter E. 'The Kingdom of God in Germany: From Ritschl to Troeltsch', in idem, et al., eds, *Re-envisioning the Past: Prospects in Historical Theology.* Minneapolis: Fortress Press, 1992, 257–80.

Bibliography

— 'Rethinking the Christian Doctrine of Sin: Schleiermacher and Hick's "Irenaean Type"', *Journal of Religion* 74:2 (1994): 199–217.
— 'Review of *Sin and Self-Consciousness in the Thought of Friedrich Schleiermacher*', in *Religious Studies Review.* 22:4 (1996): 334.
Yang, Sung Chul. *Korea and Two Regimes: Kim Il Sung and Park Chung Hee.* Cambridge: Schenkman, 1981.

INDEX

Aaron 107
Abelard, Peter 34, 110
Abraham 127
Adam 18, 22, 148
Ahlstrom, Sydney 49, 61, 64
Ahn Byung Mu 166–72, 177–8
Alfaro, Juan 7, 97, 105–109, 182
Aristotle 147
Arminianism 64, 68
Augustine 18, 34, 38, 44, 147–8

Balasuriya, Tissa, 162
Barnes, Albert 51
Barth, Karl 8, 9, 11, 15, 41, 134–5
Bauman, Zygmunt 123
Beecher, Lyman 51
Boff, Leonardo 92, 97, 101–105, 107, 182
Bornkamm, Günther 166
Brandt, James 33
Brunner, Emil 8, 11, 15
Bultmann, Rudolf 8–9, 11, 166
Bushnell, Horace 67, 70

Calvin, John 30, 32, 35, 44, 61, 71, 131–6
CDF (Congregation for the Doctrine of the Faith 92–3, 101
CELAM (Latin American Bishops' Conference) 83, 88, 92, 96, 113
Chao, T. C 162
Chapman, Mark 43
Chopp, Rebecca 106, 111–13, 116, 182
Christian, William 145
Comblin, Jose 97
Cone, James 126

Dalits 163, 179
Daly, Mary 143
Daub, Karl 63
Davis, William 65
Dorner, Isaak 75
Dunfee, Susan Nelson 115, 143–4, 155

EATWOT (Ecumenical Association of Third World Theologians) 161
Edwards, Jonathan 64
Empiricism 74
Engel, Mary Potter 116–18, 124, 156, 183
Essenes 169
Etchegoyen, Aldo 7, 97, 105–108, 182
Eve 18, 115, 144, 148

Faus, Jose Ignacio González 96–7
Fichte, Johann Gottlieb 38, 75
Finney, Charles G. 7–8, 13, 48–61 passim, 54–9, 71–2, 77–9, 181,
Fischer, Hermann 16
Freud, Sigmund 98, 100–101

Gebara, Ivone 121–4, 16
Gerrish, B. A. 61, 62
Girotti, Gianfranco 1
González, Justo 97, 105–106, 108–11, 182
Grand Canyon (film) 1
Grant, Jacquelyn 125–6, 156–8, 183
Gutierrez, Gustavo 10, 26, 83, 85–98, 107, 111–13, 182

Hagar 127–8
Hampson, Daphne 115, 143, 155
Hart, David Bentley 179
Hefner, Philip 35, 43
Hegel, G. W. F. 17, 38, 41, 63, 71, 75
Heidegger, Martin 103
Hewitt, Glenn 59
Hildegard of Bingen 114
Hodge, Charles 62, 64, 77
Holifield, E. Brooks 51, 55, 61, 73, 75,
Husserl, Edmund 5, 13, 122

Irigary, Luce 134
Isaiah 85–6
Islam 33
ITC (International Theological Commission) 92–3